A World at Sea

THE EARLY MODERN AMERICAS

Peter C. Mancall, Series Editor

Volumes in the series explore neglected aspects of early modern history in the Western Hemisphere. Interdisciplinary in character, and with a special emphasis on the Atlantic world from 1450 to 1850, the series is published in partnership with the USC-Huntington Early Modern Studies Institute.

A WORLD AT SEA

Maritime Practices and Global History

EDITED BY

Lauren Benton and

Nathan Perl-Rosenthal

PENN

UNIVERSITY OF PENNSYLVANIA PRESS

PHILADELPHIA

Published by
University of Pennsylvania Press
Philadelphia, Pennsylvania 19104-4112
www.upenn.edu/pennpress

Printed in the United States of America
on acid-free paper

10 9 8 7 6 5 4 3 2 1

Library of Congress Cataloging-in-Publication Data

Names: Benton, Lauren A., 1956– editor. | Perl-Rosenthal, Nathan, 1982– editor.
Title: A world at sea : maritime practices and global history / Lauren Benton and Nathan Perl-Rosenthal, editors.
Other titles: Early modern Americas.
Description: First edition. | Philadelphia : University of Pennsylvania Press, [2020] | Series: The early modern Americas | Includes bibliographical references and index.
Identifiers: LCCN 2020001884 | ISBN 9780812252415 (hardcover)
Subjects: LCSH: Ocean and civilization—History. | Navigation—History. | World history. | Globalization—History. | Naval art and science—History. | Maritime law—History.
Classification: LCC CB465 .W67 2020 | DDC 551.46—dc23
LC record available at https://lccn.loc.gov/2020001884

Contents

Introduction: Making Maritime History Global

Nathan Perl-Rosenthal and Lauren Benton

The oceans are a dangerous place for human beings. Our land mammal bodies make us poor swimmers; we are prone to drowning and hypothermia. Ships and their crews bring organisms to shore, from the tiny bacillus to the Eurasian horse, that can quickly disrupt our communities. Yet for all their dangers, oceans have always been essential to human life. From time immemorial they have served as a source of food, a path for news and trade, and a medium for mobility.

The tension between the dangers of the ocean and our collective reliance on it became visible on a global scale in the formative period from 1450 to 1900. Ships and sailors in this period knitted together the parts of the world in a "first globalization." Unprecedented transfers of people, ideas, microbes, and goods across aqueous spaces generated new wealth and initiated or deepened networks of exchange across regions. With connection also came the startling human misery created by overseas conquest, the spread of disease, and coerced migration. In these transformative centuries, the seas became truly global—a condition reflecting not just worldwide connections but also the composition of a global regulatory order rife with inequality and violence. Even though most early modern populations never got anywhere near a coast, let alone onto the water, the maritime world reached them: the seas lay at the geographic margins of the land, but they were at the heart of global conflicts and transformative processes.[1]

This volume seeks to sharpen and expand our understanding of how the maritime world, broadly construed, contributed to the early modern era's global transformations. The chapters build on familiar stories about the growth of maritime commercial endeavors and the regional integration of ocean basins, but they move well beyond the usual topics and approaches to maritime history. They have multiple points of departure: the shared properties of early modern maritime spaces, seafarers' need to adapt to the hazards and perils of the sea, and the challenges of controlling and governing aqueous space, among others. But all of them probe how processes spanning land and sea shaped new patterns of global ordering in the early modern era.

Our volume identifies several kinds of processes as particularly important in anchoring maritime worlds to broader transformations. First, we highlight ways in which the regulatory order of the seas emanated from strategies of land-based polities and their agents, while at the same time responding to shifting patterns of conflict at sea. The section entitled "Currents" presents chapters that explore the imperial institutions and structures organizing maritime life and reacting to challenges to order. By "institutions" and "structures" we refer not only to phenomena that historians usually describe with those terms but also to patterns of cultural practice and legal engagement that gave rise to informal and unofficial regulatory processes. Second, we draw attention to the importance of the changing information order of the seas. The second section, "Dispatches," comprises studies of documentary practices that bundled and conveyed information about sea voyages, encounters, and conflicts. The emphasis in this section is on how maritime contexts adapted existing terrestrial routines and genres while also adjusting to the explosion of new information gathered on and about the seas. Third, the volume highlights change and conflict at the water's edge. The final section, "Thresholds," features chapters that examine the relationship between littoral geographies and the transformation of sociolegal practices spanning land and sea. They probe, too, the political symbolism of the land-sea divide as a threshold of power. Each of the three sections contains perspectives from multiple ocean regions, and every chapter is either explicitly comparative or situated within a multioceanic frame.

Together the chapters chart a new course for thinking about maritime history as global history. They show how practices in different maritime contexts around the early modern world forged significant convergences in processes organizing trade, labor, violence, geographic knowledge, and law. These convergences often took shape around attempts to manage and regulate—or cross—the divide between the sea and the land. Efforts to extend terrestrial governance onto the water, or to manage and police the shoreline, for instance, reconfigured states and societies everywhere during this period. Variations in physical geography, legal culture, and socioeconomic structures put their stamp on fundamentally similar maritime trends, including the formation of land-sea regimes, across regions and polities.[2]

This variation-in-unity makes maritime history an especially powerful lens through which to examine processes of global ordering in the early modern era, encompassing everything from the remaking of political communities to the refashioning of individual lives.

Maritime History's Global Turns

Since maritime history emerged as a recognized area of study in the late nineteenth century, it has taken multiple transnational, global, and oceanic turns. These turns are part of what gives the field such potential as a lens on global transformations. Yet the sheer multiplicity of global engagements that point in many compass directions at once can also be an impediment to moving the field forward. Reckoning with previous attempts to write global history on the ocean is the first step of charting a new course for maritime history.

Most maritime histories of the nineteenth and early twentieth centuries highlighted two subjects: navies and commerce. Naval history tended to be the province of nonprofessional scholars—stereotypically, an aging retired naval officer writing the history of his own ship or service—though this body of scholarship also included serious amateur monographs, detailed naval biographies, and significant collections of naval history documents that remain valuable references to this day.[3] Naval history had a conservative bent overall. Important nineteenth-century studies of the French revolutionary navy, for instance, presented a thoroughly counterrevolutionary argument that the Revolution had nearly destroyed French naval power.[4] But the field's conservatism was often tempered by a serious interest in the life of ratings (nonofficers) and curiosity about the technological dimensions of shipbuilding and provisioning that would not be unfamiliar to social historians today.

A second powerful current in nineteenth- and early twentieth-century maritime history writing flowed from studies of seaborne trade. Before the advent of professional history in the United States, a robust amateur tradition already existed of histories of local and regional commercial ventures.[5] When professional history of early modern empires developed around 1900, it took the history of overseas commerce as one of its primary subjects, alongside the topics of imperial politics and administration. Scholars such as Charles Boxer and J. P. Oliveira Martins placed maritime ventures at the center of narratives of Iberian expansion, for example, and G. L. Beer, Charles McLean Andrews, and Arthur M. Schlesinger Sr., among others, devoted considerable attention to maritime matters in their broader treatments of the first British empire.[6]

In the postwar decades, a more specialized scholarship on maritime commerce began to appear. Some, like influential studies by Bernard Bailyn and Richard Pares, connected commerce to imperial and interimperial currents of colonization and warfare, while other works explored oceanic patterns of trade, such as Huguette and Pierre Chaunu's *Séville et l'Atlantique* and, later still, K. N. Chaudhuri's pathbreaking *Trade and Civilisation in the Indian Ocean.* Unlike naval histories, studies of commerce rarely probed the lives of seafarers, in part reflecting the limitations of merchants' records in this regard. Yet many of these works were highly attuned to questions of law and jurisdiction: Pares and the Chaunus, for instance, highlighted tensions over illicit interimperial trade, and Chaudhuri insisted that Indian Ocean seaborne trade formed part of a broader phenomenon of Asian commercial capitalism.[7]

These two oldest strands within maritime historiography had the virtue—from the vantage point of contemporary scholarship—of being oceanic in scope, and even precociously global. Naval history, though firmly inserted within national historiographies in one sense, was in another sense resolutely border crossing. Naval historians followed vessels, officers, and enlisted men wherever they traveled, revealing connections not just within but also across oceans. Many naval historians, too, regarded their subject with a comparative eye: an empire or nation's sea power could only be understood, after all, in relation to other naval forces. Many historians of maritime commerce were also decidedly global in their orientation. Some of the earliest works closely examined the high-value, long-distance operations of European trading companies, such as the Dutch East and West India Companies, the French Levant Company, and the British East India Company.[8] Such studies sketched world-spanning histories a century before "global" became a byword among scholars.

The twenty-five years from about 1970 to 1995 saw the emergence of a third strand within maritime history, the social and labor history of seamen. The historiography on this topic developed roughly simultaneously on both sides of the North Atlantic as part of the social history turn of the 1960s and 1970s, with counterparts in other world regions. In Anglo-American scholarship, Jesse Lemisch's pathbreaking 1968 *William and Mary Quarterly* article on mariners in the coming of the American Revolution remains widely cited fifty years later. A similar turn took place in Europe during the 1970s: in France, Alain Cabantous undertook painstaking work on the seamen of northwestern France. Jaap Bruijn, holder of the Netherlands' only university chair in maritime history, began to publish on social history topics (though initially for a popular audience).[9] These forays opened into wider social histories of the sea in the 1980s and early 1990s. In the United States, Marcus Rediker and Daniel Vickers studied the lives of English merchant seamen and Massachusetts fishermen, respectively. Pablo E. Pérez-Mallaina, whose early work had focused on traditional naval topics, produced an important study of daily life aboard the Spanish galleon fleet. Toward the end of this period, some scholars on both sides of the Atlantic began to take an interest in the lives of women connected to the maritime world and to study the lived experiences of enslaved and freed people in the Atlantic and Indian Ocean worlds.[10]

Much of the new social history of mariners was strikingly regional, even local, in orientation. Mariners in these studies were mainly rooted in local communities, and the research typically stayed within a single ocean. A burgeoning literature on Polynesian mariners and coastal Southeast Asian communities, for instance, broke the mold of European-centered histories of seafarers but remained regionally inscribed.[11] For some scholars of the Atlantic world, focusing on the everyday lives of mariners served to illuminate local, small-scale communities. Cabantous and Vickers, for instance, drew on probate inventories and vital statistics, types of documents deeply rooted in place and of a kind that imparted a strong local flavor to their histories even when they studied populations that were mobile by profession. Rediker's turn toward representing Anglo-American mariners as protoproletarians advanced a view of shipboard life as a crucible of class struggle, an emphasis that had its own provincializing effect as it inscribed an Anglocentric model of industrial labor within a global narrative of radical opposition to capitalism and modernity.[12]

The past twenty-five years have seen a dramatic expansion of maritime history, but also a powerful renewal of ocean regionalism. The appeal of oceanic frameworks can be traced in good measure to the persistent influence of Fernand Braudel's two-volume masterpiece, *The Mediterranean and the Mediterranean World in the Age of Philip II*, first translated into English in the mid-1970s.[13] Braudel's work traveled in so many directions, from environmental to material to cultural history, that we often lose sight of its central innovation: an ocean-centered approach to cultural and social history. The enduring power of this approach is visible in the Atlantic and Indian Ocean historiographies, Mediterranean studies, Pacific history, and literatures on scores of smaller sea regions. In each of these areas, the Braudelian perspective positions maritime flows within regions as central to cultural and political developments. Even as practitioners in these fields have critiqued Braudel's notions of regional cultural unity, ocean regionalism has still proven a powerful organizing principle for research in maritime history.[14]

The renewed ocean regionalism has, in the first instance, given us a far richer understanding of the social history of the sea. We now have a far better view of the complex seafaring communities that flourished before European contact in the Caribbean, Polynesia, East and Southeast Asia, and the Indian Ocean. We know, too, that the practices and commercial-military networks of these communities did not recede in the face of European intrusions.[15] Robust new histories of maritime bondage and the relationship between enslavement and maritime life has taken shape in multiple ocean basin contexts, especially the Atlantic and Indian Oceans.[16] Building on the early work of Chaudhuri and others, older oceanic histories of commerce have reemerged as histories of capitalism and its regional variants, including innovative global commodity studies and credit histories connected with maritime trade. There has also been a limited cultural turn in the social history of mariners, with gender and race gaining greater analytic power and the cultural worlds of maritime workers coming into sharper focus.[17]

New areas of inquiry within maritime history have also opened up through (and occasionally against) the focus on ocean regions. There is innovative research on imperial practices, movements of coerced labor, and maritime environmental change.[18] Another new strand of research has followed the circulation of information and currents of vernacular knowledge.[19] Still another area of sustained focus, only dimly perceived in the field's earlier iterations, is the history of law at sea: recent works explore oceans as legal spaces, analyze ships as "vectors of law," and uncover the way distinctive legal regimes took shape as jurists and mariners turned an arcane arena of jurisprudence, prize law, into an element of regional and global ordering.[20] Maritime violence, especially piracy, emerges in these law-framed histories as deeply connected to contests over imperial power. Meanwhile, naval history, much enriched and not a little transformed by the infusion of social history, and now increasingly expanded to incorporate forms of privateering and strategies of governance, remains a mainstay of the field while becoming more attuned to the cultural currents and political movements shaping the views of naval personnel.[21]

Maritime Practices, Global Processes

Building on these foundations, this volume seeks to capture maritime history's still-unrealized potential as a vehicle for world history. A growing list of research topics and an explicit ambition to connect histories of ocean regions do not yet equate to a clear collective enterprise. The chapters in this volume reveal the value of making three additional analytic moves in order to forge a truly global maritime history. The first analytic move is an explicit focus on the contributions of maritime practices to patterns of change on a planetary scale. In the category of maritime practices, we include social, economic, and cultural actions on the seas (such as sailing techniques) as well as practices that extended into oceans but originated or reverberated in landed communities (for example, maritime commercial regulations). Our emphasis on practice embraces the promise of maritime social and cultural history from below, while encompassing institutional change and interpolitical contexts. A second move is to insist on a comparative dimension to the study of practice, in order to reveal the links between local and regional histories and global trends. This work has already commenced with a series of recent edited collections offering comparative takes on topics such as governance, trade, piracy, and forced migration across the seas.[22]

The third analytic move involves sustained attention to processes spanning land and sea, with an understanding that the influence extended in both directions. The approach brings into view, for example, both efforts to cast imperial power over the seas and the regulatory effects of ubiquitous maritime routines. The oceans were certainly distinctive places in many respects. Yet as the contributions in this volume show, the people on them were closely and intimately tied to land-based societies, polities, and cultures. Many regional historians stop their research at the water's edge; some have mistaken the heightened drama of conflicts at sea for a difference of kind. The specialized vocabularies, conventions, and legal practices of maritime pursuits have given further impetus to a view of the world beyond the shore as radically different from that of the land. More than a few maritime historians, meanwhile, have wandered into a version of maritime exceptionalism, staking unexamined claims that global change originated on the seas or that the origins of particular strains of radical politics or labor solidarity emerged first among sailors. Recovering the close linkage between processes on land and sea is crucial if we are to position maritime history as a significant part of the new global history.[23]

Studying maritime practices on a planetary scale with a focus on the ways in which such processes by their nature span the land-sea divide has the potential to transport maritime history from its relatively quiet corner into an analytically central position within world history. The practices of seafaring, if we are willing to extend our vision to be able to see it, were that rarest of rare things: truly global phenomena constitutive of deep structural change at vast scale in the early modern world.

We organize this volume in sections corresponding to three sets of especially formative processes spanning land and sea. "Currents" takes as its subject processes of institutional change that organized maritime actions in increasingly global dimensions. Unsurprisingly, given the importance of empires in this period, the structures are first and foremost imperial or para-imperial. The section opens with Carla Rahn Phillips's chapter on maritime recruitment in the Spanish empire. Phillips explores the range of impetuses that led young men to go to sea, from financial rewards to social pressure. Her essay shows that maritime recruitment, though it had its particularities, was not radically dissimilar from other forms of labor mobilization in the early modern world. In the second essay, Adam Clulow and Xing Hang offer an intricate study of how two Southeast Asian kingdoms sought to navigate a struggle for maritime power and authority between Dutch and Chinese actors in seventeenth-century East Asia. At issue in their chapter is the troubled process by which metropolitan regulatory systems were pushed outward into maritime spaces, where they composed new, still uneven regulatory processes. Matthew Taylor Raffety's essay provides an overview of trends in European maritime law as a phenomenon with global influence. Using a genealogical approach that views European maritime legal regimes as having common roots, his chapter explores how this multifaceted legal regime developed in Europe's proximate seas and projected its complex and uneven influence around the globe.

The three chapters explicitly track institutional connections across the putative divide between land and sea. Maritime labor practices and recruitment, as Phillips shows convincingly, developed in close relation to broader labor legislation in seafaring polities. Her essay draws evidence primarily from the Mediterranean and Atlantic ports of Spain but clearly suggests that similar stories could be told about every region that made significant use of maritime labor. The contribution reminds us of the intricate institutional layering that went into the rise of increasingly global processes for finding, deploying, and disciplining maritime labor. Raffety's chapter centers not on the spread of law in the abstract but on the ways in which a transoceanic legal order emerged from shared medieval legal practices and specific metropolitan institutions (especially British admiralty courts) to become the preeminent law of the sea. Raffety in part follows other studies seeking the origins of oceanic legal ordering in projections of metropolitan law and uneven treaty regimes, but his chapter cautions that European ambitions to design a universal law of the sea, however fitful and uneven, must remain part of this story.[24] Clulow and Xing offer a particularly vivid illustration of how maritime matters crossed the land-sea divide: their chapter focuses on two early modern states, Cambodia and Ayutthaya (Siam), that did not have significant maritime domains. Yet as the authors show, both states sought to stretch their regulatory authority into maritime spaces in order to manage trade relationships and control potentially destructive conflicts among trading partners.

The chapters in this section sketch the emergence of an oceanic regulatory order that was being woven and projected through intersecting state practices spanning land and sea. The new global history is intent on avoiding the kinds of diffusionist narratives characteristic of earlier histories such as stories of the British or French or Dutch empire penetrating and integrating the globe. Current scholarship aims to recover instead a polycentric and polyphonic history of early modern global transformation. One of the puzzles created by this polycentric view of the early modern world is how to explain the emergence of global regulatory orders. How did diverse polities come to share so much—not just in their external relations but also in how they functioned internally? These essays emphasize the ways in which systems of maritime labor recruitment, seafaring legal institutions, and regulatory authority over maritime spaces crossed the divide between early modern states' internal and external operations. As states of all stripes (and many kinds of state-like bodies) competed with one another for authority and control in and around the water, they found themselves pulled internally in similar directions. The projects of regulating oceans and projecting power onto them did more than just order the oceans; they emanated from domestic political change and also rebounded onto political communities. Efforts to control the seas, including through maritime warfare, had some distinctive properties, to be sure: claiming a patch of water was not the same as claiming a patch of land. But the larger story, as these chapters convey in different ways, is that polities had to integrate the military, technical, and social logics of the maritime world into the heart of their policymaking if they hoped to survive and thrive.

The second section, "Dispatches," explores the intersection between distinctly maritime forms of knowledge and trends in the use and deployment of knowledge in the early modern world more broadly. The three chapters in this section approach their shared problem from different empirical bases. Margaret Schotte's chapter examines navigational science and the development of education for the maritime professions. Her focus is squarely on mariners and the administrators who sought to channel and replicate their knowledge.

David Igler explores visual and ethnographic knowledge through the story of a Pacific Ocean voyage and the friendship that grew up on the seas between two shipmates, one Polynesian and one European. Igler examines the way intimate, cross-cultural maritime exchanges fostered the production and transmission of useful knowledge. Nathan Perl-Rosenthal's chapter analyzes the complex processes by which eighteenth-century mariners used a particular kind of document—the private letter—to develop knowledge about the national identities of crews and ships in the wartime Atlantic. Here "official" knowledge came to reflect the categories known to captains, mariners, merchants, and captives describing the origins of men on ships and the political affiliation of voyage sponsors.

The trends traced in this section unfolded against the backdrop of twin revolutions in government and science that swept the European world during the eighteenth and nineteenth centuries. This period saw the birth of new forms of politics and bureaucracy that had distinctive demands for specialized kinds of knowledge and informed the rise of new sciences (including racial science and forms of "big science"). Vernacular knowledge about the seas was entering these circuits—though historians have only begun to understand the connections.[25] As Schotte and Perl-Rosenthal suggest, maritime knowledge-making in this period could act as a forerunner or testing-ground for the development of new forms of knowledge in and for early modern states. Navigation was one of the first areas in which European empires, eager to develop powerful naval establishments, sought to encourage the recognition and application of "useful" knowledge. The need for knowledge in this area went well beyond the technical information required to build and repair warships. Official interest in knowing the nationalities of ships influenced the development of tools for identification at sea that could be deployed in courtrooms and custom houses. New problems of knowledge at sea led to the creation, in multiple instances, of new epistemologies.

Maritime knowledge-making was not just a precocious case of what would later become common on land. The three authors in this section examine closely the ways in which maritime vicissitudes put European documentary practices, broadly construed, to the test and altered them in the process. Perl-Rosenthal shows how commercial and personal letters—technologies designed for communication over long distances—were adapted by privateersmen and admiralty courts to the new and unintended purpose of identifying nationality. Schotte analyzes how states sought to codify and render accessible mariners' practical knowledge of ships, seafaring, and geography—and, as her opening anecdote suggests, the ways in which systems of record-keeping imagined for terrestrial processes proved unequal to solving problems at sea. In his examination of the cross-cultural interaction between Kadu and Choris, Igler reveals how the technologies of illustration and ethnographic description, thoroughly established on land and in the metropole, became subject to experimentation once they were deployed on a Pacific Ocean voyage.

A fresh picture of European empire and its knowledge practices begins to emerge from these essays, which cover a wide geographic swath, from European waters to the Caribbean to the Pacific. Early modern European empires are often depicted as weaker versions of their later incarnations: too feeble, in this period at least, to effectively exercise power or acquire reliable information at a distance.[26] These chapters show not weakness or lassitude on the part of European states or actors but a kind of hyperactive pursuit of knowledge in multiple arenas. This supercharged knowledge-making and knowledge-seeking posed its own challenges. New ways of packaging navigational information, identifying ships, and depicting native peoples, often developed on the fly, clashed repeatedly or combined with older ways of accomplishing the same goals. Governments and bureaucracies often had difficulty assimilating the resulting information in a useful manner. The results hampered imperial governance in many cases, not just because of the state's incapacity to manage so much information but also through the hyperactivity of the very actors who were supposedly charged with creating and collecting useful knowledge.

The third section, "Thresholds," homes in on the link between maritime or littoral geographies and the transformation of sociolegal practices in the early modern period. In this section, the physical interface between land and sea moves to center stage. In general terms, the "threshold of the state" was a significant site of early modern political thought about the constitution of communities and their relation both to external relations and to nature.[27] The shoreline and littoral gave physical form to the idea of the state's threshold. Coastlines, beaches, sea passages between proximate shores, bays, and estuaries—these spaces were at once barriers and transitional zones, often styled as places of cultural encounter and unstable political control.[28] As later studies of the creation of borders have shown, practices of crossing such zones shaped their political meanings, not the other way around.[29] These chapters probe such processes in the early modern world. The authors also open questions, now increasingly familiar from environmental history but still emergent in maritime history, about the constraints and effects of the natural world on human behavior. They suggest the possibilities of studying the synchronic formation of types of maritime liminal zones, with attention to distinctive local sociolegal worlds they helped to create.

Thresholds—of the state and of geographies—feature in several chapters as projections of political power along coastal corridors and in proximate seas. Catherine Phipps examines debates and practices in Japan during the long nineteenth century aimed at control of coasts and coastal waters, and considers how such strategies fit within the broader politics of fashioning Japanese sovereignty and confronting the perceived dangers of European and American imperial power. Her chapter asks us to look away from Commodore Perry's arrival in Japan, the usual set piece for probing emerging views of Japanese sovereignty, and to consider instead how policies aimed at the control of coastal waters shaped Japan's borders and strategies for extending and consolidating state authority. Jeppe Mulich, in his essay, analyzes maritime marronage (the escape of enslaved people by sea) as both a social phenomenon and a political problem in transimperial borderlands. Grounded in local sources from the Danish Caribbean, his study shows how competing polities sought to control and channel such mobility to their advantage. The third essay in this section, by Lisa Norling, offers a global survey of "women who got wet" in the early modern fisheries. Norling provides a geographically sweeping yet also granular look at the kinds of work these women did and their relationship to the working worlds of land and sea. Her emphasis is on enduring and widely shared divisions along gender lines of the vast labor force whose work spanned ships and various kinds of shore communities.

All three chapters emphasize the complex sociopolitical character of coastlines and littoral zones in the early modern world. Phipps, picking up some of the same threads as Clulow and Hang, argues that coastal waters represented a crucial area for the definition of sovereignty by the nineteenth-century Japanese state. She suggests that the nature of the marine space itself—at the junction between a terrestrial sphere controlled by the Japanese state and maritime spaces under effective European control—made it central to the negotiation of Japanese sovereignty. Mulich's essay centers on the particular set of sociolegal and administrative problems posed by the archipelago geography of the Caribbean. Its patchwork of jurisdictions, with contradictory rules regarding property in persons, created an interpolity borderland, one whose character was partly shaped by the movements of enslaved people. This marine sociolegal geography, in turn, stimulated the formation of unexpected cross-polity relationships among colonial elites. Lisa Norling emphasizes the role of the littoral as a particularly sharply defined example of an ecotone—a transitional area from one environment to another. The typically rich natural resources of these zones combined with repeating practices of gendered labor to produce a socioecological pattern of global reach and local variation.

The littoral was not only a distinctive social space, these contributions suggest: the recurring processes that formed the shoreline contributed to elements of global ordering. The interpolity relationships in coastal waters and politically divided archipelagoes existed in settings beyond Japan and the Caribbean. In other island chains in the Mediterranean, the Indian Ocean, and elsewhere, thickening interactions simultaneously gave form to borders and made them porous in specific ways. Coastal waters were crucial to the formation of sovereign power in regions as diverse as colonial North America, South Asia, and the English Channel. The ecotone of the water's edge, too, represented a global phenomenon. As Norling shows convincingly, the bodily needs of families and the physical properties of the seashore led families in seafaring coastal communities around the world to organize their labor by assigning women particular, often strikingly similar, roles.

A World at Sea

Individually, the contributions of this volume develop new insights and topics in global maritime history; collectively, they point the way to a new perspective on the maritime world's significance in global history. The authors affirm the value of using the thickening processes of information sharing, navigation, and conflict (for instance, over captives or natural resources) as starting points for studying ocean regions. When we do so, instead of beginning from seemingly familiar oceanic labels—Pacific, Indian, Atlantic, Mediterranean—we uncover surprising regional formations, corresponding to overlooked but historically significant forms of geographic imagination, regulation, and capital accumulation.[30] A second insight that emerges from these essays is the promise of focusing on the institutions and practices used to extend control over ocean spaces, and their interaction with efforts to collect and communicate knowledge generated on the seas. These practices engaged imperial agents as well as families or companies dependent on seafaring, and they encompassed the actions of vulnerable and destitute groups, from slaves engaged in maritime marronage to struggling shipboard and coastal laborers to women workers. As several of the chapters in this volume suggest, we still have much to learn about the cultural, institutional, and informational practices of these laboring worlds and the global processes they generated.

But the chapters make clear that these processes compose a framework for analysis that is both global in reach and socially intimate. Finally, several chapters call for renewed attention to the ways in which the maritime world contributed to paradigmatic shifts in the period such as the development of "big science" and novel patterns of political association (such as interimperial collaboration). Moving beyond a view of ships or ports as vectors and points for transmitting political ideas makes it possible to see how maritime practices left their mark on the political formations of the period, including empires, micropolities, confederations, nation-states, and regions.

Studying the oceans and seas as sites of experimentation, innovation, governance, and disruption promises to produce a truly global history of maritime change. Transformations on the seas did not take place only in a few familiar ways, such as through long-distance trade, cross-cultural relations, migration, and war. Seafaring itself generated global processes and patterns that stitched together regions, spanned the land-sea divide, and profoundly influenced terrestrial polities and societies. These processes made the early modern world, in ways both tangible and metaphorical, a world at sea.

Part I

Currents

Chapter 1

Why Did Anyone Go to Sea? Structures of Maritime Enlistment from Family Traditions to Violent Coercion

Carla Rahn Phillips

> Anacharsis, the Scythian philosopher, said, "There are three kinds of people: *the living, the dead and those who sail the sea in ships*." That was in the Heroic Age and, at a later date, Dr Johnson said, with equal authority and force, that it passed his comprehension why anybody with the wit to steal enough money to get himself decently hanged should ever go to sea.
>
> —Richard Armstrong, *The Early Mariners*

Anacharsis in the early sixth century BCE and Samuel Johnson in the late eighteenth century CE were in complete agreement about the unnaturalness of seafaring for a land-based species such as ours. Nonetheless, countless generations have gone to sea, and some individuals have made a career of seafaring, which begs the question, "Why?" This essay will address that question, focusing primarily on the ways and means that European shipowners and governments in the early modern period found crews and officers, although it will include some evidence from other times and places. The focus will be on individuals engaged in seaborne occupations, rather than members of seafaring communities on land or the broad range of humanity that traveled by sea at one time or another through choice or necessity. For that reason, women will be absent from the story, although they were important participants in families and communities earning their living from the sea and as heads of state setting policies for the enlistment of mariners and the regulation of seaborne commerce.

The ways and means of maritime enlistment ranged widely from enthusiastic free choice to the most violent forms of coercion. Geographical location, personal inclination, family traditions, and economic incentives influenced many individual decisions to go to sea, at the positive end of the spectrum. Kidnapping someone for sea duty with no legal justification anchored the negative end of the spectrum. Between the two extremes lay a wide variety of personal, economic, legal, and other considerations that induced men and boys to go to sea for the first time. Other incentives, both positive and negative, influenced the decision to continue with a maritime life.

Historians frequently distinguish between civilian and military seafaring, especially after the late eighteenth century, as the merchant marine came to be largely separate from official navies. For the early modern period, that makes little sense. Both civilian and military voyages drew from the same pool of vessels and potential crewmen, and the same individuals and ships could serve at different times in fishing, trade, piracy, or warfare. As a Spanish merchant marine captain noted as late as the nineteenth century, "the merchant marine and the navy have identical interests to promote, and instead of divorcing themselves they complement one another. They are like two bodies with a single soul."[1] Less romantic and more pertinent to this essay, sailors in the merchant marine were the primary source of additional labor for navies. Perhaps the most important difference between civilian and military recruitment was that the former relied primarily on economic incentives, whereas the latter relied primarily on legal incentives, especially during wartime.

I have been studying Spanish shipbuilding and seafarers in the early modern period for some years now, focusing on the sixteenth and seventeenth centuries. Oddly enough, Spain is not usually considered among Europe's seafaring powers, though the global Spanish empire depended on seaborne trade, communication, and defense for more than three centuries. My current research deals with Spanish galley service in the Mediterranean, based on newly restored registers in the archive of the Naval Museum in Madrid.[2] The officers, sailors, soldiers, and oarsmen arrived on the galleys for a variety of reasons. Examples from their experiences and those of sailors on oceangoing vessels form a major part of this essay. The argument also draws on fifteen studies about European seafarers in various parts of the world from 1570 to 1870,[3] and another recent collection devoted to seafarers' lives, though not all of the authors deal with enlistment.[4]

To establish a framework to consider the many modes of maritime enlistment, one helpful approach is a lengthy philosophical article by Scott

Anderson that discusses the concept of coercion from St. Thomas Aquinas to the present. Among other issues, Anderson considers the extent to which coercion or attempted coercion can influence a decision to act, and how that decision relates to free will.[5] In other words, if an individual decides to act based on some degree of positive or negative coercion, to what extent can that act be considered voluntary? Such questions have engaged philosophers and ethicists much more than historians, but it is useful to be aware of them in studying maritime enlistment, in part because the degree of free will in the decision to enlist could easily affect an individual's subsequent experiences and behavior at sea.

To keep in mind the full range of reasons that men and boys went to sea, this essay will consider the various influences on maritime enlistment along the same spectrum, beginning with the positive and ending with the negative. The discussion will fall under several general headings, although some overlap is unavoidable: Proximity to the Sea; Family Traditions; Economic Incentives; Legal Requirements; and Beyond the Law. A brief conclusion will gather the various threads of the argument together. The examples will focus primarily on Europe, in the hope that European patterns over several centuries can suggest questions and issues of relevance to governments as well as individuals trying to crew vessels in other times and places.

Proximity to the Sea

The most obvious positive incentive for going to sea was geographical location. It is reasonable to assume that a population living on or near a coastline would develop a seafaring tradition. Portugal faced the Atlantic Ocean, with numerous ports large and small, and drew on virtually every region for its seafaring population.[6] In northeastern North America along the Atlantic coast, seafaring was an essential part of local economies in early colonial times. Daniel Vickers noted that all of the sailors from the region grew up no more than five miles from the sea.[7] Nonetheless, geography was not destiny. Norway, for example, has an extensive coastline and depended on the sea for trade and communication in the early modern period, but after the Middle Ages foreign shippers and crews dominated Norwegian trade and fishing.[8] Finland has an extensive coastline on the Gulf of Bothnia, but a very small number of ports. Farther south, although the Southern Netherlands included the major port of Antwerp, the local population was not known for seafaring in the early modern period.[9] Even Iceland, surrounded by the sea and with a population heavily dependent on fish for food, relied on outsiders to supply the fish and provide seaborne transport. Only the northwest coast of Iceland had a seafaring tradition before 1800.[10] In short, geographical proximity did not necessarily induce a population to develop a seafaring tradition.[11]

One reason is that agricultural productivity was so low in the early modern centuries that the vast majority of Europeans had to work the land to provide enough food to survive. Even in coastal areas with a strong seafaring tradition, the percentage of the population earning a living from the land was nearly always much larger than the seafaring population. That was also true in colonial New England, where many seafarers began and ended their working lives as farmers.[12] In another example, Spain has extensive coastlines on the Bay of Biscay, the Mediterranean Sea, and the Atlantic Ocean. Nonetheless, the men listed in an official registry of mariners in 1740 comprised less than 1 percent of the population of the coastal provinces, most of them in the port towns, and an even smaller percentage of the total Spanish population.[13]

On the other hand, limited coastlines did not prevent some areas from developing a robust seafaring tradition. The Holy Roman Empire was largely landlocked, but the active ports in the German states on the Baltic and the North Sea linked the empire as a whole to seaborne trade and fisheries and attracted sailors from surrounding regions as well.[14] Some sailors from inland areas of the empire may have been attracted to seafaring because they lacked sufficient access to farmland; others may have viewed life at sea as a more exciting prospect than farming or as a surer way to make a living. In short, the incentives—both positive and negative—of geographical location cannot fully explain why men went to sea, though they undoubtedly played a role in many individual decisions.

Family Traditions

Another obvious example of a positive incentive for going to sea was family tradition. For residents of coastal areas, a career at sea would have been a logical choice for men and boys, generation after generation. Presumably, many could not have imagined another way to make a living and gladly followed their fathers, uncles, and brothers to sea. We should realize, however, that not every male in every generation would have been suited or attracted to a life at sea. Would unwilling boys have nonetheless been persuaded to go to sea by their families? The degree to which family expectations and pressures can be considered coercive is open to argument. Reluctant maritime recruits may have followed family tradition without considering that they were being coerced to do so. Scott Anderson's discussion of philosophical debates about coercion rules out "by stipulation, such things as mere disapproval, emotional manipulation, or wheedling."[15] Those very attitudes and behaviors, however, are favored weapons in the emotional arsenal of family relations. Anderson himself acknowledges that coercion "seems also to be an indispensable technique in the rearing of children."[16] Historians looking at family traditions of seafaring should consider that emotional coercion—both positive and negative—may have influenced some individual decisions to go to sea, and we cannot assume that all such decisions were made with a full heart.

One of my recent projects dealt with a Spanish armada dispatched in 1581–84 to fortify the Strait of Magellan and drive pirates and interlopers from Brazil.[17] King Philip II formed the armada after Francis Drake's peacetime raids in the Americas and his own successful claim to the vacant throne of Portugal. The armada was designed to prevent other opportunists from following Drake's example and to demonstrate the king's resolve to defend Portuguese Brazil as well as Spanish territories in the Americas. The commander of the Armada of the Strait, Diego Flores de Valdés, was a nobleman from Asturias on Spain's northwest coast and a member of a distinguished seafaring clan. The head of the clan, Pedro Menéndez de Avilés, had ousted the French from La Florida in 1565 as the capstone event in a career at sea. Flores had served with distinction in that encounter, and an array of nephews, brothers, sons, and in-laws of the Menéndez clan enlisted to serve in Flores's armada in 1581. There is no question that family tradition was a positive factor in their enlistment, perhaps the most important factor. The disproportionate number of Asturians in the armada, and their family relations, are not apparent from their names alone, but the career trajectories of individual men, as well as their marriages and other documented interactions, emphasize the importance of familial connections. Pedro Sarmiento de Gamboa, who accompanied the armada as the governor-designate of the colony he hoped to plant at the Strait of Magellan, wrote lengthy complaints to the king about the horde of Asturians who were loyal to Flores and wanted to destroy plans for the colony. It is easy to dismiss his complaints, because Sarmiento accused nearly everyone of turning against him at one point or another. Nonetheless, the horde of Asturians was real, and they undoubtedly had both geographical and familial incentives to enlist.

Virtually all of the 722 mariners recruited for the expedition came from a seafaring tradition, but those not connected to the Menéndez clan were difficult to recruit. Although the destination of the armada was not made public, everyone in southwestern Spain seemed to know that it was going to the Strait of Magellan. The terrors of sailing in the South Atlantic were well known to the maritime community, and there were other disadvantages as well. An ordinary voyage to New Spain (Mexico) or Tierra Firme (South America) would have provided the men with an opportunity to engage in minor trade on their own account, but the Armada of the Strait had a purely military and diplomatic function, with few opportunities for profit. Moreover, given Drake's raids and rumors of other fleets being sent from England and France, the armada would almost certainly encounter enemies. Some may have viewed the possibility of encountering enemies in a positive light; if they distinguished themselves in battle, they could earn royal favor and advance in rank and pay. Overall, however, the officers of that particular armada had to work hard to recruit sufficient sailors and soldiers, despite seafaring traditions.

Like Spain, many other states benefited from geographical location and family traditions in recruiting sailors and other maritime workers. In Portugal, the crown relied on family networks to provide shipbuilders and seafarers generation after generation. During the period of Habsburg rule (1580–1640), the crown rewarded the families of pilots, masters, and officers with social benefits, which tended to reinforce family traditions of seafaring.[18] Similarly, in the Netherlands' provinces of Holland, Zeeland, Friesland, Groningen, and the Wadden Islands, an internal labor market for sailors focused on maritime communities with long-term relationships between sailors and employers. This internal market, based on established familial and other networks that were more or less closed to outsiders, dominated the important posts in the whaling industry, the navy, and Dutch trade to the East and West Indies. In the big cities of Holland and Zeeland, family traditions among the permanent population presumably played a role in maritime recruitment as well. Still, those cities were part of what is often called the external market for maritime recruitment, dominated by foreigners from the Germanies, Scandinavia, and elsewhere. Sailors in the external market signed on mostly for short-hauls in northwest Europe, in part because they were largely excluded from the internal market that controlled longer assignments in the navy and overseas trade.[19]

Geography and family also played a role in maritime enlistment in the British Isles. Peter Earle found that nearly three-quarters of the sailors in the late seventeenth and early eighteenth centuries whose origins are known came from coastal areas, including London and the Thames estuary, and he assumed that the sailors were embedded in local and familial networks connected with the sea.[20] In New England, family traditions of seafaring continued from colonial times into the nineteenth century, though the percentage of outsiders increased over time as the merchant fleets grew in size.[21] Even where local and family traditions were strong, however, we cannot assume that the choice of a life at sea was entirely voluntary for every individual, for the reasons discussed above.

Economic Incentives

For the majority of men and boys who went to sea, economic incentives both positive and negative were also an important part of the decision to enlist. Such incentives covered a wide range of situations. Relatively high wages or profit-sharing contracts were traditional methods of attracting officers and sailors to the sea in many venues.[22] Even in the late nineteenth century, some 20 percent of the crews on Finnish ships deserted in foreign ports, presumably to seek higher wages than they could obtain in Finland.[23] Two centuries earlier, the Dutch Republic was already famous for attracting foreign sailors with higher wages than they could earn at home.[24] In 1610, some 33,000 sailors, including foreigners, served on ships based in the Dutch Republic, attracted by the wages paid at the peak of Dutch seaborne trade.[25] In the Southern Netherlands and elsewhere, service in the merchant marine was nearly always better rewarded than in the navy. Even allowing for added benefits in the navy such as health insurance, sailors in the merchant marine earned wages that have been called "remarkably high" when the Ostend Company and other mercantile ventures flourished in the late seventeenth and early eighteenth centuries.[26] The Dutch East India Company (VOC) also hired maritime laborers in China, Bengal, Surat, and elsewhere, many of them to serve in intra-Asian trade but some for voyages back to Europe.[27] Like the European sailors, they signed multiyear contracts as free laborers, but once under contract they were often subject to more violent and arbitrary treatment than their European counterparts.[28]

The British East India Company (EIC) also recruited a limited number of Chinese mariners in the nineteenth century for voyages to England, despite legal prohibitions by the Qing government.[29] Some European states also tried to thwart market forces by barring mariners from emigrating, especially in wartime. England issued such prohibitions from the late sixteenth century.[30] Norway did the same in the mid-seventeenth century to prevent Norwegian sailors from moving to the Dutch Republic to seek higher wages and avoid conscription.[31] In the most severe case, the Tokugawa shogunate in seventeenth-century Japan prohibited all of its subjects from leaving the country, on pain of execution.[32] Not surprisingly, men who emigrated to serve on foreign ships despite legal prohibitions were afraid to return home and face punishment. In short, although higher wages or long-term contracts provided positive economic incentives for going to sea, there could be negative consequences in taking advantage of such incentives.

If higher wages pulled some men toward the sea, poverty surely pushed others in that direction. Discussing economic motives solely in terms of "pull" or "push" factors is misleading, however, as is the notion that poverty accounted for the recruitment of most common sailors. In colonial New England, for example, sailors came from a range of economic situations.[33] Moreover, it is not clear that maritime enlistment was always a good economic choice for a poor man. There may have been other opportunities for employment that kept him closer to home and family, albeit in a miserable situation. Even if a poor man went to sea, enlistment did not necessarily end his poverty. Research has shown that about 87 percent of sailors based in the major port of Antwerp in 1584–85 "were too poor to pay taxes," and the wage gap between captains and crews was wide on merchant vessels as well as navy ships throughout the early modern period.[34] Some philosophers use the notion of a 'baseline' state of affairs in considering the degree of coercion at play in making a decision. In other words, they consider an individual's situation prior to a decision to act.[35] For maritime enlistment, would an individual be better off economically if he enlisted? Would he be worse off if he did not enlist? Would his economic situation remain essentially the same, whether or not he decided to go to sea? In looking at economic factors in maritime recruitment, historians would do well to ask those questions.

Other factors besides an individual's situation should also be considered in examining economic influences. For example, despite widespread poverty in the Southern Netherlands, the population was simply too small to provide sufficient sailors for civilian and military vessels in the early modern period, because much of the population had to work the land. Scholars estimate that only about one-third of the men required for the navy in the Southern Netherlands were locally recruited. The rest of them came from outside the area—as close as Holland and as far away as Scandinavia—and the outsiders tended to be the best sailors.[36]

In late sixteenth-century England, a rising population and increased competition for employment is assumed to have facilitated recruitment for both the navy and the merchant marine. Poverty in inland areas drove some men and boys to coastal areas to seek work, adding to the maritime labor pool and making maritime recruitment easier—the classic "push" mechanism. When conditions for the poor improved in the late seventeenth century, recruitment for the sea reverted to its traditional coastal venues.[37] The overall picture was somewhat different in Scotland, which had mostly small ports except for Glasgow. Recruitment for seafaring tended to be local, based on geographic and economic factors, without much long-distance migration of potential mariners, though recruits came from farther inland with the growth of trade and population in the eighteenth century. If smaller ports had more ships and men than they needed, it was common for Scots to shift among fishing, crofting, whaling, and the merchant marine, rather than migrating. Overall, that meant that service at sea in Scotland relied on casual labor, rather than a dedicated maritime labor pool, subject to the rules of supply and demand.[38]

Depending on time and place, the relative importance of various economic incentives for enlisting—both positive and negative—undoubtedly varied. In my research, the wages offered to potential crews on sailing ships and free men serving on galleys were higher in wartime than in peacetime, and other conditions affected the labor market as well. The 1581–84 Armada of the Strait is particularly relevant here. It was pulled together at the same time that Spain's transatlantic trade was approaching a peak, with some two hundred ships at sea simultaneously. According to Pierre Chaunu, the Armada of the Strait stretched the technical and logistical capabilities of Spain to the utmost.[39] The crown had to offer higher monthly wages to persuade men to enlist, and even so, recruiters found it impossible to sign up enough men voluntarily. In desperation, royal officials resorted to conscription, discussed below, which was very rare in Spanish maritime history.[40]

A similar range of positive and negative economic incentives also affected Spanish maritime recruitment in the Mediterranean. Although active warfare between Spain and the Ottoman Empire greatly diminished after the Battle of Lepanto in 1571, the Spanish crown still maintained several galley squadrons in the Mediterranean. In fact, they reached their peak in about 1575, comprising some 150 vessels and upward of 21,000 men.[41] By then, most of the galley oarsmen were slaves (mostly Muslims), prisoners of war, or convicted criminals, who will all be discussed later. However, the officers, sailors, and soldiers, known collectively as the *gente de cabo* (people in command), were free men recruited through a combination of geographic, familial, and economic incentives. Men from noble families formed a notable segment of the free men on Spanish galleys. After Lepanto, the government decided that it would be advantageous to recruit more noblemen to serve as galley captains, given the extraordinary challenges of keeping order on board as well as encouraging the best performance from all hands. Noblemen, raised from birth as leaders, were thought to be naturally suited for such command.[42] By all accounts, some Spanish noblemen fulfilled their duty to the crown by serving on the galleys willingly and with distinction, certainly until Lepanto. Thereafter, however, many of their number seem to have decided that the disadvantages of service on the galleys far outweighed the benefits. According to one classic critique, serving as a galley captain challenged not only a nobleman's abilities as a leader, but also "his finances, his sense of honor, and perhaps even his soul."[43]

In deciding whether to serve on the galleys, a nobleman had to consider the same cost-versus-benefit analysis that faced a man from an impoverished family. Given his current situation, would be he better or worse off if he enlisted? Would he be better or worse off if he failed to enlist? In the late sixteenth century, to encourage more noblemen to serve on the galleys rather than some other venue, the Spanish government decided to use economic inducements. In a series of debates in the Galley Committee (Junta de Galeras) of the Council of War (Consejo de Guerra) in 1584, Philip II's councillors proposed a sizeable increase in the basic pay of galley captains, both noble and nonnoble. They reasoned that this would attract more noblemen to serve and eliminate the need to pay galley captains large supplements for exemplary service.[44] The incentives were not entirely positive, however. Noblemen who did not serve the crown in some desired capacity—or send their sons to do so—could not expect to be rewarded. Retaining royal favor was crucial to the prospects of a nobleman's immediate family and even his entire lineage. If the sovereign withheld that favor, it could have a very negative impact on the chances of good marriages for the young females in the family and the career ambitions of the males.

The Spanish crown's strategy to attract more noblemen to the galleys seems to have been successful in the long term. Noblemen represented a significant proportion of the men serving on the galleys as free wage earners in the mid- to late seventeenth century.[45] Of the 373 men whose records are legible, 142 (or 38 percent) were noblemen, designated by the honorific "Don" before their names and other indications of high status.[46] Among the 142 noblemen, 47 served as galley captains, or 59 percent of all the captains listed from 1649 to 1681.[47] It is noteworthy that a 30-year-old son of one of the most illustrious families in Spain—the ducal house of Medina Sidonia—served on the galleys for a year in the late seventeenth century. The unexpected death of his older brother forced him to return home and assume the title, or he might have made a career of it. Other noble lineages also staked their claims to continued royal favor by serving on the galleys, though it is not clear whether all of the individuals involved undertook that service gladly. Even more interesting, the noblemen serving as galley captains received no higher compensation than their nonnoble counterparts, at least in their initial postings, and exemplary service still earned bonuses for captains of whatever social status. In England, noblemen who served as naval officers usually disdained the commoners in their ranks.[48] That attitude presumably existed to some extent in Spain as well. However, the government's decision to attract and retain competent galley captains by positive economic incentives cut across the divide between nobles and nonnobles and may have encouraged better acceptance of the latter by their social superiors.

Moving toward negative economic coercion, the Spanish government often pressured men to reenlist when it owed them money. In the late sixteenth century, government finances were stretched to the limit. This often meant that the sailors, soldiers, and officers serving the crown at sea were not paid in a timely fashion, and sometimes they were not paid at all during a voyage, apart from their rations. Returning sailors often had to petition the House of Trade (Casa de la Contratación) in Seville, or the government in Madrid, to collect their back pay, and many of them lacked the resources to do so effectively. Their main recourse was to reenlist, so that they could collect another enlistment advance on their wages and receive daily rations of food and drink. That was certainly the situation for the 800 men who returned with the Armada of the Strait in 1584. Their rations ceased the day they arrived back in Spain and were dismissed from service, and most of them had not been paid for the duration of the three-year voyage. In September 1584, the president of the House of Trade wrote that men were roaming the streets of Seville in angry groups, demanding their wages.[49] In response, King Philip told the officials to offer them reenlistment, so that they could collect rations while they waited to be paid the monies owed them. Men who enlisted under those circumstances, one could argue, were economically coerced. Those who did not reenlist—the majority of the returnees—were not necessarily worse off, however. They presumably would be paid eventually, and in the meantime they were free to pursue other opportunities. In 1584, there were many opportunities for experienced sailors in the transatlantic merchant fleets. Moreover, rebellion in the Netherlands and other military actions in Europe provided ample opportunities for seaborne soldiers as well.[50]

Naval officers faced a more complicated choice. Those who had ambitions to advance in royal service found it to their advantage to reenlist if the government owed them money. Like the sailors and soldiers, the officers who had served in the Armada of the Strait petitioned for the wages owed them when they returned, but the government had little cash on hand. It was not immediately clear when they might be paid, and there was a long line of suppliants ahead of them. In 1586, at least a dozen of the officers from the Armada of the Strait signed on for service in the Indies fleets in exchange for part of the monies owed them and the promise to receive the balance in the near future.[51] Though economic coercion played a role in their decision to reenlist, presumably they had decided that they were better off returning to sea duty than continuing to wait for reimbursement. Moreover, they furthered their careers in royal service by doing so.

Other sorts of economic influences are more difficult to document than ambition or poverty, but they nonetheless provided incentives for men to go to sea. For example, some men may have signed on for naval service to please a powerful patron. In southwestern Spain, the ducal house of Medina Sidonia was responsible for raising crews for royal ships in times of peace as well as war. When government recruiters signed up men in the area, the ducal house often paid the advance on their wages, to be reimbursed by the crown later, and tacitly took responsibility for overseeing the welfare of the men's families during their absence at sea.[52] Local men may well have enlisted as a way to reinforce the patron-client relationship that linked them to the powerful house of Medina Sidonia.

Other recruits in various times and places may have signed up for service at sea to escape burdensome financial or familial obligations, as well as to better their economic situation. A particularly interesting dynamic occurred among slaves who went to sea in North America. In the eighteenth century, some slave owners essentially leased their slaves to seagoing merchants, who were always short of good hands. Some slaves escaped during those voyages, and the mere experience of life at sea weakened the psychological bond between them and their owners.[53] After the American Revolution, some southern slaves fled to the north where slavery was abolished, others fled to the sea, and many slave owners stopped leasing out their slaves for seafaring, a pattern that was especially strong in the Chesapeake region. Nonetheless, black sailors continued to go to sea, and seafaring rermained a crucial economic resource for free blacks and their families in the northeast as late as the aftermath of the Civil War.[54]

Over time in some maritime labor markets, recruitment by individual merchants and captains was replaced by the use of brokers or middlemen who provided crews on demand for both commerce and official navies. In the nineteenth century, brokers or middlemen came to dominate the recruitment of sailors in England, for example, and they flourished in other labor markets as well. Many of the brokers ran boardinghouses in port towns for sailors between voyages. The men who lived under the patronage of such brokers could benefit by being assigned to good berths at sea, but they could also run up debts that kept them in a kind of servitude.[55] Moreover, they often had to lodge at the broker's boardinghouse to get an assignment at all.[56] In sum, economic influences in maritime recruitment occurred in many forms, both positive and negative.

Legal Requirements

The same can be said about the legal framework for maritime recruitment. One positive example was the temporary immunity from criminal prosecution that the Portuguese crown granted common sailors who were willing to go to India in the sixteenth and seventeenth centuries.[57] Moving toward negative legal influences, a man might go to sea to escape criminal or civil prosecution, though such cases are often difficult to document unless the individual wrote some sort of memoir or autobiography.[58] Official legal pressure or coercion in its various forms is much easier to document, simply because it was carried out by the state or its surrogates. Although such coercion was most often used for naval service, it was linked very closely with trade, because both the men sailing on commercial vessels, and the vessels themselves, were often commandeered for state service when the need arose.

First to consider was the legal requirement for mariners to register for future naval service—in other words, inscription rather than conscription, which will be discussed later. The classic form of inscription was developed in late seventeenth-century France under the government of Louis XIV and his talented minister Jean-Baptiste Colbert. Like many other powerful states, France recognized the need to regularize naval recruitment, instead of conscripting sailors from the merchant marine in wartime, which was an unpredictable and disruptive process. As a solution, Colbert instituted a mandatory system of registration or inscription (the *système des classes*) for sailors and petty officers. Once inscribed, individuals were liable to be called up for naval service when the government needed them. Inscription was required for male citizens—in other words, it was legally coerced—but there were rules about how long and how frequently individuals could be called up to serve in the navy.[59] In peacetime, they were free to return to the merchant marine, because the navy needed only about 2,000–3,000 men. The French system of mandatory inscription included about 43,000 individuals by the end of the seventeenth century, and perhaps 55,000 by 1789, which gave the government enviable flexibility in manning its warships.[60]

Spain also instituted a system of inscription for maritime labor, called the *matrícula*, but it differed from the French system in several ways.[61] First, there was a strong tradition in Spain that service in the navy should be voluntary. Moreover, some of the best Spanish sailors came from the fiercely independent Basque regions on the Bay of Biscay. Anything resembling legal coercion to serve in the navy provoked strong resistance.[62] As a result, during the Middle Ages and the Habsburg centuries (1500–1700), the government worked with local officials and military commanders to enlist crews by relying on geographical location, family traditions, and economic incentives to man naval vessels. Even with local officials in charge, there was an element of legal coercion involved, because each district was often assigned a specific number of sailors to recruit, based on the total number of households. Local officials then recruited (and presumably sometimes pressured) the men to enlist. When military commanders were in charge, economic incentives were more often used to encourage enlistment. However, traditional methods became increasingly unreliable as Spain's global responsibilities grew. In 1605 and again in 1607, the government ordered the registration of all mariners in the Basque regions, but the effort met with such outrage from local residents and officials that the orders were rescinded. Then in 1625 the government initiated a system of registration for all maritime labor, which would have functioned somewhat like the later French system, except that inscription was voluntary. Mariners were encouraged to register with local officials and to let them know when they planned to be absent. In exchange, they would receive an attractive list of benefits, including exemption from arrest for debt, freedom from the billeting of troops and government officials, and preferential treatment at sea over nonregistrants on both merchant and naval vessels.[63] Despite the promise of these and other benefits, almost no one signed up, and the effort was quietly abandoned. For the rest of the seventeenth century, the government continued to rely on levies run by local officials and recruitment by naval commanders to man its ships, aided by financial inducements and moral suasion. Abroad, officials hired foreign vessels and crews (as long as they were Catholic or claimed to be), many of them from Genoa, Naples, Ragusa (modern Dubrovnik), and Malta.[64]

In the early eighteenth century, with the accession of the Bourbon dynasty, the Spanish government began a concerted effort to exercise more centralized authority. For naval recruitment, that meant repeated attempts to induce all maritime laborers to register, or matriculate; all of the efforts failed. Although the government remained committed to the ideal of voluntary registration, officials finally acknowledged that no purely voluntary system could succeed. A royal decree of February 9, 1737 once again ordered local officials to establish a marine registry of all the sailors and shipwrights in their districts, including foreigners of the Catholic faith who were willing to settle in Spain. Whereas registration remained voluntary, the men had little choice but to comply. Virtually all maritime activities, including ocean fishing and commerce, became the exclusive preserve of those willing to register and thereby agree to serve the crown when the need arose. In July 1738 the king ordered naval commanders and bureaucrats to see that registered mariners were "treated with sweetness and good form, and that the strictest orders be issued to captains and senior officers to very particularly fulfill their duties in seeing that ships' officers lay aside the rigor with which they customarily treat mariners."[65] It would be naïve to believe that official policies were always followed, but the royal decree nonetheless accorded the men more respect than we might assume, especially when harsh discipline was becoming the norm in most European navies. For example, Peter Earle mentions "the reported savagery of the [British] navy of the 1790s," compared to the "brisk paternalism" of the Commonwealth navy in the mid-seventeenth century.[66]

With a long list of benefits and blandishments to make registration more palatable, the 1737 decree finally succeeded in establishing a marine registry in Spain, despite initial problems. In the first few years officials registered some 39,000 men and boys in 300 ports and estimated that there were 3,500 more in the Basque regions, which remained apart from the national registry. Basques continued to serve in the navy with distinction, but on their own terms. A revised set of rules for the marine registry in 1751 defined the system for the rest of the century. By 1775, the *matrícula* included some 47,000 men, and in the 1790s some 65,000, all technically inscribed on a voluntary basis. Although the Spanish system of inscription clearly involved a degree of legal and economic coercion, it remained more voluntary than its French counterpart.

Farther along the spectrum toward negative legal coercion was conscription, or mandatory enlistment, with penalties for failure to comply. When mariners in a national registry, such as those in France and Spain, were called up for naval service, they were technically being conscripted—generally from the merchant marine. Their prior inscription and the legal guarantees that pertained thereto set the system apart from simple conscription without such prior guarantees. Nonetheless, once an individual on a registry was called to naval service, he was subject to serious punishment if he failed to appear or deserted, along with the possible loss of the benefits that his registration had provided. In the Spanish example, only those who had been inscribed in the marine registry for thirty years without desertion from naval service could collect retirement benefits.

In many other European navies, conscription without prior inscription was the norm, due to the inability to recruit sufficient volunteers. This was especially common in periods with low population growth and more attractive employment opportunities in the merchant marine. For example, the small number of career officers and sailors in the Danish navy was supplemented by conscription in wartime, and Danish sailors were also legally barred from serving in foreign navies.[67] Forced enlistment might also occur in the merchant marine. In the second half of the sixteenth century, Portuguese merchant ships going to India often had to resort to forced recruitment with or without legal guarantees to fill out the crews, as the government periodically did for naval vessels.[68] Naval service nearly always paid worse than mercantile service, and the gap widened in wartime, when merchant shipping often raised wages to attract crews.[69] An individual had limited options in such circumstances. He could sign on to a merchant vessel and hope it departed before government agents arrived to demand his service. He could flee his home country altogether. He could sign on and then desert if the opportunity arose, despite the risk of dire legal consequences. Or he could simply accept his fate and serve as a conscript, although the circumstances of his enlistment would presumably have made him a less willing sailor than his voluntary counterparts.

Given wartime exigencies, legal coercion in the form of conscription was often combined with physical coercion or "impressment." As mentioned above, a state might rely on brokers and labor agents, known as "crimps," to enlist crews. They in turn often hired so-called press gangs who physically compelled or impressed men and boys to sign up. Whether the legal coercion occurred before a man enlisted, through a decree of conscription, or after he had been physically coerced to sign up (through impressment), his enlistment was legally binding. England tried unsuccessfully to establish a maritime registry at the beginning of the eighteenth century but fell back on impressment as the most efficient means to enlist crews.[70] When a man or boy accepted an advance on his wages, known as "taking the king's shilling," either voluntarily or through force, he became liable for serious punishment should he subsequently desert.[71] Scholars working on the British navy generally accept that impressment, including the use of press gangs, was standard practice for enlisting crews in wartime.[72] That, in Peter Earle's words, "explains why sailors took such pains to avoid the press."[73] They knew that impressment, however legal it might be, took away their freedom of action and likely forced them to take a cut in pay as well. In short, impressment exemplified legal, economic, and physical coercion at the same time, all of which fell toward the negative end of the coercive spectrum.

Impressment was not standard practice everywhere, even in the absence of a system of marine registration. In the Dutch case, according to Karel Davids,

> The Dutch navy never resorted to impressment. In times of acute need, the authorities chose to attract additional labor by offering bounties, introducing wartime wage increases, imposing temporary embargoes on merchant shipping, whaling or privateering, or recruiting fixed numbers of men by private ship owners (under threat of embargoes) rather than outright coercion.[74]

Despite these claims by Davids, embargoes and legal threats could justifiably be considered "outright coercion" in a legal and economic sense. In the Spanish case, impressment was never the norm but it did occur under extreme circumstances. For example, in filling out crews for the twenty-three ships of the Armada of the Strait in the summer of 1581, some 280 of the 2,408 men and boys in the armada were forcibly reassigned from the returning Indies fleets and were held in local jails until the armada sailed.[75]

With regard to the galleys, the recruitment of oarsmen evolved over time. In the late medieval centuries, Mediterranean galley fleets in a number of states were crewed by free men, some responding to economic pressures both positive and negative, and others serving as citizen conscripts in times of need. During the sixteenth century, the oarsmen began to include more unfree men and boys. After the Battle of Lepanto (1571), the trend toward unfree oarsmen increased,[76] and many studies of the maritime labor market exclude galleys and their oarsmen from consideration. In discussing Louis XIV's galleys, for example, Jacques Le Goff notes that, "With the exception of the officers and petty officers, it is difficult to think of these as a normal part of the maritime labour force."[77] For the purposes of this essay, however, the enlistment of galley oarsmen provides a classic example of legal and physical coercion.

By the late sixteenth century, virtually all of the oarsmen (*galeotes*) on Spanish galleys in the Mediterranean were coerced into their situation with clear legal justification: capture in a "just war," purchase as slaves, or conviction as criminals (*forzados*). The criminals served for a fixed term; none of the 1,000 or so records I have noted so far involved a sentence longer than ten years. Even the men convicted "for life" or "in perpetuity" were released after serving ten years if they were still alive.[78] The available records do not allow for a full statistical analysis of the survival rates on the galleys. It is interesting to note, however, that of the 440 convicted criminals whose complete records I have noted, some 89 percent survived to the end of their sentences.[79] Galley slaves may truly have served for life, or until they were deemed unfit to continue, but I have not yet examined their registers in detail. A few free oarsmen, often from Sardinia or Sicily, might sign on voluntarily. Known as *buenas boyas* (a corruption of the Italian for "good will"), they received wages as well as better food. The unfree oarsmen earned no compensation for their labor except food and clothing and were collectively considered slaves of the crown. Moreover, they were held at their posts by force, generally chained to the benches on which they rowed while the vessel was at sea. On shore, carefully supervised by soldiers, they washed their clothes and carried out various assigned duties.

The French galley fleet under Louis XIV in the late seventeenth century had similar characteristics.[80] The Ottoman Empire and its subsidiary states in North Africa also used galley squadrons in the early modern period, and a cursory survey suggests that the Ottomans manned their vessels in much the same way as France, Spain, and the various Italian states. Galleys did not play a major role in the fleets of other European powers, though various states experimented with their use in the early modern period. Because of the reasons for their service and the conditions under which they served, the enlistment of galley oarsmen from the late sixteenth century onward represented a more rigorous form of legal and physical coercion than did impressment.

Beyond the Law

At the extreme negative end of the coercive spectrum were the men and boys forced to labor at sea with no legal justification. They were captured and conveyed to ships simply because they were unlucky enough to be in the wrong place at the wrong time. In modern usage, we often refer to their capture as "shanghaiing" or "being shanghaied." The origin of the phrasing seems to date from the mid-nineteenth century, usually referring to the seizure of men and boys to serve on merchant ships going to the Far East. Force, threats of force, drugs, and/or alcohol often aided in their seizure, and they were generally treated harshly and set to work doing ships' maintenance and other onerous tasks if they were not suited to be sailors. The concept and the words "shanghaied" and "shanghaiing" have taken firm hold in popular culture in the West, featured in a film starring Charlie Chaplin (1915), a cartoon starring Mickey Mouse (1934), and more recently an episode of the animated television series *SpongeBob SquarePants* (March 9, 2001). The words and the concept continue to crop up from time to time in popular films and music. For the purposes of this essay, shanghaiing represents the most extreme form of negative coercion, compared to the voluntary and even enthusiastic decision to go to sea at the positive end of the spectrum. What set shanghaiing apart from the often violent practices attending impressment was the absence of state involvement or any sort of legal justification.

Conclusions

Throughout history, anyone involved in trade, as well as the leaders of states that used ships to defend their territories, fight their enemies, profit from overseas commerce, and project their power, had to concern themselves with the maritime world to some degree. For Europe during the early modern period, when trade and international rivalries expanded to encompass the world, maritime matters became crucial elements of business decisions and statecraft alike. In that evolving context, traditional sources of maritime labor often fell short of the needs of both commercial and military voyages. Whereas the private sector largely relied on economic incentives to attract ships' crews, governments could also rely on legal compulsion when the need arose. The unavoidable tension between public and private needs sometimes allowed individual mariners and seaborne soldiers to improve their lot when the demand for maritime labor exceeded the supply. More often than not, however, they were simply pawns in a game that was beyond their control.

By considering the spectrum of maritime enlistment from positive inducements to the most violent forms of physical coercion, we can gain valuable insights into maritime life in early modern Europe, which was inextricably linked to life on land. Those who enlisted because of positive incentives, local and family traditions, or hopes for economic betterment were presumably willing seafarers, easier to manage on board. By contrast, those who enlisted because they were compelled by legal or physical coercion would likely have required harsher discipline and closer supervision to carry out their assigned tasks.[81] In short, the circumstances of maritime enlistment had implications for the selection of officers, the size of crews, general conditions at sea, and other matters of concern to those in power, both in the private sector and in governments. This brief survey has raised various issues that characterized maritime enlistment in early modern Europe. It seems likely that some of the same issues characterized maritime enlistment in other times and places as well. By considering these issues, historians can understand a bit more about why human beings went to sea and what awaited them when they got there.

Chapter 2

Between the Company and Koxinga: Territorial Waters, Trade, and War over Deerskins

Adam Clulow and Xing Hang

In 1662, a grand embassy from Taiwan arrived in Ayutthaya in Siam. Dispatched by Zheng Chenggong, a famed Chinese maritime commander also known as Koxinga, it carried letters, lavish gifts, and, most importantly, news. Landing in the bustling port city, the ambassador announced the "scandalous surrender of the famous island Formosa" and its supposedly "unconquerable fort Zeelandia," which had fallen to Zheng troops just a few months earlier.[1] The arrival of the embassy opened another front in the ferocious commercial, diplomatic, and military struggle that was being waged between the Zheng maritime network and the Dutch East India Company (Verenigde Oostindische Compagnie or VOC) across East and Southeast Asia.

Both organizations had been drawn to Ayutthaya by the booming trade in deerskins, hundreds of thousands of which were shipped out each year from Southeast Asia to Japan. Alongside his tales of Dutch defeat, the ambassador was there to buy as many deerskins as he could find. Soon after the envoy's arrival, VOC officials received news of a clandestine shipment coming down the river intended for transport to Taiwan and then on to Japan. The company acted quickly, sending out its own boats to arrest these goods and hold them until Ayutthayan officials could reaffirm their monopoly rights to the skin trade within their borders, rights that had been formalized in a series of treaties signed between successive kings and Batavia. Any expectations that local authorities would side with the Dutch were dashed, however, when a large crowd of armed Chinese surrounded the VOC trading lodge, threatening to cut off the ears and noses of all inside "as had been done to the Dutch in Tayouan."[2] With the tacit consent of key officials within the court, the crowd proceeded to seize the captured skins, ignoring VOC complaints about the privileges guaranteed to the company by the crown.

Such episodes form one part of a much larger war that was fought across East and Southeast Asia between the two dominant maritime powers in the region: the Dutch East India Company based in Batavia and the Zheng maritime network headquartered in Taiwan after 1662.[3] In recent years, a wave of innovative scholarship by Tonio Andrade and others has made it clear just what a formidable adversary the Zheng network was for the Dutch East India Company.[4] Not surprisingly, the bulk of this work has focused on Taiwan, where long lines of soldiers and fleets of ships faced off against each other in an extended military campaign.[5] But while the island served as the central arena for this conflict, the struggle between the Zheng network and the VOC also spilled out, as Cheng Wei-Chung has shown in his groundbreaking 2013 monograph, across the region.[6] Like two massive tectonic plates, the company and the Zheng collided at multiple points distributed widely across East and Southeast Asia. For rulers across the region, the presence of two maritime powers with ambitions to dominate the same markets presented clear opportunities. Koxinga and his successors offered new sources of revenue as well as a potential counterbalance against aggressive Dutch attempts to enforce monopoly rights over commodities like deerskins. But the ongoing conflict also presented significant hazards as a range of polities attempted to steer a precarious middle path between the company and the Zheng network, both of which possessed formidable naval resources and a readiness to use force to cut through potential difficulties.

This chapter explores how two Southeast Asian polities, Cambodia and Ayutthaya, navigated the rivalry between the Dutch East India Company and the Zheng network in the aftermath of the fall of Taiwan in 1662. Although neighbors, Cambodia and Ayutthaya were very different polities. The first was a weak state with a fractious government that made it vulnerable to outside intervention, the second a regional power under the control of an expansionist monarch, Narai (r. 1656–88). They faced, however, a similar challenge: how to manage an escalating conflict that sprawled across sea-lanes, coastal waters, and port cities. In this chapter, we argue that a conflict between two maritime powers, the VOC and the Zheng network, triggered a process of legal improvisation and innovation on land as territorial rulers with limited naval resources sought to guard their interests by extending protection over ships, waters, and people. Such examples show that, even if they could not challenge the Zheng network and the VOC on the open ocean, local rulers retained a formidable set of legal weapons.[7] But, as we also demonstrate here, the use of these weapons could play out very differently: Cambodia was torn apart by both external and internecine conflict after an attack by Zheng allies on a VOC trading outpost, while Siam was able to weather the storm of a VOC naval campaign to emerge with new trading links in place.

Studying such conflicts pushes beyond the conventional Taiwan-centric frame to show the ways in which the competition between the VOC and the Zheng played out across the wider region. They also tell us something about how maritime space was shaped in the early modern period. As has been well documented, the sixteenth and seventeenth centuries saw the rise of new seaborne powers capable of projecting power across vast distances. But as we show here control over coastal waters and trade routes did not pass freely to these new powers. Instead, it became the product of an ongoing negotiation between territorial polities that retained a degree of influence over the waves, private merchants eager to find protection, and maritime enterprises that were compelled to navigate a complex jurisdictional seascape.

The Asian Deerskin Boom

Although deer had been hunted for millennia for their meat and hides, seventeenth-century Asia witnessed an unprecedented boom that turned deerskins into one of the most heavily traded commodities across the region.[8] Fueling this sprawling trade was a seemingly insatiable demand for deer leather in Tokugawa Japan, which had entered a prolonged period of stability and economic growth after decades of endemic warfare. Deer leather was vital to the production of various kinds of military equipment prized by Japan's warrior class. In comparison with other kinds of leather, deer leather was both soft and pliable, and therefore especially well suited for use in the fingers of archery gloves and the parts of samurai armor that rubbed against the skin. As Japan's urban population expanded, the locus of demand shifted from the samurai to a wider swathe of the population as the inhabitants of Edo, Osaka, and a host of castle towns rushed to purchase vast numbers of two-toed socks (*tabi*), coin purses (*hayamichi*), and other items made of deerskins.

Recognizing the lucrative nature of the exchange, the Dutch East India Company moved aggressively into this trade after it occupied part of Taiwan in 1624. In a good year, VOC administrators could ship over 100,000 deerskins from Taiwan, making this a reliable source of income in a world of tight margins.[9] With the surrender of its Taiwan hub in 1662, the company had to look elsewhere to make up for its lost supply. The result was that Siam and Cambodia, both of which had significant deer populations, became important supply sources.

While its push into these kingdoms escalated after 1662, the VOC had been active there for years. From the beginning, however, the company faced stiff competition from a range of groups. The first challenge came from Japanese merchants and migrants. One Dutch official complained that the "head of the Japanese [community] in Siam . . . has increased his wealth and strength greatly so that with his own or his associate's capital he can send out a junk with 1000 piculs of sappanwood and 50,000 deerskins to Japan."[10] An attempt to send an empty vessel to purchase all available skins was sabotaged when Japanese merchants purchased 160,000 deerskins, leaving only "few and bad" deerskins for their competitors.[11] In response to such episodes, company agents lamented that the Japanese monopolized the "top quality" goods, leaving them to buy up the "refuse."[12]

When maritime restriction edicts promulgated in Japan in the 1630s undercut the capacity of the Japanese community based in Southeast Asia to trade directly with the archipelago, Chinese merchants moved to fill the gap.[13] The VOC responded to such competition by deploying a standard template it had used for other commodities. At its center were monopoly agreements that were signed with local rulers handing over control of key goods. In Ayutthaya, for example, the Dutch concluded a series of agreements with successive kings in 1634, 1645, and 1646.[14] Although such agreements supposedly ceded monopoly rights over the deerskin trade, they proved highly porous in reality, opening up gaps that could be readily exploited by rival merchant groups and local officials.

While frustrating, such problems could be papered over as long as the company retained access to Taiwan and the infrastructure of hunters and deerskin traders it had built up there. Because of this, the surrender of Fort Zeelandia represented a double blow. The VOC not only relinquished a secure supply of deerskins; it also handed over a strategic gateway to the depots of Southeast Asia and the Indian Ocean to the one rival most capable of exploiting it, the Zheng network.[15] Its defeat on Taiwan came at a difficult time for the company, which was already contending with falling profits prompted by the decline of the silk-for-silver trade that had long formed the key dynamic underlying East Asian trade. For decades, China had supplied the majority of silk, which was exchanged for Japanese silver at Nagasaki, but draconian Qing maritime prohibitions, which included the evacuation of ports and islands along the southeastern Chinese coastline, severely curtailed exports.[16] Although the Dutch over time found effective substitutes in silk from Vietnam and India, the Tokugawa *bakufu* moved as well to restrict the flow of precious metals abroad.[17] This combination of factors meant that VOC profit margins in the Japan trade declined sharply in the 1660s compared with those of a decade earlier.[18] Within this overall context, Southeast Asian exports, especially deerskins, acquired an even greater significance. One place where the company saw an opportunity to replace lost supplies was Cambodia, where VOC agents pushed to secure monopoly rights over the trade.

The "Pirate" Piauwja

The company had a long-standing but difficult relationship with Cambodia. The VOC had established a Cambodian factory in 1636 but suspended operations after its factors there were attacked and killed in 1643.[19] Relations were reinstated in 1656 but soon collapsed in the spasm of violence that convulsed the country. The accession of a new king, Paramaraja VIII (Barom Reachea, r. 1658–72), with plans to expand foreign trade offered the promise of a fresh start and in 1665, three years after Taiwan changed masters, negotiations commenced aimed at producing a new treaty to regulate interactions and provide a basis for an ongoing VOC presence in Cambodia.[20] Negotiations centered on two predictable sticking points: monopoly concessions to the deerskin trade and rights to attack Zheng shipping sailing to and from Cambodia.

As it had done in Ayutthaya, the VOC insisted on an expansive concession in the form of full monopoly rights to the deerskin trade for twenty-five years, although its representatives later agreed to drop this to just twenty years.[21] The company demanded, moreover, the right to attack all Chinese junks sailing north of Cambodia. The desire for such a wide-ranging mandate was propelled by concern over the increasing spread of Zheng influence. Acting with the help of piratical groups, the Zheng network had established smuggling outposts off the coast of Guangdong Province before extending its operations into the Gulf of Tonkin and the South China Sea, with Zheng-sponsored merchants sailing to Cambodia in significant numbers. Equally worrying for Batavia, Zheng ships had started to aggressively enforce their own rights over maritime traffic in ways that looked strikingly similar to VOC practices. Besides trading on their own account, Zheng forces plundered ships caught without a pass and provided armed protection for those that had purchased one.[22] Given the expanding nature of the maritime threat, Duch officials were insistent that the Cambodian king give them full rights to attack Zheng and Zheng-affiliated vessels wherever they encountered them.

The company's demands placed the king and the court in a difficult position. Not surprisingly, they were reluctant to undercut a valuable source of income by allowing VOC ships such expansive rights to attack Chinese shipping. But Cambodian officials recognized as well that the company was in a state of open conflict with Zheng merchants and that the Dutch were determined to wage war along the trade routes connecting Cambodia with the wider region. Their solution was to carve out a secure maritime space in coastal waters. Rather than permitting such an expansive mandate for violence, the court decided the best way to respond was by designating a maritime belt where all shipping would be protected against VOC privateering by the king's authority. Similar tactics had been deployed in other parts of Asia, including in Japan where the Tokugawa shogun had designated a band of secure maritime space, vaguely defined, around the archipelago for the same basic purpose of curtailing maritime violence by Dutch vessels.[23] In the Cambodian case, these waters were defined with a relatively precise triangular designation, running from a promontory in the north, Cincotjagas (Cap Saint Jacques/Vũng Tàu), to two islands in the south and east, Poulo Condor (Côn Sơn) and P'Oubij (Hon Khoai), that constituted, Cambodian officials insisted, the "limits and boundaries of our realm."[24] Predictably, the two VOC officials tasked with the negotiations protested, explaining that "it does not seem within reason to us because those are distant, remote quarters and that according to our usual custom we never refrain from taking a prize, even if it is just outside the mouth of the river." Yet they had little choice but to accede, and the new treaty was signed on February 1, 1665.

The agreement generated immediate resistance from Chinese merchants trading in Cambodia. In a petition to the monarch, they argued that they had already invested considerable sums in that year's trade and hence must be granted at least one third of the deerskin trade.[25] At the same time, these traders insisted that the twenty-year monopoly should be scaled back to just ten years. In response, VOC officials mobilized to defend the bounds of their newly acquired monopoly. An immediate flashpoint presented itself in the form of two Chinese junks that were readying for departure with a cargo of deerskins. When Dutch officials attempted to inspect the cargoes of these vessels, they were prevented from doing so by the vessels' crews. In his diary, the local *opperhoofd* recorded the great "arrogance of the Chinese" who had, he explained, resisted the company's lawful attempts to claim total monopoly rights over the deerskin trade.[26]

The result was a precarious equilibrium in which neither the VOC nor the Zheng network could claim dominance. The VOC had a paper monopoly over the deerskin trade, but Chinese merchants retained a significant degree of access. At the same time, Dutch vessels could attack Zheng ships traveling to Cambodia but could not lie in wait in coastal waters where it was easiest to locate their prey. This arrangement proved fleeting, however, and within two years it had collapsed. The catalyst for this change was provided by the appearance of a powerful military force tied to the Zheng maritime network that threw the king's arrangements into disarray. In February 1667, a Chinese maritime commander named the "pirate Piauwja" (*rover Piauwja*) in VOC records and identified in Chinese sources as Xian Biao arrived in Cambodia with a force estimated at several hundred soldiers and sailors.[27] Although much is unknown, Chinese local gazetteers suggest that he was a native of the Leizhou Peninsula, on the extreme western end of Guangdong.[28] During the 1650s, he had joined forces with a local anti-Qing resistance movement based in the islands and ports along the littoral. There Piauwja remained until relentless attacks from Manchu forces forced him to flee with his allies across the border. Once in Tonkin, they took refuge with a Vietnamese warlord, whose protection gave Piauwja the opportunity to regroup by drawing refugees fleeing from the Qing evacuation into his depleted ranks. With this enlarged band, he ravaged the Gulf of Tonkin unchecked and seized several outposts on the island of Hainan.[29] These raids resulted in retaliation from authorities on both sides of the border. Qing forces moved against him, while the Dutch, acting in their capacity as allies of the Tonkinese court, impounded Piauwja's ships.[30] Under intense pressure, Piauwja and his adherents escaped to Taiwan, where they joined forces with Zheng Jing and became incorporated as a regular military division in his armies.

Given their background and experience, Piauwja and his men were a natural choice for Zheng Jing's southward push. Their arrival in Cambodia in 1667 was watched nervously by a small group of VOC officials led by Pieter Ketting who were based in an unfortified trading outpost with minimal military resources.[31] By contrast, the Cambodian king, Paramaraja VIII, enthusiastically welcomed Piauwja as a potential ally and appointed him head or *shahbandar* over the Chinese community.[32] In the unstable political environment of mid-century Cambodia, Piauwja's unattached contingent of experienced fighters presented a valuable weapon. Since the 1620s, Cambodia had been an arena of fierce rivalry between Cochinchina and Ayutthaya for influence over the throne. Cochinchinese immigrants, mostly convicts and soldiers, had begun to pour en masse into the Mekong River Delta on the Cambodian kingdom's eastern frontier, enticed by the promise of fertile land and with tacit encouragement from the Nguyễn lords at Huế. Paramaraja VIII had come to power in 1658 with Nguyễn backing, but had begun to bristle at the influence of his more powerful neighbor. More disturbingly for him, the settlers had started to form a separate power base organized around their main patron and protector, the crown prince Ramadhipati.[33] The arrival of Piaujwa presented a useful opportunity for the king to reassert his authority domestically and in external relations. He did so by authorizing a bloody assault on the Cochinchinese community, with Piauwja and his men massacring, according to Dutch accounts, as many as a thousand men, women, and children.[34]

If Piauwja was a weapon to be turned against the king's enemies, he also had his own grievances to pursue against the company. At first, it seemed as if he was only interested in a perceived debt owed to him, he claimed, as a result of a VOC naval blockade and the subsequent confiscation of his ships. Eager to defuse the situation, the company's chief official in Cambodia, Pieter Ketting, decided that some sort of bribe was necessary to ensure his outpost's security. When one of the king's advisers suggested that the Dutch give Piaujwa 2,000 taels, he responded with a counteroffer of 1,000 taels. Unwilling to accept such a low figure, Piauwja opted to raise the stakes by demanding six times Ketting's offer. As justification, he explained that he was owed a significant debt by a Chinese merchant based in the company's headquarters in Batavia and hence that any payment made in Cambodia could simply be extracted there. Refusing to hand over such a large sum, Ketting attempted to bribe several court officials who he hoped would intervene on the company's behalf. Instead, things quickly escalated as Piauwja seized a group of VOC personnel, who were only released when Ketting agreed to hand over 4,837 taels, a total that supposedly reflected the original debt owed to Piauwja. As this process was unfolding, a VOC ship, the *Schelvis*, arrived at the mouth of the river near the Cambodian capital. While the cannon mounted on the *Schelvis* might have swung the military equation in favor of the Dutch, the low water level meant that it was not possible to fire over the river's banks.

The king of Cambodia saw Piauwja as an ally. In fact, he was increasingly dependent on these Zheng partisans as the main source of support for his throne. But this was an ally over whom the king had little actual control. Although Cambodian officials had successfully banned violence between the company and the Zheng in their territorial waters, they proved unable to halt the use of force on land. On July 10, matters came to a head when Piaujwa launched an assault on the VOC outpost.[35] In the subsequent attack, Ketting was killed along with three servants, while another employee, a surgeon, died later of his wounds.[36] The company's remaining staff including Jacob van Wijckersloot, who would later produce a detailed report on the incident, fled into the nearby jungle where they sheltered nervously until they were able to reach the relative safety of the *Schelvis* a few days later.

For the Cambodian court, the attack proved disastrous, severing promising trading links with the Dutch East India Company while emboldening a volatile new political actor on the domestic scene. Eager to placate Batavia, the king attempted to wash his hands of responsibility and persuade the VOC to return to his lands. In service of this goal, he dispatched a remarkable document to Batavia dated October 28, 1667, just a few months after Piauwja's attack on the VOC lodge in July.[37] The letter began with an exaggerated expression of contrition with the king writing that "I cannot emphasize enough how sore my heart is" over the attack on the lodge. He swore that he would not rest until he had brought the attackers to justice. As proof of this good faith, Cambodian soldiers had arrested three VOC employees who had supposedly betrayed the company by defecting to Piauwja's side just before the attack. At the same time, the king claimed that he had "done justice" by executing Piauwja and six of his principal followers. Such actions were motivated, he insisted, by a desire for the Dutch to consider the king a "good friend" and to reestablish the trading relations that had been so violently severed by Piauwja's actions.

It was certainly true that three Dutch merchants were arrested—they turned up some years later in Batavia—but Piauwja's fate is far murkier.[38] Chinese local gazetteers reference him as a main instigator of raids along the Guangdong coast throughout the 1670s.[39] That Piauwja survived is not surprising as the king possessed limited military resources of his own. In fact, the evidence suggests that Piauwja's contingent continued to play a significant role in Cambodian politics for years after their arrival. In 1671, the king was assassinated by his nephew, an event that ushered in a new round of political turbulence. Piauwja's contingent supported a claimant to the throne against a rival backed by Cochinchina, and the two sides fought several inconclusive naval battles.[40] Over the same period, ships attached to Piauwja, and likely based on the Guangdong coast or Cambodia, conducted regular patrols of the South China Sea. They offered safe passage to Zheng commercial ships and engaged in a profitable exchange of products between Guangdong, Taiwan, and Southeast Asia on their own account.[41]

Even if it was not entirely accurate, the purpose of the king's 1667 letter was clear: to apologize for what had happened, to restore trade with the VOC, and to ensure that Dutch traders returned to Cambodian cities. The company did not prove sympathetic, however, and in 1670 the factory in Cambodia was finally shut down. Viewed as a whole, the Cambodian episode shows the dangers of a close embrace of Zheng affiliates. Such forces could serve as a valuable counterbalance to the Dutch and a useful weapon in the hands of local officials, but they could also add volatility to an already unstable domestic political situation. In the end, Paramaraja proved unable to navigate this rivalry. The result was not simply the loss of a potentially valuable trading connection with Batavia but also the kingdom's ultimate descent into chaos. For a weak polity like Cambodia, the rivalry between the VOC and the Zheng could prove disastrous, sparking external ruptures and internal dissent. In neighboring Siam, by contrast, the king and the court were able to navigate a fine line between the VOC and the Zheng maritime network, even as this rivalry threw up new questions that confounded easy resolution.

"Legal Subjects of the Realm"

In Siam, the VOC had worked for decades to wrest control over the deerskin trade by concluding binding agreements with successive kings.[42] Since such arrangements were never as effective or as complete as they appeared on paper, there was a perennial impetus to sign additional agreements. The accession of a new ruler, King Narai, in 1656 sparked a renewed negotiation over the company's deerskin monopoly. The result was a new treaty signed in 1659 giving the VOC the sole right to purchase deerskins and cowhides within Siamese borders.[43] While the monopoly in theory encompassed the full extent of the trade, it was undermined from the beginning. A key accelerant came in the form of an extended and hugely expensive military campaign conducted by the king's forces that required Narai to search for new sources of revenue beyond what the Dutch could provide.[44] In this environment, an alliance with Zheng merchants offered obvious advantages and a new ally who might help fill the crown's depleted treasuries.[45] Zheng ships had been trading with Siam since the 1650s, but relations intensified in 1662 when an envoy from Koxinga arrived with considerable fanfare.[46] The event marked an ominous turn for the Dutch, and VOC officials lamented what they saw as the humiliation of the company.[47] Even worse, Koxinga's ambassador was allowed to return with presents from the king and a full cargo of deerskins.

While the conflict between the Zheng and VOC followed familiar contours across the region, particular circumstances in Siam pushed it onto a different track. Rather than relying on foreign merchants to act as middlemen, Narai aimed to send his own ships to trade directly in Nagasaki, thereby securing a larger share of the profits of the deerskin trade.[48] It was an ambitious plan designed to circumvent two sets of competing merchants, but it required the king and the court to clear multiple hurdles. First, Narai needed to break from the unhappy pattern set by his predecessor, Prasat Thong, whose multiple attempts to reopen trading relations with Japan had been rejected because of questions of legitimacy stemming from the way he had originally come to power.[49] Second, someone had to actually crew these ships. According to VOC officials, the "Siamese cannot come themselves to Japan, but must use Moors and Chinese with the junks that they send there."[50] In this way, the court drew maritime labor from the well-established Persian and Chinese communities in Siam. A vessel that arrived in Nagasaki in August 1661 provides an example of the composition of a typical crew. According to the pass that it carried, which was issued by Dutch officials in Siam and subsequently recorded in Nagasaki, the ship was owned by Okphra Sinaowarat or Aqa Muhammad, the head of the Persian community in Siam. Its crew of seventy-seven mariners was drawn in part from this community with VOC sources listing twenty-three Persian sailors. The bulk of the crew, however, numbering fifty-four sailors in total, were Chinese.[51] Although it was not owned by the king and carried no Siamese sailors, the ship was nonetheless identified as a royal junk and it sailed under Narai's protection with part of the profits flowing directly to the throne.[52]

Such vessels show how Chinese mariners became the indispensable participants in these voyages. Their role was not simply as maritime labor. The presence of Chinese sailors made it easier for these vessels to be subsumed within the expansive category of *tōsen* or Chinese ships by Nagasaki officials. While the port was closed to a range of overseas groups like the Portuguese or the Spanish, it remained open to private Chinese merchants, who were permitted to trade in a non-official capacity.[53] But while the use of Chinese sailors made these voyages possible, it also opened up a new danger: that they could become targets in the company's wider maritime campaign against the Zheng network. As the conflict over Taiwan ramped up, the VOC was determined to attack Zheng shipping wherever such vessels were encountered. This desire to take action raised new questions about the ships from Siam. Were royal junks crewed by Chinese sailors, some of whom, the VOC suspected, might be tied to the Zheng, fair targets for capture and plunder? At first, the answer looked like it might be yes. In August 1661, a VOC vessel, the *Roode Hert*, seized a Siamese court junk in the "waters of Tonkin."[54] When questioned, Dutch officials presented multiple, often contradictory explanations as to why they had seized the vessel. The most believable was that the junk had been captured because it was "was manned by the Portuguese and Chinese, our open enemies."[55] Considering that later sources report just a handful of Portuguese slaves on board, it seems most likely that the assault had far more to do with the presence of the Chinese crew and hence the wider campaign against Zheng shipping.[56]

The seizure of the ship and the company's ongoing attempts to assert control over the deerskin trade triggered the angry response detailed at the opening of this chapter as more than 800 heavily armed Chinese merchants, sailors, and residents surrounded the VOC outpost.[57] For a while it looked as if the situation might escalate, as, for example, happened when Piauwja arrived in Cambodian territory, but eventually the crowd dissipated. In the aftermath of the *Roode Hert* incident, the king of Siam demanded compensation of 84,000 guilders from the company.[58] He also pressed the VOC to issue passes providing absolute guarantees of security for his own ships. Court officials insisted that these protective documents should be issued not only to crown junks, including two that would depart shortly for Japan, but also to Zheng-affiliated trading vessels.[59] For the VOC, issuing passes to Zheng shipping was out of the question. At the same time, company agents insisted that any Chinese mariners carried aboard royal junks must have deep roots in the country in the form of wives and children resident in Siam.[60] In this way, they attempted to slice up the Chinese population in Ayutthaya into different groups, allowing the king to draw maritime labor from a pool that stood outside Zheng influence. Only those junks with Chinese crewmembers with no Zheng affiliation could be protected by VOC sea passes.

While Siamese and VOC officials debated the fallout from the *Roode Hert*'s actions, the company's share of the deerskin trade in Siam continued to decline. There were fewer deerskins to buy and on the other end of the sea route, VOC market share in Nagasaki was increasingly under assault from Siamese crown junks arriving in Japan.[61] The situation prompted a response from Batavia, which decided it had to take action to shore up its monopoly rights over the deerskin trade and halt the king's push into Japanese markets. The *opperhoofd* in Siam, Enoch Poolvoet, was instructed to close the VOC factory there in preparation for a maritime campaign designed to force concessions from Narai. From November 1663 to February 1664, the company's ships sealed off part of the Chao Phraya River with the goal of seizing Siamese junks until the crown gave in to Dutch demands. The campaign culminated in the capture of one of the king's junks on its way back from Japan loaded with a rich cargo including a large quantity of Japanese copper.[62]

By June, the company was convinced it was in a sufficiently strong position to reopen negotiations, and a representative, Pieter De Bitter, was dispatched from Batavia with instructions to sign a new treaty. The subsequent talks centered on two familiar issues: the deerskin monopoly and the use of Chinese sailors. The company wanted an iron-clad monopoly over the trade: full purchasing rights but also the capacity to confiscate any deerskins found in non-VOC vessels. At the same time and bolstered by its successful demonstration of maritime might, Batavia was determined to halt the crown's ingress into the deerskin trade in Japan. Rather than prohibiting the practice outright, the company decided that the easiest way to do this was by making sure that the king could no longer rely on Chinese sailors to crew crown junks. In this way, such voyages would not be prohibited outright, but without access to a key labor source they would either be greatly diminished or effectively halted. But how to limit access to Chinese mariners? VOC officials presented a straightforward but strikingly radical proposition: the king should banish all the Chinese residents from his kingdom.[63] Any Chinese migrant, merchant, or resident within the borders of Ayutthaya and regardless of ties to the country should, company administrators insisted, be "expelled and banned" from the country.[64] If the king acceded, the move would resolve a string of problems for Batavia. Narai would not be able to draw sailors from this community, hence making voyages to Japan essentially impossible, while Zheng Jing would be deprived of allies or a potential power base in the Chinese community in Siam.

Siamese officials pushed back aggressively against the demand. There were "many thousands of Chinese spread through the entire realm" who had been there for generations and "had married and mixed with the natural

Siamese." They had been admitted under the protection of the king's forefathers and were "legal subjects of the realm" (*wettige onderdanen van 't ryk*).[65] Given their status, "His Majesty was obliged to maintain them and not to cast them out." Rejecting any notion of a connection between the Chinese community and Koxinga, Siamese officials insisted that these were the king's subjects and hence could not possibly be expelled. The result was a clash: the company insisting that all overseas Chinese were somehow tarnished and should be expelled, and Ayutthayan officials attempting to erase any distinction between the Chinese community and the larger Siamese population.[66] In this way, the conflict between the VOC and the Zheng triggered a dramatic process of claiming. Just as Paramaraja had attempted to mark out Cambodian waters, so Narai now moved to pull his Chinese subjects within his protective embrace and hence to remove the threat of VOC violence.

In the end, the king and the company agreed on a compromise and a new treaty was signed on August 22, 1664. The document gave the VOC total rights over the trade in "deerskins and cowhides" to the "exclusion of all other merchants."[67] The king did not agree to expel the Chinese, but he did consent to no longer make use of Chinese sailors on Siamese ships. The treaty thus handed over expansive privileges to the Dutch. If VOC ships encountered vessels dispatched by the king or his subjects that were "manned with Siamese," they would allow them to pass freely and unhindered.[68] But the king, his subjects, as well as any residents of Siam regardless of level or station were prohibited from employing "Chinese on their junks, ships and smaller craft." If a ship was discovered with these mariners on board, it could be seized immediately and its goods confiscated.[69]

Almost before the ink was dry on this document, the king began to push back against the prohibition by seeking to reclaim Chinese sailors. A letter dispatched to Batavia attempted to modify the key clause by stipulating that Chinese sailors would be allowed on the king's vessels, but only if they were from "great China and Canton," "were not subjects of Koxinga," and were resident in Siam.[70] In this way, court officials attempted to draw clear lines distinguishing a loyal from a potentially suspect Chinese population. The VOC protested by pointing out that the treaty had already been signed and that it contained within it a blanket ban on Chinese sailors regardless of origin or affiliation. Negotiations intensified in 1665 when ambassadors from Ayutthaya arrived in Batavia. They had been dispatched for the express purpose of renegotiating the clause forbidding Chinese mariners from sailing on Siamese vessels. Deploying a familiar argument, they proceeded to explain that the Chinese were not tied to Koxinga but were rather the "king's subjects and vassals."[71]

Faced with sustained resistance, VOC officials offered a compromise. Chinese sailors would not be allowed on the king's ships, but Batavia would lend some Dutch mariners, including a pilot, to the king's voyages, thereby enabling them to go ahead in a much reduced and more controllable form.[72] It seemed to offer a workable alternative, but a first attempt to put this system into practice proved disastrous. A crown junk with a Dutch pilot did depart, but the vessel was unseaworthy and started to leak as soon as it reached the open ocean.[73] The result was that the voyage was cancelled and no royal vessels reached Japan from Siam that year.

Faced with such an unsatisfactory situation, the king of Siam started first slowly, then more aggressively, to bend the rules of the treaty. Although the VOC had staged a successful blockade in 1664, it did not have the resources to repeat the tactic year after year, and beginning in 1665, Narai enthusiastically welcomed Zheng traders to his shores. During that year, out of a total of twenty vessels dispatched by the Zheng network to ports across Southeast Asia, half of them visited Ayutthaya with the remaining ships trading at Siamese dependencies on the Malay Peninsula such as Ligor.[74] King Narai would later recall that his kingdom and the Zheng enjoyed "a deep friendship" during this period.[75] The following year, Narai went further by dispatching a junk manned by Siamese, Moors, lascars, and "short-haired Chinese" to Japan.[76] The last group were mestizos born in Siam and hence did not, according to one reading, violate the 1664 treaty. Soon after this voyage, even this pretext was abandoned and the king's junks started arriving again with Chinese sailors onboard.[77] By the late 1660s, the king was back in the deerskin business, leaving the VOC with little recourse unless it wanted to stage another expensive blockade.

Influence on Land, Influence on Water

The war between the Dutch East India Company and the Zheng was a regional struggle that pulled in polities across East and Southeast Asia. The conflict was fiercest in territories where the most lucrative trading opportunities presented themselves, in places like Cambodia or Siam that offered access to high-demand commodities like deerskins. As the company and the Zheng fought over trade routes, capturing ships, goods, and people on the sea, they forced a response on land. This chapter has considered the ways in which two territorial polities reacted to the aggressive expansion of the VOC and Zheng merchants into Southeast Asian markets. Both Cambodia and Siam attempted to use these dueling rivals to counterbalance each other, while at the same time engineering legal frameworks capable of neutralizing the damaging effects of their conflict.

The triangular relationship that developed between the Zheng, the VOC, and territorial polities like Siam or Cambodia was particular to seventeenth-century Southeast Asia, but the broader dynamic should be a familiar one. In the cases discussed here, territorial polities with few or no naval resources sought to develop solutions on land for problems that developed in coastal waters, on sea-lanes, and in the deep ocean. As their primary weapons, they could make use of mechanisms such as the designation of secure maritime spaces (Cambodia) or the laying down of protection over vessels or mariners (Ayutthaya). On the other side, maritime powers like the VOC or the Zheng sought to leverage their influence on sea to control the land and with it trade in key commodities such as deerskins. To do so, they relied on threats, blockades, and attacks on shipping. Only in very rare instances could they move directly onto land to exercise military force as Piauwja did when he attacked a VOC outpost in Cambodia in 1665. All of this churn created a shifting balance that in turn generated legal improvisation and innovation. In Cambodia, the struggle between the VOC and the Zheng prompted a relatively precise definition of territorial waters; in Siam the conflict led to the aggressive delineation of the Chinese population as the king's subjects. In both places, rivalries over valuable maritime trade reached deep into local politics and structured the relation of political power on land and sea.

Chapter 3

"The Law Is the Lord of the Sea": Maritime Law as Global Maritime History

Matthew Taylor Raffety

From the fifteenth-century emergence of the "Atlantic world" through the eighteenth- and nineteenth-centuries' "Age of Revolution," maritime law occupied a critical place at the intersection among different empires and legal systems. European empires used law to order the movement of people and goods around a complex and connected world, to bring regulatory clarity to the seas, and to establish jurisdictional boundaries.[1] Maritime law operated in juxtaposition to other, competing systems in ways that most terrene law did not. Litigants contested jurisdiction over maritime cases, and their actions shaped even the essential components of definitions of citizenship: the national "character" of vessel, crew, and goods aboard ships.[2] Most polities, as a result, regarded maritime law as operating differently from law on land. The Romans, for example, did not claim dominion over the waters the way they did ashore.[3] Byzantine emperor Justinian declared in 533, "I am, indeed, the Lord of the World, but the Law is the Lord of the sea."[4]

The central role of maritime law in European empires makes it a valuable tool for thinking about the processes of globalization in the early modern era. Maritime law played a key role in the growing Northern European dominance of the globe after 1500.[5] Though the dream of a unifying international law of maritime transport and commerce still eludes modern diplomats, the story of the seventeenth through the nineteenth centuries is one of growing coherence and organization of interactions on the seas. Someone's law would prevail; the questions were largely about whose law to use.[6] Examining how the law went to sea—that is, how systems of legislation, regulation, jurisprudence, treaties, convention, and tradition developed to bring order to life at sea—can give historians new purchase on empires' and states' role in the process of globalization.

Yet a narrow focus on the growth and development of European maritime law and regulation risks being simply a return to imperial history under another name. An older generation of legal historians recounted the development of maritime law in separate ocean basins as a tale of growing coherence around two basic principles: (1) all nations may access the sea, and (2) "the state of the ship's nationality has exclusive jurisdiction over the ship on the high seas."[7] More recent research has explored Northern European incursions into the Mediterranean,[8] the rise of the Atlantic systems of the emerging colonial powers, and finally the development of legal structures that bound the world and its commerce ever more tightly to those Atlantic colonial powers as the tendrils of their commerce and control reached around the globe.[9] Yet even as it crosses oceanic basins, such research risks reinscribing differences among oceanic spaces rather than identifying processes and properties shared among them.

To globalize the history of maritime law and fulfill its full potential as a window into the history of global empires, scholars need to focus not just on the expansion of European legal structures but also on the places and times where those expanding systems overlapped, met with resistance, or became hybridized by local pressures. These zones of contestation offer some of the best opportunities to break the hold that empires and basins have held on historians and free scholars to take newer, more global approaches. Using a combination of historiographic synthesis and analysis of primary sources, this essay examines five areas of maritime law in which such contestation became particularly visible or important during the early modern era. By focusing on sites of contestation, the essay seeks to identify arenas where developing legal systems came into conflict, and where scholars can study the overlapping, disputed, and hybridizing character of sea law. The intent is to offer a roadmap to historians who aim to challenge Eurocentric narratives of maritime law and empire.

The essay first surveys the roots of European maritime law and regulation in order to understand the antecedents of the systems that expanded their reach globally from the sixteenth to nineteenth centuries. This section challenges the common idea that this process took place in a clear and linear fashion. We then turn to the philosophical tension between the development of maritime law as an expansion of various municipal/national traditions across expanding empires and a conception of the aqueous realm as a distinctly "international" sphere, where international law, predicated on shared assumptions of natural law or universal understandings, prevailed. The suppression of piracy, the practice of privateering and prize law, and the nineteenth-century pressure to end the Atlantic slave trade all reflect the tensions between nationalist and internationalist impulses in the law. Third, the essay explores the role of custom: the idiosyncratic processes of negotiation and renegotiation that framed the governance of each individual ship. Seafarers defended the traditions of their craft against the incursions of law. During the eighteenth century, seamen also fused these preexisting customary rules of their craft with emerging Enlightenment ideas about natural rights and their roles as citizens. The chapter then turns to the roles of nonstate and semistate actors in the creation of maritime law. It was not just the various imperial metropoles that sought to bring legal order to the waters: private and semiprivate corporations often began the process of ordering empire before the state, leading to competition and collaboration between state and corporate structures. Finally, the essay considers the hybrid structures that developed between the legal systems of the major colonizing powers and indigenous, colonial, or emerging polities. By the nineteenth century, a nation's domain over its own maritime affairs became an essential aspect of independence; simultaneously, a complex set of capitulations, treaties asserting extraterritorial rights, and other semicolonial structures offer yet another site of complexity in the application of law to the waters.

The Development of European Maritime Law

The origins of European maritime law can be traced back to ancient Greece.[10] The Athenians established the earliest known maritime commercial code. Around 320 BCE, as Athenian power waned, Rhodes expanded upon these earlier regulations. Even in the classical period, however, what developed was a patchwork of practices and customs rather than a single unifying system built on a core logic or legal philosophy. As Roman power engulfed the Mediterranean, the Romans created "a distillation of the customs and usages of the seafaring people they conquered."[11] Thus, even the Pax Romana left in place competing traditions and practices to govern the seas. Roman dominance brought a degree of legal coherence to the Mediterranean that to a significant degree withstood the empire's decline.[12]

Alongside the durable Roman system, however, Northern European seafarers developed their own approaches to maritime matters. Legal scholars in the eighteenth and nineteenth centuries, seeking coherent origins for maritime practice in their own eras, often pointed to the rise of the Hanseatic League, which developed as a trading consortium of small Germanic polities in the late twelfth century. By the mid-fourteenth century, these trading ports crafted increasingly uniform rules to govern waterborne trade between member states. However, these same scholars often overstate both the reach and uniformity of the Hanseatic League's control. In fact, Scandinavian, French, and Hanseatic practices diverged in significant ways by the mid-thirteenth century.[13] Thus even the story that is sometimes told of a general Northern European consensus on maritime governance, which developed as an admixture of classical Mediterranean and Germanic medieval law, is difficult to sustain.[14]

Well into the early modern period, local regulation and national law, each specifically aimed at governing the waters, remained in conflict. Codified "town laws" often prevailed, as opposed to "customary sea laws," which "were adhered to only when they were accepted by an undefined group or enforced by a national authority as in England or in France."[15] In England, the first major work of maritime law appeared in the early 1400s as the *Black Book of Admiralty*, less a synthesis than a compendium of existing local and national regulations and custom.[16] By the seventeenth century, conflict between common law courts and the newer admiralty courts represented an important step in undoing the overlapping jurisdictions and local practices that governed maritime matters.[17] The "town laws" of the medieval period died hard in some jurisdictions, as local polities jealously guarded their power over local waters and seafarers. Indeed, "the pluralism of classical European learned law" remained a significant barrier to uniformity in maritime practice well into the early modern period, and in many cases, well beyond.[18]

The seventeenth-century rise of transoceanic empire forced Western European states to seek greater coherence both in their own maritime affairs and in their interactions with other polities on the water. António Manuel Hespahna suggests that scholars need to divide the maritime legal history of European colonization into key phases. Early colonialism remained "rooted in the pluralism of classical European learned law."[19] Just as European powers were still sorting through their own jurisdictional quandaries, maritime regulations promulgated for colonial realms in the seventeenth and eighteenth centuries continued to accommodate overlapping bodies of law.[20] In other words, though European jurisprudence was moving from a conception of law as a "gamekeeper" (who keeps order) to that of law as "gardener" (implanting that order systematically), the transformation was never complete in practice or in principle. In its colonial realms, European jurisprudence continued to have to negotiate with both indigenous and commercial entities.

As Europeans extended their reach across the waters, they adapted older legal traditions to novel settings. When England began to expand its commercial and colonial interests in the early 1600s, English jurists began compiling various editions of the *Lex Mercatoria* as a body of law wholly distinct from the common law.[21] French maritime law took a somewhat different path. The French borrowed the terminology of "admiralty" from the Arabic *amīr al baḥr* during the Crusades,[22] shortly before creating the first and most influential European articulation of maritime law, the *Rôles d'Olerón*, in the middle of the twelfth century. Building on commercial law from the ancient world that had governed aspects of Mediterranean trade for centuries, the Oleronic codes influenced the maritime law of many seagoing powers. It was, however, far from a uniform or coherent system, and overlapping authorities, jurisdictions, and practices remained. Despite numerous attempts to centralize maritime authority under the crown, it was not until the Ordonnance de la Marine, in 1681, that the French truly sought to "put an end to jurisdictional conflicts that bogged down the courts."[23]

As European states struggled to order their internal maritime structures, they also encountered one another on the seas more often, which forced to the fore the question of which polities had rights to which waters. Supporting the upstart Dutch's claim to maritime access, Dutch jurist Hugo Grotius made the case in *Mare Liberum* for universal entrée, a principle that argued for the seas as shared international space. In practical terms, however, Grotius's argument permitted multiple nations' legal systems to coexist on the waters of the world, as each vessel became understood as a small floating patch of sovereign territory wherever it traveled. Several nations, however, sought to extend their legal control unilaterally over specific bodies of water. "The Sea, by the Law of Nature or Nations," argued Grotius's greatest critic, the English scholar John Selden, "is not common to all men, but capable of private Dominion or proprietie as well as the Land."[24] Both Grotius and Selden grounded their claims in the confusing and incomplete claims of Roman *imperium* over the Mediterranean.[25]

While Grotius and Selden debated over right of access to the seas, and expanding empires fretted over the regulation of trade and ships on the water generally, relatively scant attention was paid to the regulation of individual vessels until the end of the eighteenth century. Despite several centuries of rapid legal proliferation that saw "early modern seafarers . . . embedded in a thick web of legal regulation, often across multiple jurisdictions," vessels, and seafarers, attempts to articulate uniform rules governing maritime labor lagged.[26] Britain did not begin a serious effort to codify such laws until the second quarter of the eighteenth century, and the United States did not promulgate a major law governing shipboard labor until 1835.[27]

Pirates, Prizes, and the Slave Trade: Internationalism in Maritime Law

The eighteenth and nineteenth centuries saw the Atlantic powers developing a more robust corpus of law particular to each nation, yet maritime law remained singularly international in its practice. Among major maritime powers, jurists referred to cases and practices from other nations far more regularly than in other areas of legal practice.[28] Scholars acknowledge the "bipolar history of early modern international law," particularly regarding how nation-states alternated between support and suppression of piracy and other forms of private waterborne violence, as pragmatic considerations required. [29] Piracy, privateering, and the regulation (and, later, suppression) of the Atlantic slave trade represent the three most internationalized aspects of maritime law from the seventeenth through nineteenth centuries. While nations sought to order their own maritime trade, piracy and its close cousin privateering necessitated a more universal approach. In the early nineteenth century, antislaving actions by British and others further expanded the internationalist claims over maritime law.

Under the law of nations, piracy represented a rare universal crime. Seeking classical origins for international law, early modern Anglo-Italian legal scholar Alberico Gentili argued that Roman law classified pirates as *hostis humani generis*, or enemies of mankind as a whole, rather than criminals who offended only against the nations of victims. Piracy has drawn tremendous scholarly attention and been used to serve wildly divergent analyses. Most scholars have not acknowledged complex, fraught legal understanding of piracy. As Lauren Benton notes, "calls for universal jurisdiction for the punishment of pirates were always combined with more practical approaches that defined piracy as a crime under municipal law," and legal structures struggled to contemplate and cope with the always-changing world of piracy. Even today, jurisdictional overlap and statutory confusion bedevil piracy cases. Different conceptions of what constitutes piracy in different eras and regions make it useful to examine both the successes and limitations of the reach of both international and national law over the waters.[30]

The curious world of prize law is another rich opportunity for scholars to examine the complex evolution of maritime legal development.[31] Although encouraging raiding of enemy vessels is ancient in origin, European custom and law governing the practice began to solidify by the fifteenth century.[32] The letters of marque and reprisal that licensed vessels as sea raiders first appeared around 1300, "to bring the anarchy of retaliation under the rule of law."[33] Grotius himself sought to justify Dutch privateering on internationalist principles.[34] Privateering offered warring nations an inexpensive way to expand maritime power quickly by hiring a navy on commission. Even as Britain's Royal Navy expanded and professionalized in the mid-1700s, a strong political countercurrent argued that reliance on privateers as a sort of sea militia would not only protect imperial interests more cheaply but would also prohibit the navy from becoming a threat to liberty.[35] Younger and less powerful states in particular relied on privateers. The U.S. Constitution explicitly grants Congress the right to issue letters of marque, which had been essential during the earlier Revolution and remained important into the War of 1812 and even the American Civil War.[36]

Yet privateering was always messy in practice, as one nation's privateer was an enemy's pirate. Even in peacetime the temptations of sea-raiding often lured men and vessels into the trade under another nation's flag, further blurring legal and national lines. American seafarers frequently found themselves, willingly or otherwise, serving as privateers licensed by upstart Latin American revolutionary states. In 1806, the U.S. Circuit Court in New York took up the case of a Revolutionary War veteran, George Martin, who had taken for himself the name and rank of "General Francisco de Miranda" (who was at the time the leader of a rebellion in Venezuela) and sought to outfit an American vessel to join the conflict.[37] Thomas Gibbs, the most infamous American pirate of the 1830s, claimed to have started the nefarious side of his career after organizing a mutiny of his fellow Americans aboard an Argentine privateer on which he illegally served.[38] The *Niles Register* describes U.S. naval forces intercepting a vessel, alternately named *Wilson* and *Bolivar* and "having several flags—Buenos Ayeran, Artigan, Venezualian, *et alias*," but with a largely American crew and a cargo of slaves.[39] Indeed, it seems that many vessels split their time between filibustering for breakaway republics and the illicit slave trade.[40]

South American privateering in the early nineteenth century represented a new site of contestation in a centuries-old debate over legitimacy as defined through maritime prize law between established and upstart states. To South American revolutionaries, not only did the issuance of letters of marque increase their military power against Portuguese and Spanish naval might, it also represented an important assertion of the rights of nations for these fledgling republics. By issuing letters to American vessels with (partially) American crews, however, these revolutionary states put their assertion of legal control over the waters in conflict with the young United States' neutrality laws and status in the world. Moreover, their actions continued a debate about which states could effectively assert control over the waters through the application of maritime law. Portuguese diplomats, for example, rejected the legitimacy of privateers from Banda Oriental (modern Uruguay) not just because the rebellion was invalid but because the rebel leader, Jose Gervasio Artigas, "had possession of no sea-port." In the end, established powers became more concerned about the ways privateering undermined the increasingly structured legal world of the sea than they were eager for the strategic advantages of these naval subcontractors. Because "privateers could don and doff national affiliation as easily as their tunic," by the second quarter of the nineteenth century they had fallen out of favor among established powers.[41]

Ultimately, privateering largely came to an end by treaty, itself an assertion of the internationalist approach. The Paris Declaration Respecting Maritime Law, signed in 1856 by fifty-five maritime nations at the end of the Crimean War, curtailed the issuance of letters of marque in times of war, although nonsignatories (including the United States) still maintain the theoretical right to commission privateers.[42] It has even been proposed that the United States might issue letters of marque to help curtail modern piracy off the Somali coast.[43]

The British-led international effort to curb the slave trade in the early nineteenth century marked another important move to internationalize and make uniform legal practice on the water. However, how to interpret this move toward "international law" remains contested. While some scholars see in the international cooperation against piracy and later the slave trade an expansion of shared legal principles and structures, others including Lauren Benton and Lisa Ford suggest that "attempts to order oceans . . . and Britain's role within this process, were significant precisely because they developed in the absence of broad-based legal principles," relying instead on "an awkward combination of bilateral treaties, municipal law, admiralty law, and diplomatic negotiation."[44]

Forecastle Law: Custom, Resistance, and Venue Shopping by Sailors

Whether municipal or internationalist in origin, the development of maritime and commercial law is only one side of the legal world of seafaring in the early modern period. Amid the worlds of expanding regulations and overlapping jurisdictions, "sailors were themselves 'lawyers,' spinning the webs of imperial jurisdiction by justifying their own, often violent actions in terms of empire,"[45] a practice that was continued strongly among American seafarers' extension of an informal, racially charged definition of empire in the nineteenth-century Pacific.[46]

The diverse, mobile men who made up the maritime workforce presented national and jurisdictional dilemmas, and the international and fluid nature of maritime labor was (and remains) a double-edged sword. On the one hand, seafarers have been unusually free among workers at times in their ability to choose between not just employers but also regulatory and legal regimes, negotiating for higher wages and desirable berths in harbors with a strong demand for labor. On the other hand, laws against desertion sought to check this practice, and in some cases, Atlantic seamen likened the antidesertion rules to fugitive slave laws.[47]

Custom, or "forecastle law," was an important aspect of the legal environment of the ship, and, as Richard Blakemore argues, "must be understood within the legal system, not outside or against it; and that, due to the importance of custom, seafarers had more agency in the development of both maritime law and employment practice than is usually supposed." Court documents and contracts alike regularly referred to "manner and Customes" or "lawes and Customes of the Seas," and in many cases those customs had the force of law in court.[48]

While *Lex Mercatoria* guided maritime trade, it was largely silent on the governance of ships themselves. To fill that gap, seafarers helped build a legal world out of custom rather than the medieval texts like *Oléron* favored by jurists, at least prior to 1729.[49] Marcus Rediker sees the rise of the contract and the growing power of maritime legislation in the eighteenth century as part of the proletarianization of shipboard labor, subsuming the more expansive custom within a legal structure that favored masters and merchants over seafarers. In British legislation from the eighteenth century and American legislation from the dawn of the constitutional era forward, however, the law sought to protect the rights of seafarers as well as officers and owners.[50] In the American context, "forecastle law" remained significant both as customary practice and legally enforceable law, much like the laws that sought to supersede it.[51]

If scholars need to acknowledge both the legitimate and extralegal force of custom on the legal world of the sea, they also need to note how readily seafarers used jurisdictional overlap and confusion to their advantage. Within the Mediterranean, "The presence of ships and seamen of different nationalities . . . and the trail of litigation left behind in local courts of justice, brings to light substantive differences in maritime 'usages and customs' between different countries."[52]

Seafarers, who often moved between vessels of different nations, certainly understood and made use of these distinctions, maneuvering themselves to more favorable flags when possible and articulating the distinctions in court.[53] Interacting with sailors steeped in "different labour and legal traditions" meant that Mediterranean seafarers "developed flexible occupational and economic strategies" in the seventeenth century.[54] Malta operated its maritime law under a complex confluence of judicial traditions and jurisdictions, utilizing a "subtle mix of local and Rhodean maritime customs which often overlapped."[55] Its strategic location in the Mediterranean made it an important node for trade and a frequent site for the airing of seafarers' grievances, as sailors could ply their claims at either Maltese courts or the consuls of their own countries.[56]

Although these various national legal traditions—and a growing body of law—did seek to spread systems of uniform control around the globe, the lived worlds of sea and waterfront were never legally tidy. The tangle of regulations that maritime powers promulgated throughout the eighteenth and nineteenth centuries can be seen as an attempt—desperate at times—to bring the power of the nation to an ungovernable realm and to undo the inherited chaos of overlapping jurisdictions and legal traditions. Indeed, attempts to bring systematic legal governance to the water were an essential part of the transformations of the early modern era. Notions of nation and the relationship between citizens, the body politic, and the law all took shape in meaningful ways on the water.[57] Although crimping, press gangs, and regulations limited the freedom of seamen to move between berths and ships at will, desertion remained both a main point of resistance and a form of pragmatic economic opportunism throughout the world's oceans into the modern era. Particularly in diverse ports of call, sailors traded not only berths but also legal environments and, in many cases, even national identities. British and Dutch mariners shopped their complaints between local authorities and whatever emissaries their own national governments had installed in early modern Mediterranean ports,[58] and sailors in the Anglo-Caribbean ducked press gangs to remain in the more lucrative merchant service.[59]

Perhaps the most significant way in which seafarers in the Age of Revolution were truly "citizens of the world"[60] is reflected in the utilitarian approach they took to their own national identity. Faced with impressment into the Royal Navy, Scandinavian-born seafarer Nicholas Isaacs protested first that he was an American citizen, but when the British officer was unmoved, Isaacs "showed him both my Danish and American protections, but it mattered not."[61] Thus, despite most Atlantic states' efforts to maintain the national character of a country's merchant marine service by statute, the sea remained a singularly diverse and mobile workplace from the sixteenth through the nineteenth centuries.

Company Law: Nonstate and Semistate Actors in Maritime Regulation

At the growing edges of colonization, corporate regulation rather than imperial law often prevailed. Early Portuguese colonization in East Africa was not the work of state actors, but rather of traders in loose affiliation with the state, through "a process of empire-building which frequently escaped the control of the Portuguese crown."[62] These early ad hoc Portuguese traders set the model for the complexity and jurisdictional might of vast entities like the Dutch East India Company. Despite occasional calls for order and accountability from the metropole, every major colonial power farmed out aspects of colonial governance, both ashore and at sea, to private or semiprivate entities. Long-distance trading companies, often tasked with semijudicial authority over maritime matters, were founded in Sweden, Prussia, Portugal, Spain, and France, in addition to the English and Dutch firms that have drawn most attention from historians.[63]

Corporations handled a great deal of the early British empire's maritime regulatory business. The Royal Africa Company on the West African coast, the Levant Company in the Mediterranean Ottoman realm, and the East India Company in India and the Ottoman territories bordering the Persian

Gulf and Indian Ocean all handled maritime cases with quasi-state authority.[64] Distance, lack of legal training, and the temptation of officials to seize the main chance made the operation of this corporate law even more localized and idiosyncratic.[65] Considering that men often served simultaneously as a British consul and as an official of the Levant Corporation, the mixture of corporate and state law becomes all the more confusing.[66] In the Americas, the Hudson's Bay Company governed northern waterways with somewhat less autonomy than the eastern British corporations, perhaps in part because its founder, Prince Rupert, was also Britain's Lord Admiral and preeminent naval commander.[67] Even when state authorities were present, they competed with corporate entities for legal control. In Havana in the 1830s, for example, the U.S. consul struggled against locally entrenched American merchants who believed his primary role was to serve their interests, rather than those of the American state.[68]

Corporate entities wielded nearly unfettered legal authority in the Indian Ocean. Both the Dutch and British East India Companies were effectively governments unto themselves in the Indian Ocean, and European, African, or Asian seafarers toiled in a legal environment made by the corporation, not the state.[69] Non-European employees of the Dutch East India Company were primarily "subject to Company law and discipline," rather than Dutch law.[70] Beginning in the late seventeenth century English vessels employed "lascar" sailors, a catchall legal category for the seafarers of non-European origin who straddled imperial and corporate regulatory authority.[71] Imperial authorities turned control over the crewing of vessels in the East to the British East India Company, which created "Asian Articles" under different (less favorable) rules than those governing other British merchant vessels.[72] These Asiatic Agreements varied considerably and were controlled by individual steamship companies, with little direct imperial oversight.[73]

By the nineteenth century, British dominance in the Indian Ocean had created "a paradise for traders working under the protection of the British or Indian crowns."[74] So long as trade benefited empire, the specific rules under which it operated were often left to local, traditional, or corporate entities. As lascar sailors crewed British ships in greater numbers and farther beyond the Indian Ocean, the British finally begin to develop rules governing white and nonwhite mariners in the late nineteenth century.[75] The Dutch also acted to gain greater racial control of their imperial trade in the mid-nineteenth century. Under an 1866 law, the Dutch labeled the Hadhrami traders who crisscrossed their empire as "*vreemde oosterlegen*" ("foreign Orientals"), creating for these maritime traders "a category [legally] distinct both from Europeans and the indigenous people," which complicated and undermined the ancient trading routes and maritime conventions of the Hadhrami.[76]

Warfare frequently challenged the loyalty of seafarers and shipowners. During the Napoleonic Wars, British ships adopted the nominally neutral Omani flag as a means of evading the conflict in areas the Royal Navy left underpatrolled, only to return to British registry with the arrival of lasting peace after 1815.[77] Like the Omanis in the Indian Ocean, Americans sought to profit from their neutrality during the early years of the Napoleonic Wars, but fled to British and French flags during the Embargo of 1807 and, later, in anticipation of the War of 1812.[78] Five decades later, the American Civil War decimated U.S. shipping as American ships and masters fled to neutral flags, most commonly Britain's.[79]

In wartime and at peace, ultimately, capital rather than labor most deftly engaged in legal arbitrage between national regulatory structures. In what would become a model for offshoring capital, Greco-Ottoman traders in the Low Countries began alternating between Dutch and Ottoman citizenship as suited their commercial interests in the second half of the eighteenth century.[80] As the fortunes of the Spanish empire declined in the early nineteenth century, Cuba experienced a "de facto invasion" of foreign merchants seeking to profit from lax Spanish enforcement, especially in the illicit slave trade.[81] Despite the 1835 treaty giving the British extraterritorial powers to search Spanish shipping suspected of "blackbirding," the practice continued under Portuguese and American flags, and, briefly, that of the independent Texas.[82] Given that the same man served as U.S. and Portuguese consul in the mid-1830s, it became easy for investors to purchase American ships, switch them to Portuguese registry at Havana, and then switch back again once they returned with their illicit cargo. This "flag foolery" to obscure the slave trade presaged the rise of "flags of convenience" in the twentieth century.[83]

As it became harder for seafarers to slip between nationalities and legal systems, capital's ability to do so expanded dramatically, constituting "an exact reversal of sovereignty's intent and a perfect mockery of national conceits."[84] The legal uncoupling of vessels from their logical national connection may ultimately be the most significant aspect of maritime legal developments for the modern era. Flags of convenience vastly increased the ability of capital to move around the globe unfettered, shopping among various legal regulatory regimes. The rise of a globally mobile "transnational capitalist class,"[85] beginning in the eighteenth century and forming in earnest in the twentieth century, "captured the agenda of key global institutions," including systems of international and maritime law.[86] The "capital exodus to nowhere"[87] reflected in the global shipping of the twentieth century was underway much earlier. Labor historian Leon Fink sees loosening national control and the rise of flags of convenience as "neoliberalist globalism" that today "threatens national social sovereignty in the name of worldwide market forces."[88]

"Semicolonization" and Hybrid Legal Structures at Sea

A global study of maritime law also needs to engage with the "semicolonial phenomenon"[89] that developed as Atlantic powers fashioned "fuzzier 'areas of influence'" in lieu of explicit colonial control.[90] Extraterritorial control through expansive legal efforts (and particularly maritime jurisdiction) was one of the first means of drawing noncolonized states into the maritime legal world framed by Atlantic powers. An examination of European treaties granting extraterritorial rights within the Ottoman, Chinese, and Siamese empires suggests that military, diplomatic, and commercial pressure rather than conquest created complex legal structures fusing British, indigenous, and external regulatory concepts.[91]

Crafting and enforcing more uniform maritime law was, for leading powers, part of building the symbolic structures of the modern state. For countries that lacked the power to control their own destiny, however, the maritime law of other nations encroached in complex and powerful ways. Whether by treaty or by force (threatened or explicit), powerful nations inserted their legal constructs and institutions within smaller states, particularly in the realm of ships and sailors. In the Mediterranean, "British military power played an important persuasive role with 'weak states' such as the Republic of Genoa and the Grand Duchy of Tuscany."[92] Local authorities worked with the British "informally or as an exception, always seeking to avoid creating a dangerous precedent."[93] Thus, both sides sought to solve specific maritime legal crises including the operation of naval press gangs in foreign ports without creating clear or lasting rules, favoring instead quiet case-by case negotiations between local authorities and British diplomats.[94]

Ottoman maritime trade straddled several systems and legal structures, and therefore represents particularly rich examples of overlapping and competing legal systems.[95] As the decline of Mongol hegemony made terrene Eurasian trade routes more fraught in the mid-fourteenth century, trade and its regulation shifted to the water. As such, the Islamic states of the Middle East straddled "two major maritime commercial systems, one in the Indian Ocean, and the other in the Mediterranean," bound together by the Red Sea.[96] Looking at the structures that underpinned Ottoman sea power problematizes the periodization and loci of the early modern world, and even forces a reconsideration of what a "world power" is.[97] Although Western sources often describe an Ottoman retreat from the sea after its fleet's defeat at Lepanto in 1571,[98] the Ottomans remained a major maritime power, even if they did cede a growing share of trade—and legal control thereof—in the ensuing years. The increasing presence of European traders and officials beginning in the late fifteenth century ushered in a "transitional stage in the articulation of the Ottoman system with the world economy."[99]

The operation of maritime law for European vessels in Ottoman waters serves as a model for the mixed-jurisdictional aspects of later semicolonial regimes marked by partial incursions into a nation's sovereignty rather than outright control.[100] Sultanic capitulations—essentially extraterritorial grants of maritime and commercial access for outsiders to operate within the Ottoman sphere—began to appear in the thirteenth century and continued to guide maritime interactions until World War I.[101] These capitulations, which began as "concessions voluntarily bestowed by the Ottoman Sultan on non-Muslim foreigners," developed into a system whereby a foreign ambassador and his staff, rather than Ottoman courts, possessed extraterritorial rights to handle "both criminal and civil cases."[102] Before 1800, European merchants handled nearly all trade leaving or entering Ottoman lands via water and had even captured the majority of intra-Ottoman marine trade.[103]

If the capitulations meant that European vessels operated under their own laws and had jurisdiction over their own seamen even when in port, Ottoman-flagged vessels were governed by a substantively different system that diverged from the developing European systems in important ways. Islamic states like the Ottoman Empire and Oman did not turn maritime issues over to specialized courts, nor did they develop a distinct body of regulations to govern them. Some scholars argue that Islamic and European law is so different at "the deepest conceptual levels" that any direct comparisons become difficult.[104] Basic practice, as well as the conceptual underpinnings of law, differed too. Despite a sizeable fleet in the nineteenth century, both Oman and the Ottoman states lacked any specific body of maritime regulation; cases that, in the Western understanding, would have been "at Admiralty" or "Maritime" in nature were instead handled by the the regular sultanic courts.

In addition to conceptual and logistical differences between western and Ottoman maritime legal practice, Ottoman control over its own marine domain was often fractious and incomplete, particularly at the empire's western edges. Not only did distance weaken the sultan's power, but jurists in North African ports operated under Maliki traditions, a fundamentally different school of Islamic jurisprudence than the Hanafi school that predominated in the Ottoman core. This legal disconnect had enormous implications for the interactions between North African corsairs and vessels from Atlantic states, but it also had important implications for regular Ottoman vessels, which were often targets of raiding *korsanlars*.[105]

From the sixteenth century into the nineteenth, the Western Mediterranean was, like the Caribbean, a site of incomplete maritime control, and the operation of corsairs, privateers, pirates, and raiders of various legalities made both regions particularly complex from a legal standpoint, although the interplay of European and Islamic legal traditions extends the confusion in the Mediterranean.[106] The complexity of the line between privateer and pirate in European terms is more than matched by the confusion over *korsanlars* and *levendlers* in the Islamic Mediterranean.[107]

Omani control of the Swahili coast represents another understudied example of a non-Atlantic state removing a European power in favor of its own imperial advancement. In the seventeenth and eighteenth centuries, Oman transformed itself from a religious state focused away from the water on the Arabian peninsula, to a raiding maritime state, to the dominant commercial power in the region, brushing aside Portuguese and Dutch interests and subjugating the Swahili region.[108] By the end of the Napoleonic Wars, Oman had become a semicolonial client state that supported British power in the region, but the still substantial number of Omani-flagged dhows meant that, however contingent its independence, Oman remained an important maritime presence in the Indian Ocean. Indeed, smaller sultanates and polities along Africa's east coast negotiated their own diplomatic agreements governing the legal organization of maritime labor and trade well into the nineteenth century.[109]

For new and weaker nations, control over their own maritime matters became a central pillar of true independence, particularly as powerful nations forced extraterritorial concessions from weaker ones as the cost of avoiding complete colonial subjugation. From the start, the United States' approach to maritime matters was in response to, and to an extent a rejection of, British practice, in particular the expansive powers afforded the vice-admiralty courts.[110] As a result, the new nation began creating maritime regulation "writing on a somewhat clean slate."[111] In the nineteenth century, independent Texas briefly asserted its maritime autonomy, both in its constitution and in subsequent legislation.[112] The Kingdom of Hawai'i, seeking to halt encroachments from both British and American law, issued its own corpus of law to register and govern its vessels on the waters and to reassert control over the foreign seafarers overrunning the island.[113] Similarly, as Siam sought to modernize at the start of the twentieth century, it issued a detailed criminal code, which explicitly included maritime crimes.[114]

Conclusion

Scholars of the early Atlantic have long identified the ocean as a site of both the expansion of and resistance to new systems of power.[115] Expanding state authority and accompanying tighter categorizations of class, nationality, and race sought to define the role of everyone and everything within this evolving sphere. A growing body of maritime law, built on both classical and medieval Northern European precedents, allowed for a series of colonial and commercial powers to organize the sea (and movement of vessels, people, and goods across it), creating practical means by which the authority of the state took to the water. The Atlantic powers that perfected this transformation, especially Britain, France, the Netherlands, and, later, the upstart United States, spread versions of their maritime law across the world. In this manner, one can see the rise of increasingly coherent bodies of maritime law, relatively similar across these nations, as a firming up of the systems of imperialism and world trade—a process that culminated in a major, if not wholly successful attempt to bring consistency to maritime law around the world that continued until the early twentieth century.[116]

The rise of globe-encircling commerce and empires that linked far-flung locales in hierarchical chains of authority made for a complex and rapidly changing seascape, and legal systems played catch-up, as the metropole sought to bring uniform coherence while simultaneously adapting to ever-changing local conditions. Such regulation was always incomplete, always contingent, always beset by challenges and resistances. These contests came both from within, as when a European crew mutinied, or without, as when colonizing and trade powers negotiated by force, compromise, or treaty how to manage the dramatic and commonplace challenges of commerce, transit, and labor.

Does a "legal turn" help, either in bringing coherence to maritime history as a field, or in breaking out of the parochial fetters of single-ocean categories like the Atlantic world? Or does a focus on sea law add yet another subspecialty to the already woefully diffuse discourse on maritime history?[117] The globalization of maritime history must do more than simply reconfigure tales of the Atlantic world to fit other oceans. The reach of Western powers from the fifteenth through nineteenth centuries may be indisputable, but concentrating just on how the maritime law of a handful of powers spread throughout the globe leaves too much out. Whether positioned as a triumphal tale of "global progress" or a grim accounting of the violence, coercion, and oppression by which the law sorted people into fixed categories for the benefit of imperial masters, this approach remains too unidirectional, too Eurocentric a view.

Certainly, there are challenges and shortcomings to looking to the law as a means of globalizing scholars' understanding of the maritime world. Yet, despite all these concerns—narrowness, Eurocentrism, Whiggishness, ahistoricism, and logical incoherence—maritime law remains a useful tool by which to globalize the historical study of the oceans. A focus on how law went to sea, both conceptually and practically, offers a valuable, concrete approach to explore structures of globalization as they form and the resistances those systems encountered.

He who could invoke the power of law (whether custom, corporate, imperial, or international) brought to his argument a powerful intellectual framework into which he could fit his claim or grievance. Intersections between competing and overlapping systems of legal knowledge and authority are rich with interpretive possibility. Individual incidents are linked to the multifaceted, global conflict for both physical and conceptual control of men, vessels, and cargo at sea.

Focusing on maritime law's global character allows scholars to study in new detail the limitations of these emerging systems of Western hegemony, both from within and without. Acknowledging that these systems often shared space, so that vessels, corporate officials, consuls, and seafarers from several nations interacted at sea and in port, offers useful comparative opportunities. Even as jurists and legislatures sought to create national and international systems, these globalizing conceptual frameworks also had to contend with local realities. Seamen, vessels, and capital moved pragmatically between systems, shopping for favorable regulation with nuance and aplomb. The interaction between national law and corporate regulation for the major international trading companies of the colonial age and the wholly unmoored multinationals that followed in their wake is rich terrain for scholars to mine, both individually and with an eye to comparison and grand synthesis.

Part II

Dispatches

Chapter 4

Reading Cargoes: Letters and the Problem of Nationality in the Age of Privateering

Nathan Perl-Rosenthal

It did not take the sailors of the British privateer *Molly* very long to find ten bundles of letters aboard the *Vertumne*, a vessel they captured off the coast of France in August 1778. Letters played a vital role in the social and commercial life of empires, and they were ubiquitous on deep-sea vessels in the early modern era. The correspondents who put their letters on board the captured ship, bound from Saint Domingue to Le Havre, had hoped to remain connected to distant friends, family, and business partners. But the privateersmen who found the missives had other plans for them. The letters' wrappers bristled with the addresses of senders and intended recipients. Their closely written pages were thick with nuggets about current events and business opportunities. All of this information, in the eyes of the *Vertumne*'s captors, promised not a window into the lives of the correspondents, but valuable clues about the legal identity of the vessel and its cargo.[1] The *Molly*'s officers examined the bundles of letters and then brought them back to England, where they became a key part of the evidentiary record in the captured vessel's trial before an admiralty court.

Privateers like the *Molly*—private warships licensed to capture enemy shipping—had a central role in early modern European military strategy and constituted a substantial sector of the maritime economy.[2] The empire-states that licensed these vessels, while eager to benefit from the vessels' activities, intended also to prevent them from engaging in indiscriminate raiding (i.e., piracy). In order to do so, each European state in the early modern era created a specialized jurisdiction, prize courts, to govern privateering. Its core principles were, first, that only the property of enemy subjects could be deemed a valid "prize" and "condemned" to the captors' profit and, second, that prizes had to be formally adjudicated before they could be condemned. These rules made the determination of the "national character" or nationality of vessels and their cargoes a central element of privateering enterprise.[3] Yet in spite of its importance to state-sponsored commerce raiding, no definitive method existed in the eighteenth century for determining the national character of ships and cargoes.

Correspondence found aboard captured ships offered a rich but troublesome trove of evidence to solve the riddle of nationality at sea. Captured correspondence of all kinds had the potential to reveal a great deal about a ship's course, cargo, and identity. Letters among imperial officials, which were often carried by merchantmen, could provide clues about the empire to which a ship properly belonged. The elaborate epistolary networks of merchants, which underpinned Atlantic commerce, could give hints about the ownership of both vessel and cargo.[4] Even private correspondence, which had expanded in both volume and social reach during the eighteenth century, could be put to use by privateersmen.[5]

Yet letters, in part because of their very richness, could be a difficult source to use for the determination of nationality. Letters conformed to complex, idiosyncratic literary conventions that varied by country and circumstance. They came in many languages, and the use of codes could make them doubly unintelligible to unintended readers. To make letters testify to the validity of a prize, then, privateersmen and jurists had to get creative. They read letters "against the grain," looked for clues from the language in which they were composed, considered how correspondence had been handled, and (once they were in jurists' hands) subjected them to close reading informed by judges' understanding of the norms of mercantile practice and imperial economies.

Exploring the use of letters as proof of nationality deepens our understanding of how eighteenth-century privateering worked and sheds light on wider questions about the relationship between land and sea in the early modern era. The struggle to turn letters into evidence highlights the transitional quality of national identity in the eighteenth century. The maritime context starkly reveals the improvised, fragmentary nature of nationality-in-the-making. The troubled efforts to use letters as evidence of nationality in privateering enterprise also point to the futility of creating artificial analytic boundaries between land and sea. Private letters are usually imagined by historians as a piece of the terrestrial world, as a means of connection between those who stayed home and those who traveled abroad. Letters' transit over the water has usually been ignored, for this reason, in maritime histories. But eighteenth-century privateersmen and admiralty judges perceived a tight connection between owners on land and what happened at sea. By looking beyond the land/sea divide, they transformed instruments of terrestrial communication into instruments of power and knowledge on the water.

Prize Law and the Problem of Nationality

The late seventeenth century marked the beginning of the end for freelance commerce raiding—or, as it was pejoratively called, piracy. All of the major European states took steps, both military and legal in character, to tame and domesticate piracy. In the decades surrounding 1700, every European empire elaborated and strengthened the legal framework governing state-sponsored commerce raiding. These efforts included the codification and dissemination of guidelines for legal raiding, intensified policing of commerce raiders, and the expansion of tribunals to administer and adjudicate prize cases.[6]

The core of the new regulation of privateering was "prize law": a set of procedures, under the jurisdiction of admiralty tribunals, that governed the capture of enemy vessels and the determination of which seizures were legitimate ("good" or "valid"). Prize law drew on a shared European tradition of maritime law, stretching back to the Middle Ages, that had significant commonalities across the Euro-American empires. In each empire, prize law was concerned entirely with property: its objects were ships and cargoes, not legal persons. This meant that it could apply to human beings who were transported as cargo—the enslaved[7]—but did not govern criminal behavior at sea, such as piracy, which was dealt with under a separate body of maritime law. Like most forms of maritime jurisprudence, prize law fell within the jurisdiction of specialized admiralty tribunals distinct from ordinary civil or criminal courts. These tribunals, which also existed in each empire, had a narrowly circumscribed jurisdiction limited to ships, sailors, cargoes, and matters related to them. The individuals who staffed eighteenth-century admiralty tribunals included some highly trained legal specialists—such as those who served on the High Court of Admiralty in Great Britain—but many lower-level judges had little formal training in the law of prize.[8] In some jurisdictions, of which the United States is an example, the regular courts doubled as admiralty tribunals. However, whenever courts sat as admiralty tribunals they followed admiralty procedures and rules of decision that were distinct from their usual practice.[9]

Both privateersmen and admiralty jurists had responsibilities in the process of determining whether a prize was valid. Privateersmen had to make an initial determination about the likely nationality of vessels that they encountered at sea. The captain's duty was not to muster definitive proof of nationality; his obligation was to determine whether the vessel or cargo was probable enemy property (and if not, release the ship promptly).[10] The decision had to be made speedily but with care: if a merchantman were taken without good reason, the owners of the ship and the cargo could demand that court costs, expenses, and even damages be charged to the captors.[11]

Once a captured ship arrived in port, admiralty judges assumed the task of making a final judicial determination of the national character of ship and cargo. The British High Court of Admiralty underscored the importance of the courts' determination in a 1757 case issuing from the capture of a ship off the coast of India. A lower court had excused the captors from completing regular prize proceedings. But the High Court judge, George Hay, reversing the decision, added an admonition in the strongest terms: "the maritime law of nations *universally received*," he declared, "requires a judicial determination in the Court of Admiralty" of whether a vessel was "the property of enemys only, and that no ally or neuter hath any share or interest therein."[12]

Unlike privateersmen at sea, admiralty judges were obliged to determine the actual ownership of vessel and cargo. The courts almost always made their decision about whether to condemn a vessel and its cargo on the narrow grounds of whether its owner was an enemy subject.[13] To adjudicate this question, they conducted adversarial trials drawing on a prescribed body of evidence, normally limited to the papers taken from the captured merchantman (including any private correspondence it carried) and testimony gathered from individuals on both vessels.[14] In rendering their verdict, the judges could condemn all or part of the captured ship and cargo as a valid prize, or they could find that it was not a valid prize at all. In cases where there were allegations of misconduct, the judges could also assess penalties against one or both of the parties.

Letters as Evidence: Privateersmen

Prize law was surprisingly imprecise about what constituted good cause for a privateer to seize a merchantman at sea. A vessel obviously "pretend[ing] to be neutral," or carrying cargo without the proper papers, or with false or suspicious papers, was probably subject to seizure.[15] But one could not rely too heavily on official paperwork as proof, given the relative ease with which these documents could be falsified or altered. Ships' papers also regularly got lost, damaged, or destroyed at sea.[16]

Given the unreliability of paperwork, and faced with the need to make quick, high-stakes judgments about the legal identities of vessels and cargoes at sea, captains of privateers looked for additional evidence of nationality that was both readily accessible and easy to "read." The construction of the vessel and cargo were one source of information: privateersmen could sometimes tell that a ship or barrel was the typical work of shipwrights and coopers in an enemy region.[17] Many captains in the eighteenth century came to rely on a "common sense of nationality": because there was an emergent connection between sovereignty and regional cultures, they could often infer the likely nationality of a ship and cargo from the language spoken by the crew. Yet this practice was hardly foolproof, as many captains discovered to their chagrin after 1776. American independence, by creating two enemy polities whose inhabitants shared "the same language, the same habits, the same manners," added a new layer of difficulty to the already challenging process of discerning nationality at sea.[18]

Letters offered the captains of privateers an important additional way to quickly assess the nationality of a merchantmen they had stopped. The most straightforward use that privateersmen made of captured letters was to search them for indications of illicit activity or ownership. In effect, mariners sought to use letters as a kind of informal ship's paperwork that could supplement (or contradict) a merchant vessel's official documents. The *Ravens*, for instance, with a cargo belonging in part to the New York firm of Greg & Cunningham, was captured and condemned during the Seven Years' War after a concealed "letter of instructions to the supercargo" revealed that the ship had engaged in illicit trade with the French.[19] Nearly forty years later, at the end of the eighteenth century, a British admiralty court cited a letter that the ship *Minerva* carried as evidence that the ship was engaged in illicit trade with enemy subjects—even though its official papers were in order.[20] In each of these cases, privateers used the correspondence found aboard the stopped vessel to muster crucial evidence that the ship or cargo contained enemy property.

Letters that demonstrated some connection between a ship and enemy subjects, even if the letters did not have any direct bearing on the voyage, could also lead to a ship's seizure. Consider the case of George Folger during the first year of the American Revolution. The Nantucket-born captain of the brig *Richmond*, secretly loyal to the rebellious American Congress, was trying to navigate safely in 1776 from the British island of Nevis to rebel-held Massachusetts. Folger had managed to acquire false official paperwork for the ship and cargo, which he had used to get past the British customs agents in Nevis. But he worried that if he encountered a British ship, a search of his vessel would reveal highly incriminating "Letters and Dispatches from the Friends of America in England" to the U.S. Congress. Though these concealed letters had no direct connection to the cargo, he worried that they would strongly suggest to a suspicious privateer or naval officer that that the *Richmond* was a rebel ship and provide sufficient cause for its seizure by the British—even though the ship's papers were formally in order.[21]

Yet privateersmen had more ways of using letters as evidence than just reading them for clues to illicit activity. One potential source of information was the language in which letters were written. In the international world of eighteenth-century trade, commerce took place in many languages, and privateersmen sometimes could not even read the letters that they captured: what, for instance, did the captain of a French privateer make of a trove of letters in Yiddish that he captured aboard a British vessel in the early nineteenth century?[22] But privateersmen knew that there was often a link between the language that individuals in the Atlantic world spoke and their allegiance. This linkage was, after all, the basis for the "common sense of nationality" that mariners used to good effect before 1776 to discern the allegiance of other mariners. Private letters could be made to testify in a similar manner: the language in which a letter was written was a valuable, though hardly infallible, guide to the allegiance of those who had written the letters—and thus could provide a clue to the legal ownership of the vessel and cargo.

During the 1790s, British privateersmen treated the discovery of letters in French aboard an American ship, addressed to a French colony, as strong evidence for suspecting that the ship was engaged in illicit trade "covering" for the French—and thus carrying French property. This was the gist of the story told by Josephine du Bourg, a mulatto woman from Saint Domingue, who happened to be aboard the American ship *Molly* when it was seized by a British privateer in 1793. Under questioning, du Bourg revealed that the *Molly*'s American captain had taken some of her correspondence from her. She had complained to him about it, she reported to the admiralty examiners, but "he told her that those Letters would be enough to cause them to be taken by the English" and had destroyed them.[23] In that case, the captain was probably wise to avoid excess scrutiny: when the ship was stopped, a search uncovered a second set of papers for the ship, which revealed that its cargo was in fact French.[24] The different ways that privateersmen read letters thus tended to intersect: seizures of ships justified on the basis of one kind of document not infrequently led to other documents or sources that confirmed the validity of the initial decision.

Individuals with something to hide, like the captain of the *Molly*, were not the only ones who worried about privateersmen reading facts into the language in which their epistolary cargoes were written. The *Nancy*, another American ship trading to the French West Indies during the 1790s, also ran afoul of a British privateer for carrying French letters. Under examination, David Florence, the *Nancy*'s master, admitted that he had thrown overboard "several Letters, in French, as he supposes." He added that he did not "recollect to whom they were addressed, as he cannot read French." The supercargo, in his examination, offered further explanation: "his Reason for wishing those Letters to be out of the Way, and thrown over-board, was, he was afraid they had no Linguist on board the Privateer, and that, as they were French Letters, it would be the Cause of carrying them into some Port, and detaining them." He emphasized that the letters were not incriminating; the only significant point about them was the fact that they were written in French.[25]

The case of the *Nancy* points to a third main way in which privateers relied on correspondence to provide evidence of a ship's national character: the destruction or attempted destruction of letters. Privateering regulations throughout the eighteenth century made clear that any effort by merchant captains to destroy papers aboard ship, including correspondence, was grounds for suspicion that the ship was engaged in illicit trade.[26] Cases in which privateers invoked the destruction of documents as cause for seizure frequently involved letters, and with good reason: if one destroyed official documents, it made the ship subject to seizure anyway, since it was navigating without papers. The semiofficial status of correspondence—not required of ships but known to be vital to trade and acceptable as proof in court—made it both the logical place to put sensitive information and the type of document that merchant captains were most likely to destroy.

Privateering captains had considerable latitude in seizing ships for having destroyed their papers. In some instances, a member of the capturing crew witnessed firsthand the destruction of papers, or saw papers or a mail bag floating in the water. In many cases, however, the destruction of letters took place out of sight of the captors and became known to the privateersmen only secondhand. The British captors of the American brig *Eagle* in 1794, for instance, heard from unnamed seamen on the prize that "papers [including correspondence] had been thrown overboard."[27] The captors of the *Nancy* and the *Molly*, similarly, found out about the destruction of correspondence from individuals aboard the prizes who had not themselves been involved in the act. The captors of the brigantine *Maryland* in the early 1790s heard from a cabin boy that the master, John Stran, had concealed a letter in his "Stocking" and then surreptitiously destroyed it. The interrogators were even told that Stran had said to the boy that "it was fortunate the said Letter had not been found, as they would have been carried into Port, and likely to have been condemned."[28]

Each of the ways that privateersmen employed seized letters at sea—looking for evidence of illicit activity in the text, inferring enemy ownership from the language in which they were written, and inferring enemy ownership from the destruction of letters—represented an effort to fill the legal gap between state sponsors, who increasingly demanded proof of nationality, and empires that still did not produce systematic official nationality paperwork for vessels and cargoes. The result was a sophisticated form of paperwork bricolage at sea, in which privateersmen used the documents that were available (in this case, letters) to make the best guess they could about the national identity of ships and cargoes.

Crucial to this process of drawing inferences from captured letters was mariners' skill in unraveling the connections between land and sea coded into correspondence. This could be as straightforward as knowing which ports and regions were under the sovereignty of an enemy power at a given moment. One needed this knowledge of the terrestrial political map to assess whether ships whose papers linked them to those places were likely enemy property. Making educated guesses about the allegiance of a ship's owners from the language in which they wrote their letters was a more demanding proposition. To do this successfully, privateersmen needed to know which languages, in which geographic contexts, suggested the likelihood of a particular allegiance for the owners of a ship and cargo. In other words, they needed a mental map of how, for merchant communities, the linguistic cartography of the Atlantic world overlapped with its political geography. This kind of knowledge, which was almost taken for granted by captains of privateers, necessarily straddled the divide between sea and land, incorporating information about both terrestrial sovereignty and water-borne commerce.

Letters as Evidence: Admiralty Courts

Admiralty judges, too, were shrewd users of shipboard letters. Prize regulations in every empire required the captors to turn over to the courts "all . . .

Letters" found aboard a seized merchant vessel.[29] In most cases, admiralty judges never had to use these troves of captured correspondence; the interrogations and official ships' papers usually offered clear and incontrovertible proof of whether a ship or cargo was a valid prize or not. But in the subset of cases that were less open and shut, especially those involving ships and cargoes with multiple owners and interimperial business partnerships, seized correspondence was a crucial type of evidence for the admiralty tribunals.

Like privateersmen, admiralty jurists looked in captured letters for both implicit and explicit clues to the national identity of the ships and cargoes that they accompanied. But the admiralty courts had a different set of obligations under prize law than privateersmen and so a different way of using captured letters. The courts' task was to determine who actually owned seized property and the allegiance of those owners. As a result, admiralty jurists were focused on a particular subset of letters, those which had a direct relationship to the ship or cargo, and unlike privateersmen at sea were interested almost exclusively in their actual contents. The jurists' first step was to gather, sort, and translate the letters that were relevant to their task, processes that required a well-developed understanding of epistolary genre that is not what one usually associates with privateering. They then relied on their deep knowledge of both maritime commercial practice and the conventions of eighteenth-century epistolarity to interpret this body of evidence.

Admiralty judges began the process of working with captured correspondence by isolating those letters that could be used as evidence of ownership. Except in rare circumstances, judges considered only commercial correspondence to have value in proving the nationality of a vessel or cargo. This rule meant that one of the first steps in prize proceedings was for jurists to sort captured letters by genre. Mercantile correspondence had come to be seen as a distinctive epistolary genre, with its own conventions and form, by the later seventeenth century.[30] Men of affairs were taught from a young age to distinguish what one epistolary manual writer called "Letters that have no other End than the Entertainment of the Correspondent" from those in which "Intelligence is communicated, or Business transacted."[31] Yet though commercial correspondence was certainly a genre of its own in the eighteenth century, distinguishing a commercial letter (with probative value) from one written in another epistolary genre (which had no probative value in court) was a matter of judgment.

A corollary to the need to sort correspondence by genre was that admiralty judges could not draw conclusive inferences from the absence or destruction of letters. Under eighteenth-century prize law, a merchant captain's destruction of letters or other documents created the presumption that he was engaged in some kind of illicit activity, making his ship subject to seizure by a privateer. But the fact of having destroyed documents did not offer any direct evidence about the nationality of the prize's owner, which was required for a ship to be condemned by the admiralty courts as a valid prize. Once a ship and cargo were on trial, therefore, the fact of having destroyed letters merely subjected the parties, as High Court of Admiralty judge William Scott explained in an 1800 case, to "the necessity of making farther proof" of ownership.[32] Thus the captain of the brigantine *Maryland*, having successfully destroyed the letter that contained evidence that the ship was engaged in illicit commerce, had both his ship and cargo returned to him by the courts when the captors proved unable to show other proof of its illegal activities.

Admiralty courts took pains to ensure that any letters entered into evidence were translated. Larger or busier admiralty courts usually had paid staff members responsible for producing translations, but even in far-flung outports, where there was not a staff translator, the courts took pains to find merchants and other multilingual individuals who could produce reliable translations.[33] Of course, the process was not always smooth: the High Court of Admiralty judge Sir William Scott, for instance, noted in his opinion on one case that the evidence of nationality was shaky because the letters in question had been "twice translated—first from Arabic into Italian, and then from Italian into English."[34] Yet the fact that this case stood out to Scott indicates just how rare it was for there to be a problem with the translation of correspondence.

Admiralty judges sought to use the captured letters that they had selected and translated to create a probative connection between a seaborne ship or cargo and the "national character" or nationality of its owner. "National character" as it was defined by admiralty jurists in the late eighteenth century was a fundamentally terrestrial characteristic. Drawing on what was by then already a long-established principle of the law of nations, the admiralty courts considered that an owner's national "character" flowed primarily from his or her domicile. This term was usually understood, in the period, to denote an individual's permanent place of residence and/or business.[35] As the chief British admiralty jurist put it in the 1770s, the "nationality of a character of a person taken in war, is with more peculiar propriety determined by *the locality* in the age we live in. This was at all times the doctrine of the law of nations."[36] By the end of the eighteenth century, British admiralty judges had added that long-term participation in enemy trade could "[stamp] a national character" on a merchant regardless of his "mere personal residence." This expansion of the rule of domicile was primarily intended to prevent residents of neutral countries from "covering" for enemy commerce during wartime.[37] When private letters were brought into admiralty proceedings, therefore, jurists were usually trying to deploy them to root the owner of a ship or cargo in a particular place—thereby making it possible to determine whether he was an enemy subject or not.

The case of the *Harmony*, an allegedly American vessel captured by the British in the 1790s, offers one illustration of the reading strategies that admiralty judges used to make captured correspondence into evidence about domicile. The case arrived at the British High Court of Admiralty on appeal: a lower court had found that the *Harmony* was partly American property, but that the portion of the cargo belonging to one G. W. Murray required further adjudication. The question before William Scott, the judge of the High Court, was how to determine Murray's legal domicile. He was an American-born U.S. citizen, and thus at least originally a neutral subject. However, his residence in France for four years prior to the seizure of the vessel meant that he could at least potentially be seen as having become an enemy subject. To resolve this question, Scott defined the problem as one of the merchant's intent: whether Murray ought to be considered to have switched his "domicile" to France and made his property valid prize, Scott stated, depended on whether he had intended to remain in France.[38] By thus defining Murray's future election of domicile as one of the essential "facts" to be proven, Scott in effect made reliance on captured correspondence essential to resolving the case: Murray's intentions could not be divined from the bills of lading that accompanied the cargo.

As he sought to characterize Murray's intentions, Scott carefully weighed and evaluated the entire collection of correspondence that had been captured aboard the *Harmony*. He devoted a good portion of his opinion to explaining how he was going to extract usable evidence from the heterogeneous packet of letters found aboard ship. He admitted that the "different letters" had "various" wording that seemed to be somewhat contradictory, even as regarded the merchant's intentions about where to live. This was, of course, not surprising, given the uncertainty of Atlantic commerce in the period and the fact that these missives were intended for different audiences. Scott even noted that there were "some passages" in the seized letters that directly "intimate a designed return to America." Taken in isolation, such an intention would have made Murray a neutral in the eyes of the court. Yet Scott was too sophisticated a reader to rest his case on a single letter. Scott went on to note that the letters "all concur" in indicating that Murray envisioned "a general, and continued commercial agency in Europe." That is, regardless of his place of residence, Murray apparently intended to maintain a permanent set of commercial interests in Europe. The letters also indicated that even if Murray did intend to return to the United States, he also "intended to return again to Europe" in the near future.[39] An affidavit from Murray's brother, allowed in as supplementary evidence, also suggested that the American merchant intended to remain in Europe for a prolonged period. Scott concluded that the preponderance of the epistolary evidence favored the view that Murray did indeed intend to remain in France and thus could be treated as an enemy subject. His property was condemned.[40]

In the case of the *Conqueror*, which came before him in the same year, Scott demonstrated another set of techniques for reading captured correspondence in order to help determine the nationality of ships and cargoes. In that case, a Danish merchant (one Mr. Peschier) claimed that he had tried to send a valuable cargo including iron and saltpeter to New York, on the account of an American merchant. The ship had difficulties and landed in France instead, where the cargo had been sold; the ship was subsequently seized in England on suspicion of engaging in illicit trade. During the course of the case, Scott requested proof from Peschier of his business arrangement with the American merchant, Mr. St. John. Peschier demurred, claiming that he had only exchanged a pair of letters with St. John, and that his copies of both the incoming and outgoing ones had been destroyed in a major Copenhagen fire of 1795.[41]

Faced with insufficient proof of neutrality but reluctant to condemn a vessel that might be innocent, Scott used his knowledge of the conventions of mercantile correspondence to shore up the thin evidentiary record. It was implausible, he observed, to imagine that a merchant would write only one letter about a major order from across the Atlantic. Surely "Mr. Peschier must have written to inform Mr. St. John of the sailing of this cargo." Copies of that letter and others must "be remaining in the copy book of Mr. St. John." What's more, Scott observed, "there must have been other letters from St. John, or other merchants . . . in allusion to these original orders."[42] The fact that none of these letters had been produced as evidence, Scott strongly implied, pointed to fraud and made him more confident in choosing to condemn the cargo.[43]

Captured correspondence could provide grounds not just for the condemnation of seized vessels and cargoes but also for their restoration to their owners by the courts. This was what happened in the case of the schooner *Hannah*, commanded by Benjamin Rice, which came before the British admiralty courts in the 1790s. The ship had been seized in the Caribbean and condemned in an admiralty court there on the basis of questionable papers and incriminating affidavits from the crew. The owners of the vessel appealed, pointing to correspondence found on board the ship that had indicated that the ship was trading to British Trinidad and Tobago. On the basis of these letters, the British High Court of Appeals for Prizes overruled the lower courts and returned the ship and cargo to its American owners.[44]

Although they have rarely figured prominently in discussions of admiralty courts' prize jurisprudence, letters were a valuable source—in some cases an indispensable one—for adjudicating prize cases in the eighteenth century. Admiralty courts found captured letters essential evidence for deciding a subset of complex cases in which the nationality of ship and cargo owners was otherwise opaque or uncertain. Courts and privateersmen approached these letters differently. Whereas privateering captains were more freewheeling in their use of letters, admiralty courts carefully delimited the set of letters that could be used as evidence of nationality in prize proceedings. They translated the seized correspondence and relied primarily on the text itself rather than features such as the language in which the letter was written. Yet like the privateersmen, judges engaged in sophisticated and well-informed readings of the captured letters. Drawing on their knowledge of terrestrial geopolitics and linguistic zones—and the norms of epistolary communication—judges formally ascribed domicile and thus nationality to mobile merchants and captains.

Conclusion

Privateersmen and admiralty jurists in the eighteenth century faced a fundamental problem in carrying out their trades: a gap between the legal obligation their state sponsors imposed on them to capture and condemn only enemy property, and the absence of reliable nationality documentation at sea. As contemporaries knew well, merchant vessels' official paperwork regularly failed to meet the legal needs of privateersmen and admiralty jurists. This shortcoming was not surprising, given that the documents were not primarily designed with the goal of proving the nationality of the ship or cargo, and in light of the difficulties in preventing forgery or loss of papers.[45]

Privateersmen and jurists alike tried to forestall legal trouble by using alternative sources of evidence to demonstrate the nationality of seized ships and cargoes. Captured letters, turned to this purpose, came to be a regular part of privateering enterprise and the legal proceedings that resulted from them in the eighteenth century. So much so, indeed, that prize law explicitly regulated how captains and judges were to handle them. Yet letters were a troublesome kind of evidence that did not readily offer black-and-white proof of a ship or cargo's nationality. In order to make use of them, privateersmen and admiralty jurists had to get creative, drawing inferences from letters informed by an array of knowledge about the political and linguistic geography of the Atlantic world and the relationship between terrestrial political borders and overseas commerce. Captains of privateers, who had only to identify a likelihood of enemy ownership, could use the presence of letters in foreign languages aboard ship, or the destruction of letters, as grounds to seize a vessel. Admiralty judges used letters, read through their knowledge of epistolary conventions, to shed light on the intentions and allegiances of property owners. In more than a few cases, judges' sophisticated readings of captured letters proved decisive in the outcome—whether to condemn or to release the seized ship and cargo.

The fate of captured letters in the hands of privateers and prize courts offers an object lesson for historians about the importance of keeping in focus the linkage between land and sea in studying the early modern era. A growing number of scholars have studied the early modern explosion of letter writing, relating it to central narratives of the period such as the formation of new political ideologies and the operation of empires. Yet little of this work has paid attention to the ways in which letters moved, and even less to the transmission of correspondence by ship. Merchants and others were well aware of the risk of ships being captured in wartime and surely knew that privateersmen and even admiralty judges might end up as the unintended recipients of their letters. There is much yet to be learned about how letter writers managed this maritime dimension of their correspondence practice. Conversely, students of privateering (and the maritime world in general) would do well to pay closer attention than they have to how letters served to connect ships to the land. The romantic image of the roving sailor or ship as disconnected from land and free of attachments is still a powerful force in this scholarship. But it is unsustainable once one realizes—as eighteenth-century privateers and admiralty judges knew so well—that the letters stashed in ships' cabins and sailors' sea chests were so many invisible cords binding vessels and their cargoes to terrestrial places, communities, and sovereigns.

Chapter 5

Sailors, States, and the Creation of Nautical Knowledge

Margaret Schotte

On November 1, 1624, the *Speedwell,* a 36-gun British galleon, had scarcely set sail from Vlissingen, a port in southwestern Netherlands, when it was stranded on a sandbar just off the coast. The mishap arose due to a disagreement between the ship's master and the Dutch pilot who had been brought aboard to guide the vessel safely beyond the coastal waters. The pilot set out on a bearing recommended by the town's *burgemeester* (mayor), but Master Manne worried, having studied a chart of the coast, that such a course would be unsafe. The Englishman was quickly proven correct when the 350-ton *Speedwell* got lodged on a shoal. The Dutch pilot, with his extensive local expertise, felt sure the vessel would be safely lifted off the sand with the next high tide. Alas, the "ship continued aground, being terribly beaten by the working of the Sea, which was so tempestuous and violent." The keel broke apart shortly after 9 o'clock that evening. A passing bark made a rescue attempt but also struck the shoal, and of the selfless crew, "all were drowned and perished with her." Master Manne remained on board the *Speedwell*, "as willing to lose his life as his credit and reputation . . ."; "hee knew if the Ship perished, hee should bee blemisht with infamie and disgrace." All together, Manne and more than one hundred and fifty mariners lost their lives.[1]

Such nautical disasters happened in growing numbers as early modern Europeans ventured further from home in the name of commerce, colonialism, and expansion. While the risks along the shoreline were daunting—submerged hazards, unfamiliar currents, dramatic tides—navigators faced even greater hurdles in the trackless open ocean. To steer their vessel safely in the midst of towering waves, from the sixteenth century onward sailors turned to new instruments, numerical tables, and mathematical calculations to track their time and position. Where they had once honed traditional skills of observation and memory during lengthy apprenticeships, in the seventeenth century they became increasingly likely to study new mathematical concepts in textbooks and schoolrooms.[2]

In many ways, this shift from deck to desk, and from practice to theory, mirrors the broader transformations that characterized the Scientific Revolution of the sixteenth and seventeenth centuries, when many early modern Europeans began to view the natural world through a lens of rules and mathematics. Sailors have rarely been included in this narrative of innovation; historians of science have deemed them insufficiently mathematical,[3] while maritime historians tend to present navigation as intuitive and timeless.[4] And yet the account of the experts on the *Speedwell*—Master Manne, with his new charts and mathematical approaches, *and* the Dutch pilot, who had developed his observational skills over years in local waters—helps us recognize and add nuance to this picture of applied science. In spite of their respective expertise, neither man was able to prevent the shipwreck. Ultimately, the best approach to navigation would be a hybrid one, blending the pilot's firsthand exploration of local conditions with the master's abstract conceptualization of space. But how did this hybrid model arise?

This chapter calls for renewed attention to the role of the state in nautical training and practice. Mariners like Manne and the Dutch pilot would both have been licensed by their respective nations, a process that involved examinations, record-keeping, and reaccreditation. However, this was not simply a top-down process. As the definition of maritime expertise evolved, land-based administrators increasingly recognized that sailors had a great deal to contribute to this fast-developing science. Opportunities for knowledge exchange—when state administrators tried to appropriate the wisdom of working sailors—gave rise to new forms of maritime knowledge and allowed them to spread. These sailors left relatively few personal records, but contemporary curricula, textbooks, and legislation can provide evidence of their training and practice. Such sources make clear that the science of navigation was generated "from below" as well as "from above."

Over the course of the seventeenth century, commercial navigational knowledge was deliberately integrated into state bureaucratic systems. This chapter will survey how authorities in England, Russia, France, and the

Netherlands faced the common challenge of generating a maritime labor force with the skills necessary to maintain a fleet, be it naval or mercantile. It begins by exploring the shifting definitions and constituent parts of the science of navigation, and considering the ramifications of codifying this knowledge in the age of print. The flood of printed navigational manuals offered lessons about new instruments and techniques, but also preserved traditional practices. The next section traces how land-based authorities (including Samuel Pepys and Peter the Great) came to respect sailors, and consequently elevate them to positions of authority—as tutors, authors, and contributors to theoretical matters such as the longitude problem. Lastly, we see how these experts and their texts operated together in a variety of educational institutions in France, England, and the Netherlands, each of which emphasized different aspects of navigational knowledge. By consulting with experts, fostering research, and developing training programs to ensure an adequate supply of practitioners in the pipeline, these early modern states treated navigation as a scientific project.[5]

A pattern emerges from these systematic responses to the challenge of crossing the open oceans: each nation developed a model that blended practical knowledge with formal, theoretical training. Yet within this common model there were significant variations when it came to disseminating knowledge. States with strong central governments, such as France and Russia,[6] established one or more institutions with clear curricular guidelines, whereas less centralized polities, namely England and the Netherlands, left many of the schools and logistical details up to innovative entrepreneurs. These differences seem to have had only a modest effect on the overall success and reputation of each nation's fleet, suggesting that the idealistic plans of landlocked bureaucrats were less influential than they might have hoped. Instead, the efficacy of these programs was indelibly shaped by socioeconomic factors. In the end, the percentage of the population that came to these schools with some degree of nautical experience, and the status of maritime men in society, had a far greater impact on the level of technical expertise reached by common mariners, and on the success of the navy. Innovation flourished at the water's edge.

Practical Science, Captured in Print

State authorities across early modern Europe considered navigation to be crucial to the success of their polities. Jean-Baptiste Colbert, Louis XIV's secretary of state for the navy, regarded "Navigation and Maritime Commerce as one of the main sources of wealth and happiness of [the] state."[7] The "pearl in the crown of the nation," navigation brought honor, success, profit, and protection to one's country, and nautical manuals were filled with patriotic calls to improve technical standards for the good of the nation.[8] At this crucial period, most naval and mercantile fleets faced a shortage of skilled mariners, and thus sought expeditious methods for training larger numbers of often inexperienced men. In light of colonial ambitions and ongoing war, there was no time to wait for the deep wisdom that gradually accrued over the course of a long career. Instead, mariners and onshore experts devised a variety of strategies for effectively replicating (and improving upon) the practices of those skilled men, producing written guides to what had once been tacit knowledge.

Over the early modern period, authors, educators, and bureaucrats debated whether to consider navigation an art or a science—a conceptual distinction that would in turn dictate how best to teach its particulars. They used the two terms interchangeably and frequently blurred the distinction between the theoretical and the practical. Some authors chose *scientia* and its cognates for its associations with learned knowledge, while others preferred the term *ars*—in terms of "artificial" calculations—to evoke the sense of man improving on nature.[9] Early treatises on the subject tended to identify navigation as an art, following the example of Pedro de Medina's pioneering *Arte de navegar* (Valladolid, 1545).[10] However, despite the cultural currency of that phrase, people still thought of navigation in what today would be called scientific terms. An early Flemish author wrote of the "science of common navigation" and "the arts of Astronomy and Cosmography,"[11] while a century later, a French author equated "the art of navigation" with "the science of pilotage"—despite the very different competencies entailed by each.[12] For some, framing navigation as a "noble" science was intended to raise the status of the inchoate field, but others simply used the term "science" as shorthand for a set of helpful rules. One English student-mariner perfectly captured this ambiguity in his classroom notebook, noting that "Navigation is a s[c]ience or arte which containes certaine Rules absolutly necessary for every man to know."[13]

The parameters of this "science of navigation" had yet to be firmly codified in the sixteenth, seventeenth, and even eighteenth centuries, continuing to represent different things to different segments of society. Authors and practitioners debated not only which technical elements fell within the field—piloting, astronomy, trigonometry, shipbuilding?—but also the best ways to learn them.[14] As traditional coastal navigation was supplanted by celestial navigation on the open sea during the sixteenth century and beyond, the navigator's daily techniques became more complicated and mathematical. Many teachers and authors set out to elucidate the theoretical underpinnings of new mathematical methods—from arithmetic and geometry to spherical trigonometry[15]—while others promised tips and tricks to avoid these same developments, instead offering simplified tables, formulaic rules, or multi-purpose instruments.[16]

During this period, the effects of the print revolution were also working their way through port cities and onto ships' decks. Mariners embraced inexpensive manuals and reference books, to say nothing of engraved charts and the close-set numerical tables that facilitated daily celestial observations and logarithmic computations. The contents of nautical textbooks are illuminating, for authors often tried to explain traditional practices to complete beginners while simultaneously presenting newer, more abstract theoretical approaches to experienced practitioners. Traditional memory rhymes for calculating the time of high tide on one's knuckles appeared alongside cosmographical definitions out of university textbooks, while "regiments," astronomical tables that represented years of collective observations, were juxtaposed with arithmetical practice questions.[17] Even as these volumes blended theoretical and practical knowledge, certain topics were omitted completely. Authors did not attempt to describe how a boat would perform under various wave conditions, nor to explicitly explain when a navigator should intentionally overestimate distances to avoid running ashore (although that was common practice).[18] These books contained no practical hints about weather prediction or tying knots.[19] No matter the power of print, there were certain truly tacit skills that could only be learned aboard ship.

These manuals nonetheless provide a window into specific aspects of the mariner's daily practice and his underlying knowledge. Authors included extensive instructions for a range of nautical instruments, even those that had long been in use. For instance, most works devoted at least one chapter to the humble cross-staff, one of the most basic tools for determining latitude. The first generation of textbooks, from the sixteenth century, included crude diagrams that depicted how to hold the instrument at noon in order to "sight the sun" (measure its altitude). They also provided detailed descriptions of the cross-staff's physical dimensions, components, and markings, for aspiring navigators would probably have had to make their own.[20] A century later, instrument makers were more likely to sell the tools ready-made—but even then, a navigator would have to calibrate his particular staff for errors, make notches for the stars he used most frequently, or even shave off a tiny portion to make the instrument more accurate. It was far from easy, one expert warned, for a navigator to switch to a new cross-staff after making all of these adjustments.[21] Although instrument makers were striving for greater accuracy, every navigator's tools remained highly personalized, delivering either accuracy or efficiency to the daily routine, but rarely both.[22]

Manuals provide additional insights into the navigator's training and practice. As the standards for daily observations, timekeeping, and calculation grew more stringent as the eighteenth century wore on, navigators were expected to be increasingly numerate and to maintain ever more detailed logbooks.[23] However, even in relatively late textbooks, simple early techniques persisted alongside more elaborate ones. As I have argued elsewhere, it was a hallmark of nautical handbooks to include multiple approaches to solving a problem. Authors would present their first choice—an innovative instrument, or trigonometry—but they would also include one or more backup methods in case clouds were obscuring the sun at noon, or pirates seized one's equipment. Within the careful routines of the navy or the merchant marine, mariners were encouraged to deploy both old and new solutions, as practitioners and theoreticians alike acknowledged the importance of flexible problem solving.[24]

Sailors—the State's Newfound Experts

Early modern Europeans viewed navigation not only as a valuable set of rules, but also recognized it as the type of knowledge that could transform states, and should thus be supported by them. With this end in mind, we can see maritime authorities pursuing three avenues that we now regard as components of a scientific enterprise.[25] In order to master the subject matter, mariners and land-based administrators alike sought knowledgeable experts to help them systematically study navigation. Governments called for compatriots to seek solutions for obstinate problems, effectively funding research. They also established facilities to train the next generation, through schools, apprenticeship programs, public lectures, and published materials. This three-pronged strategy enabled new forms of nautical knowledge to germinate and be disseminated.

National navies were usually headed by elite gentlemen. (Unlike Spain, France, and Russia, England did not require naval officers to be titled aristocrats, but men in the highest positions were generally from well-connected families.) This practice effectively linked landed power and naval power, but meant that these officers rarely had firsthand maritime experience.[26] They therefore enlisted experts to advise, adjudicate, teach, and publish treatises on the art of navigation, for administrators as well as for the broader public. Few of the earliest authors had spent time at sea; they were university-educated cosmographers, learned mathematicians, Jesuits and other clerics who traveled the world, or educators who professed their love for the subject—"Philo-mathematicus" or "liefhebbers."[27] This lack of practical experience did not initially cause concern. Rather, elites in many locales tended to discount the knowledge of practitioners, not deeming them qualified to commit their expertise to print.[28] Due to their low social status and lack of formal education, to say nothing of their reputation for insalubrious behavior, seamen were often denigrated as drunks or "frank beasts."[29]

It was well into the seventeenth century before bureaucrats and theoreticians began to reassess sailors' intelligence and capacity to be reliable informants, as they realized how many aspects of sailing could only be learned through time at sea. "Discreet saylors" and "plain illiterate seamen" were suddenly holding their own against "ye best read man of ye Age" and "men of art."[30] Sailors who had retired from the navy or merchant marine began running schools and acting as examiners, and there was increasing incredulity if men in these positions lacked personal experience of the sea. It became more common for authors to advertise their maritime credentials on their title pages—captain, "Schipper," "pilote"—a rhetorical move that occurred more frequently in England and the Netherlands, where such positions had a noticeably higher social standing than in France.[31]

The identity of a navigational expert was in flux. In the latter half of the seventeenth century, when a pair of passionate and conscientious administrators set out to learn about every element of their navies, they turned not to theoreticians or published authors but directly to experienced mariners. Samuel Pepys, meticulous British diarist and consummate bureaucrat, knew virtually nothing about the sea when he was appointed to a clerical position within the Royal Navy in 1660.[32] In his famous diary, the twenty-seven-year-old Pepys recorded his strategies for quite literally learning the ropes—and all the other technical details of naval operations. His first step was to hire Richard Cooper, the one-eyed ship's mate of the British Navy's flagship, the *Royal Charles*, to tutor him in mathematics. To learn the finer points of tar, sails, and timber, Pepys consulted with his friend Anthony Deane, a master shipwright, and with several other captains and scholars.[33] As Pepys rose through the ranks within the navy's administration over the next three decades, he assembled an extensive library of nautical material, familiarizing himself with shipyards, terminology, and daily naval operations, all while making a systematic study of nautical theory and history at home and abroad.

In his ecumenical and international approach to obtaining nautical knowledge, Pepys was not unique. Czar Peter the First pursued an intensive immersion in the final years of the seventeenth century as he prepared to establish a state navy in Russia. In 1697–98, he embarked upon a "Grand Embassy," a tour that combined politics with what would now be termed industrial research. Peter (who had studied Dutch in his youth) traveled incognito to the small town of Zandaam on the outskirts of Amsterdam and apprenticed to a Dutch shipwright.[34] It proved impossible for the young monarch, who stood more than six feet tall, to maintain his disguise, so he moved on to the Dutch East India Company's shipyard in Amsterdam. While there, Peter took navigation lessons from Jan Albertsz. van Dam, author of a popular textbook on the subject, as well as lessons—presumably in physics, mathematics, and astronomy—from the respected instrument maker and natural philosopher Nicolaas Hartsoeker.[35] The next stop on Peter's training tour was across the Channel. He and his exuberant retinue took up residence at John Evelyn's handsome estate in Deptford, where he learned about the British Royal Navy's shipyard and naval procedures when not attending audiences with William III. Peter established a national navy upon his return to Russia, laying out rules for the entire organization. He recruited young graduates of England's Royal Mathematical School to St. Petersburg to teach in the new School of Mathematics and Navigation.[36]

Elites were not the only parties interested in navigation. Peter the Great and Pepys may have had privileged access to notable practitioners—but ordinary early modern Europeans who wished to learn about the sea also had numerous options for instruction. They could purchase introductory textbooks, attend free lectures, or pay for classroom lessons, where they might well venture outside to conduct hands-on observations. As the seventeenth century gave way to the eighteenth, the definition of expert grew yet more capacious. By the 1760s, rather than apologizing for their humble sailor's vocabulary, authors advertised it as a sign of authority, further evidence of evolving attitudes regarding the intellectual capabilities of practitioners. One Dutch teacher, for instance, presented his rough language as a badge of legitimacy: "I am a Seaman and no Scribbler, and I write as I would speak on board."[37]

After consulting with common mariners and reading their books, naval authorities made concerted efforts to gather an insider's perspective from their own officers, and to solicit ideas for new instruments and procedures.[38]

Many of these men also had international experience, having crossed paths with foreign sailors on their own voyages. In 1681 the galley captain Sieur de Viviers advised Minister Colbert that the French navy should follow the example of the Dutch and set up shipboard classes and a series of exams.[39] Proposals for schools were common, although few were acted upon. In 1558, for example, Captain Stephen Borough proposed an "academy in the model of Seville," which Queen Elizabeth declined to pursue. In Paris in 1800, a French naval officer suggested anchoring a training vessel for *gardes de la marine* in the middle of the Seine.[40] A number of practitioners turned their hands to inventing instruments—or criticizing existing ones. In the 1720s, another French galley captain, M. de Radouay, recommended that the navy adopt instruments of his own invention. A generation later, Martinus Martens and Jan de Marre, a retired Dutch merchant commander and a mathematician, both of whom worked as examiners for the Dutch East India Company (VOC), successfully convinced the company to update the list of equipment that was included on every voyage to the Far East.[41]

In addition to making this type of practical proposal, expert mariners were also asked to weigh in on more theoretical problems. In the sixteenth century, a large-scale research agenda coalesced around the intractable "longitude problem." For at least three centuries, scientists and sailors were stymied over how to determine one's east-to-west position on a globe that was itself spinning west-to-east. In hopes of finding a solution that could work on a pitching deck on the high seas, three nations ran contests: Spain and the Netherlands each launched theirs in the late sixteenth century, predating by more than one hundred years the British Board of Longitude's famous 1714 competition. The two earlier longitude contests are less well known than the British case, but all involved similar stories of public-private collaboration and conflict. Dozens of competing solutions poured in from all echelons of society. Great thinkers, including Galileo Galilei and Christiaan Huygens, made contributions; university mathematicians published dense Latin treatises; and men (and women) with virtually no nautical experience submitted eccentric proposals, often embarking on voyages to test their methods and seeking endorsements from experienced practitioners.[42] The problem remained unresolved, however, until the British clockmaker John Harrison invented a reliable marine timekeeper, for which he finally received a reward in 1773.

Harrison's story has been cast as an example of a brilliant individual overcoming trials to invent something revolutionary.[43] However, more recent work on the operations of the Board of Longitude demonstrates that

Harrison's scientific accomplishments were far from solitary efforts.[44] Rather, a government-supported institution fostered systematic research, which ultimately introduced and steadily improved a technology. This latter model, where the gears of inspiration moved more slowly but spread further across society, evokes the modern-day apparatus of "big science." The defining character of so-called big science is generally the scope of the financial investment, as well as the coordination between all the involved parties, scientists and engineers as well as administration and public relations. (In the maritime setting, it can be difficult to disentangle naval budgets from larger national economies; how much of the profits from overseas trade should be credited to sailors, without whom no such trade could exist?)[45] Over the course of the early modern period, mercantilist states poured funding into each stage of the system—understanding the problem, research, training—with the expectation of receiving a good return on their investments. In large part, these programs aimed to reduce the hazards inherent in maritime ventures. It was precisely because of these sizeable risks that governments were so invested in improving navigators' skills.

The trio of longitude contests, with their substantial degree of public involvement and government support, underscore the significant place of nautical science in early modern society. Natural philosophers and mathematical practitioners of all varieties investigated numerous other problems relating to the sea, including tidal theory, climate, astronomy, and ship design. There were cartographic challenges (How could the three-dimensional world be represented on a flat surface? How could the result be used as a computational aid?) and technological ones (How could a user ensure an instrument's accuracy?).[46] The newly established Royal Society included maritime research alongside other questions of natural philosophy. In 1666 and 1667, the *Philosophical Transactions* published two lists of observations that they hoped "Masters of Ships, Pilots, and other fit Persons" would undertake on "Voyages into all parts of the World."[47] Inspired by Francis Bacon's idealized scientific society, the Royal Society expected sailors to return from distant regions with copious scientific information. They requested data on compass variation (then a leading candidate for solving the longitude problem), tides, shorelines, ocean bottoms, and (betraying an overly optimistic idea of sailors' patience for measurement) the weight of a vial of sea water at every degree of latitude.

Across the Channel, the Dutch conceived of similarly ambitious projects. In 1693, the VOC asked its employees to test-drive technological prototypes.

Eighteen ships bound for Batavia via the Cape of Good Hope were given preprinted forms upon which to record statistics about a new method of water desalination.[48] In the eighteenth century, the VOC expected their navigators to record meticulous data about lunar observations, another contender for solving the longitude problem. There were less formal research networks as well: in late sixteenth-century Amsterdam, the celebrated atlas maker Lucas Jansz. Waghenaer paid sailors to bring him new geographical data to correct his charts. (Unsurprisingly, the water-bound Netherlands was one of the first markets to view input from practitioners in a positive light.)[49] In the early 1670s, Abbé Bernou, inspired by a passing reference in a Jesuit *Relation*, asked an acquaintance in New France to send detailed observations of tides and other matters; the abbot wanted to gather data to contradict Descartes's tidal theory.[50] These moments of intersection between maritime men and natural philosophers confirm that sailors did more than simply bring raw information back to the metropole. Rather, they helped create science en route and carried it across the sea.

Contrasting Educational Strategies

Having learned the basics from practitioners and encouraged further development on theoretical and technical fronts, maritime administrators then had to determine how best to teach these materials to the next generation. It was in this third phase of the scientific program—when the principles accrued in the previous stages needed to be imparted to men of varied backgrounds—where neighboring regimes took different paths. Debates swirled not just over how much time young sailors and naval officers needed to spend on deck as opposed to in the classroom, but also about what type of character they required. Officers, it was widely believed, needed certain inherent leadership qualities, but for other ranks it might be sufficient to find young men with signs of aptitude. But aptitude for what—for life at sea or for mathematics? At the close of the seventeenth century, it was not yet obvious that they could be combined, Samuel Pepys, for his part, fretted that the Royal Navy would have trouble finding sufficient numbers of "persons furnished both for the pen and seamanship."[51] Educators were far from unanimous on whether low-status men could actually learn the complex theories of celestial navigation, or if they needed perforce to remain limited to the sphere of intuition and art.

While some administrators placed great weight on social standing and familial connections, others felt that likely candidates for naval service could be found within other maritime professions, from fishing to river ferrymen. As one early eighteenth-century commentator explained, "Men, who [were] utterly Strangers to Marine Affairs" had difficulty performing their duties. However, those who "have been bred to Sea, and have themselves made choice of that way of living, are generally so addicted to it, that one wou'd think they had been born in't, and cou'd live no where else."[52] With this in mind, administrators hoping to speed up the training process looked for any number of more or less formal "nurseries for navigators," areas where promising sailors might originate or be nurtured.[53] In the United Provinces, where such a large share of the populace worked in fishing, whaling, or cargo trades, the merchant companies (and later, the naval corps) had a substantial pool of nautical men from which to draw.[54]

In France, a far smaller group had experience on the water. Coastal cities with strong trading and fishing traditions were obvious targets, but even regions "with few boats" could develop good reputations for able men.[55] The French felt the colonial wilds were particularly promising: the fishery on the Grand Banks of Newfoundland was deemed a "most useful novitiate," while the colonial administrator Jean Talon felt that if the state were to foster the "young people of Canada," New France in general could become a nursery of "navigators, fishermen, sailors and artisans."[56] A French instructor reporting to Minister Colbert in the 1680s agreed that it made sense to seek qualified candidates from sailing centers, but he disputed whether fishermen could be adequately trained: "of every thirty of these people, there are only two" capable of mastering the material. At the same time, the right attitude or "inclination" was critically important, and when one found men of "good will," he conceded that their social origins should to some extent be ignored.[57] The constant need to recruit potential sailors led authorities to orphanages (*hôpitaux*) in port towns. But there was no unanimity: some experts noted that it was preferable to "turn to children of men of the sea" than those in the "hospitals," or, another one noted, to sons of gentlemen. At one point, a local intendant suggested that every family with three children should send one to navigational classes.[58] In all of these cases, prospective mariners needed further grooming before they could serve in the navy or merchant marine—grooming that might be intellectual, social, or practical, in institutional settings that differed by region.

Maritime nations established a spate of formal schools in the latter half of the seventeenth century. The polities in northwestern Europe were directly inspired by the pioneering schools in Iberia, particularly that of the Casa de la Contratación in Seville.[59] The English also admired the French, while the French looked to the Dutch.[60] As in modern scientific programs, it was essential to build capacity in the pipeline. These institutions differed in each local community, with variations arising due to the socioeconomic and political factors that were also at play.

France had the advantage of a strong, centralized monarchy, but its maritime traditions were limited to the coastal regions.[61] Critics contend that Louis XIV committed more attention—and consequently a greater proportion of his coffers—to his army. However, the French navy did in fact see a period of significant reform during the early decades of the Sun King's reign. This multifaceted, coordinated program can be analyzed as an effort, not to foster innovation, but to improve reliability and effectiveness in military and commercial realms.[62] Colbert introduced sweeping national legislation (the pivotal Ordonnances of 1681 and 1689), and spearheaded the establishment of nearly a dozen schools for *gardes de la marine* as well as cannoneers and carpenters.[63] The minister's plan included checks and balances to ensure consistent performance from teachers, students, and practitioners. To improve the quality of instruction in a country with a dearth of suitable teaching manuals, each new instructor had to publish a textbook.[64] Colbert and his successors solicited frequent reports on the conditions in schools, and assigned shipboard *écrivains* (secretaries) to keep track of expenses and anomalies.[65] The students could spend months or years studying, and many of their classes were paid for by the state. However, they were required to pass a series of exams during their schooling and upon returning from the sea. All merchant sailors were expected to spend every third year on a naval vessel to support their country's military and defensive objects.[66]

Under this plan, France was not aiming to improve navigational science so much as to standardize education and training. Policies about classroom incentives and punishments were refined as students proved reluctant to study.[67] Debates over the correct proportion of shipboard training reveals a nuanced recognition of the value of "experiential learning." Naval administrators repeatedly sent new trainees out to sea in order to get their sea legs, but this program proved too dangerous during wartime, and insalubrious even during peace.[68] These training institutions continued to evolve after Colbert's death, but in many ways it was his managerial abilities that enabled the coordinated establishment of this sizeable enterprise.

English officials directed similar energy toward their navy in the late seventeenth century. However, the scale and emphasis of their training program were significantly different. Instead of half a dozen schools for naval cadets, the Admiralty Board relied primarily upon a single institution—the Royal Mathematical School.[69] Founded by Charles II in 1673, the school aimed to train a select group of boys for service in His Majesty's Navy. Most of the students, graduates of the Christ's Hospital charitable school, came from modest backgrounds but showed some mathematical aptitude. Although the caliber of the trainees (and the teachers) was uneven, the school was well respected, in many ways a flagship for shaping the navy and thus the nation. (A number of "mathematical practitioners" also ran independent schools in London and surroundings, and offered tutoring in navigation and related topics, but it is unclear what proportion of their students went on to the merchant marine or the navy.)[70]

The RMS was designed to provide an elite education to talented, lower-class youth. During the first twenty-five years of the school's history, there were extensive debates over the curriculum.[71] Efforts were made to install the latest astronomical instruments—and hands-on lessons were supposed to be a prominent aspect of the school day. (Regrettably, few instruments were ever installed.) Samuel Pepys, who was a very involved member of the school's board of directors, assiduously collected details about foreign institutions, books, and inventions. Teachers who wished to apply for the position of mathematical master submitted elaborate lesson plans, and some of England's most eminent scientific minds—Isaac Newton, Edmund Halley, and the Astronomer Royal, Sir John Flamsteed—weighed in on the curricula for these aspiring mariners.[72] These men had unabashedly elevated priorities. Flamsteed disdainfully argued that a navigator's education should be anchored by mathematics and astronomy rather than menial shipbuilding.[73] Newton had particularly lofty goals: he insisted that the youth at the RMS should be trained in "inventing new things and practises, and correcting old ones, [and] in judging of what comes before him." Newton's mathematical idealism had hints of political utility: in his view, such innovative critical thinking would "furnish the Nation with a more skilfull sort of Sailors, Builders of Ships, Architects, Engineers and Mathematicall Artists of all sorts, both by Sea and Land, then France can at present boast of."[74]

Despite the Royal Navy's high aspirations for this institution, it largely failed at its original mission. The idealistic curriculum was disregarded, the exams were perfunctory, and few of the students who studied there in the early decades went on to naval careers of any note. (Nor did they become the inventors of Newton's dreams!)[75] And yet the British fleet went on to dominate the seas in the eighteenth century. This disjunction between formal training and professional performance suggests that more effective lessons must have taken place outside the classroom. Whereas the French tried to arrange a series of training cruises, the British simply placed teachers aboard many of their vessels. These lessons, increasingly structured over the course of the eighteenth century, continued to be a key venue for cementing theoretical as well as practical knowledge.[76]

Looking back across the English Channel, we can see a third example of how the science of navigation was mobilized. Curiously, the Netherlands—widely considered the apogee of maritime success in the seventeenth century—established a state-funded school only in the final decades of the following century. This was partially because of the decentralized nature of its navy, but was also due to the numerous high-quality independent schools that already dotted the coastline. In 1624, when the *Speedwell* was wrecked, the Dutch were still prioritizing local, experiential knowledge—as was the case for virtually all European mariners outside of Iberia. This model worked extremely well when much of the republic's maritime traffic was on familiar routes along the North Sea coast, through the Channel, and around the Baltic region. However, as Dutch trade expanded to Asia, the nature of their navigators' daily work changed markedly. The Dutch quickly adopted charts and instruments to help them in foreign waters. By the mid-seventeenth century, professional navigators had become comfortable with the trigonometric calculations and logarithmic tables that celestial navigation required.

To a greater extent than the French or English cases, the Dutch maritime community was shaped not just by the navy but also by two major merchant companies. Notably, neither the East nor West India Companies (VOC and WIC), which were quasi-state institutions in their own right, saw any need to open a training school of their own.[77] In order to secure a lucrative post as a navigator or captain with either of these companies, men needed to pass a series of qualifying exams that tested them on the latest mathematical techniques. They paid for private lessons to help with all of this. As early as the 1580s, entrepreneurial teachers established small schools in Amsterdam, Rotterdam, and other ports. Schoolmasters vied for sailors' business, and once the mariners had signed up for a series of lessons, they could also purchase manuals, instruments, and even blank books for their homework.[78] The curricula shared many elements, but some classes stood out. For example, an eminent author and teacher from North Holland, Dirk Rembrandtsz. van Nierop, took his students out to observe comets and other celestial phenomena.[79] (It was van Nierop's younger relative, Jan Albertsz. van Dam, who gave lessons to Peter the Great.)

The Dutch maritime community was brimming with teachers, textbooks, and diligent students clamoring for additional mathematics lessons. As much as a tenth of the adult male population made their livelihood on the water, and although they might have been sailing for years, many men wished to take classes to improve their job prospects. Such healthy competition led to high standards and innovation. If the longitude contests discussed above invited practitioners of all stripes to submit proposals, this free market system similarly encouraged teachers to be more creative in their classes, their textbooks, and their pedagogy. Many of these entrepreneurial teachers developed new instruments, sold them to their students, and then charged for additional lessons. As Jim Bennett has observed in his studies of British and French instrument makers, an open market fostered inventiveness—even more than Newton's mathematical curriculum did.[80] (England, like the Netherlands, had more independent teachers than France, and a similar diversity within its publications and instruments.) Dutch navigators, who studied in these more rigorous classrooms and were motivated by enviable wages, were early adopters of certain new instruments, and also grew comfortable at reading dense trigonometric tables and making precise adjustments to their position. Mariners in other regions were far more likely to stick with simpler—and less exact—instrumental solutions.

By the eighteenth century, however, as economic opportunities diversified and the Dutch ceded much of their maritime dominance to the English, a smaller proportion of young Dutchmen spent time working on boats. In response to this, the Amsterdam branch of the navy felt the need to establish an academy, the Kweekschool, in 1785. Their curriculum hewed closely to the leading textbooks of the day.[81] When it came to hands-on practice, they differed in a notable way from the French *collèges de la marine*: instead of making provisions for training cruises, they erected an oversized model boat *inside* the courtyard of the school, large enough for the students to clamber up to practice working the rigging. Where the French needed time to acclimate to the swell of the waves, the Dutch were likely already used to spending time on the water; they needed only to practice their rope work.

Around the same time, the VOC increased the rules governing its trading voyages, record-keeping, and examinations, a late move toward stricter regulation that seems to have had an inverse effect on the caliber of the mariners. A VOC captain, Jan Stavorinus, felt that the company's new rules "impeded and fettered [the commanders of Dutch ships] in the improvement of navigation," with the end result "that the English, the French, and others, so far outstrip us in the making improvements, new discoveries, &c."[82] This drive for higher technical standards and greater precision came at a time when many Dutch mariners were starting from a less experienced place. Where previous generations were readily able to graft technical procedures onto a traditional foundation, by the close of the eighteenth century, the training system seemed less effective at preparing experts to wield hybrid knowledge.

Conclusions

Over the course of the early modern period, maritime practitioners and administrators recognized the intertwined theoretical and applied aspects of navigation, and poured resources into supporting and expanding the field. These brief sketches illuminate very different approaches to what was essentially the same scientific undertaking: training competent officers and crews in order to launch and maintain large fleets. The fleets—mercantile as well as naval—were substantial enough, and the number of individuals involved great enough, that these projects can be considered the big science of the day. Whether the driving forces behind these programs were powerful individuals such as Peter the Great or Jean-Baptiste Colbert, or mid-level bureaucrats like Samuel Pepys or the directors of the VOC, they all shared similar strategies for acquiring and promoting scientific knowledge. Each state sought out experts, showing an increasing respect for experienced practitioners. In the drive to find solutions to problems, they enlisted the help not only of academicians but, once again, of practitioners.

Despite these commonalities, these programs for training future generations have instructive variations. These correlated roughly to a country's degree of centralization: authoritarian monarchies, like France and Russia, tended to establish schools and curricula that were more standardized—but professionalizing efforts such as theory-based examinations or stints aboard ship seem to have been less effective at guaranteeing minimum competence. By contrast, in the polities with less rigid control, namely the decentralized Netherlands and parliamentary Britain, examinations focused on applied skills seem to have been more regular aspects of professionalization. Although the relative success or failure of these programs can only be measured obliquely, by estimating changes in the rate of shipwrecks, respective international reputations, or the level of mathematics in each country's textbooks, the strongest—and most innovative—systems turn out to be those with the most connection to the water.

Both the United Provinces and England, lapped by the North Sea, featured a wide variety of maritime professions. Thanks to these ample opportunities, it was far easier to recruit men who were already familiar with open water and more likely to commit themselves to its vicissitudes in the hopes of reward. In the Netherlands, many of the men taking navigation lessons already knew how to sail, unlike the majority of the young pupils in the French schools, a disparity that certainly shaped the content of the lessons. In these nautical environments, those educating the next generation enjoyed more respect (sometimes university educated, sometimes the men who set the examinations for the broader community), and exposed their pupils to more advanced lessons. These environments where the sea facilitated extensive trade also offered sailors a reason to improve their numeracy (as investors or brokers of goods), which then allowed them to manage more complex computations at sea.

In the end, confident bureaucratic plans for implementing the advice of experts did not always have the desired result: top-down efforts could rarely overcome socioeconomic factors. In countries where few aspiring mariners had experience on the water, it was hard to speed up the process of teaching traditional knowledge. For all the well-intentioned respect for hands-on practice, brief stints on training ships were no substitute for years of careful observation. In regions with more marine connections, by contrast, a larger proportion of naval recruits had already gotten their sea legs, and once aboard could thus study new concepts and techniques unhindered. Uncovering these variations within a common enterprise also underscores the local scale of epistemic practices, and reminds us that particularity can shed light on the global picture.

This analysis helps overturn claims by earlier maritime historians that the oceans were becalmed by technological timelessness. It also destabilizes outdated teleological accounts of the Scientific Revolution. In her recent work on "Artisans/Practitioners," historian of science Pamela Long contends that the "science" that emerged during the early modern period should be conceived of as "an appreciation for the knowledge acquired by hands-on manipulation and the use of instruments; the practices of direct observation and experimentation; methods of precise measurement and other forms of quantification; and a positive valuation of individual experience."[83] This broader definition clearly encompasses mariners. In fact, navigators stand out: not only did they retain many traditional practices far later than expected, but, since their field combined elements from astronomy, arithmetic, and geometry, they engaged in significantly *more* mathematics than many other artisans.[84] For anyone seeking to understand longer-term patterns in scientific development, nautical practitioners and institutions should be considered an important bellwether. In a period given to debates over the dichotomies of science and art, head and hand, theory and practice, the example of the navigator's education demonstrates that there was a much more complex interplay between these pairings.[85]

At its heart, the story of the science of early modern sailing is not a simple one of top-down administration, nor of bottom-up influence. Here, as complex elements from traditional practice are blended with more abstract theories, we find multiple parties participating in the creation of knowledge. We should view Czar Peter, incognito in a humble shipwright's house, as part of the same enterprise as the young naval recruits sitting in a classroom working through trigonometry problems, and as well-born officers learning the finer points of masting, rigging, and wielding a cross-staff. With each new challenge from the sea—encounters with new peoples, places, or hazards—individual actors and states alike had to devise new solutions. By recognizing sailors as scientists, we gain new insights into how these practices of sovereignty, technology, and technique were generated and transformed, both on the high seas and closer to shore.

Chapter 6

Indigenous Maritime Travelers and Knowledge Production

David Igler

In March 1817, a young Caroline islander named Kadu climbed aboard the Russian exploratory ship *Rurik* for destinations unknown to him. Despite repeated warnings from his friends on shore, Kadu refused to leave the *Rurik* and he made clear his desire to sail away with this group of Europeans, all of whom appeared thrilled to have him in their company. During the next year Kadu would experience the frigid cold of the Bering Sea, visit the Hawaiian Islands and meet the great King Kamehameha I, and gather extensive knowledge of unfamiliar places and people before returning to his adopted home in the Marshall Islands. Given his role in the expedition, one might be tempted to characterize Kadu as an intrepid indigenous explorer, similar in kind to Vitus Bering or James Cook. But such a comparison would be ill-advised. Instead, Kadu represented a fairly ordinary Pacific islander and navigator—ordinary in the sense that he already possessed extensive travel experience and he was very much at home on the sea. It was curiosity that inspired Kadu to see what lay beyond the horizon, and while he had never before met Europeans, the men on board the *Rurik* seemed to amuse him with their peculiar ways, constant stream of questions, and surprising forms of knowledge.[1]

On the *Rurik* Kadu met a young man named Ludwig Choris whom we might be tempted to characterize as Kadu's cultural opposite. The expedition's wealthy Russian sponsor, Count Nikolai Rumiantsev, chose Choris to serve as the official artist for this imperial voyage. Often dressed in a vest and topcoat, Choris appeared to be an educated Russian gentleman if not a minor noble. He

Figure 6.1. "Kadu," from Louis Choris, *Voyage pittoresque autour du monde* (Paris: Firmin Didot, 1822). Courtesy of Alaska State Archives.

was neither. Like Kadu, Choris came from fairly humble origins, although his exceptional artistic gifts gained him entry to elite academies in Ukraine and Russia.[2] And similar to Kadu, Choris developed a desire to see what lay beyond the horizon and, ultimately, visually represent it for European audiences. The voyage on the *Rurik* offered him the opportunity to do just that.

Kadu and Choris spent almost a year together, in very close quarters, on a voyage that failed to achieve the goal of its sponsor: the discovery of a Northeast Passage connecting the Pacific to the Atlantic Ocean. However, the voyage did result in the publication of certain scientific and illustrated volumes that today reside in the world's great archives. One of those publications is Choris's *Voyage pittoresque autour du monde*, a collection of drawings and lithographs that document the voyage.[3] This rare 1822 book offers striking views of Pacific locales and communities during the early nineteenth century—views of species, landscapes, indigenous peoples and their seacraft. While other artists documented Pacific populations and locales during this period—one contemporary would be Jacques Arago—no artistic work compares to those images produced by Choris. However, his work is less important for its artistic value than for the way it transmitted knowledge of geographic and ethnographic concerns: ethnographic in the sense that Choris attempted to depict indigenous people in relationship to their cultures, homelands, and the historical moment.[4]

As Choris visually rendered the people, places, and cultural differences he encountered in the Pacific, Kadu powerfully informed the artist's accumulated knowledge through his stories, songs, navigational technique, and general sensibilities. The relationship of Kadu and Choris offers a view of how knowledge was produced in a maritime context of imperial and indigenous interactions. It demonstrates how knowledge was not simply acquired or invented by Europeans, but instead resulted from connections and exchanges with the indigenous groups encountered on the *Rurik*'s voyage. Furthermore, the perspectives embedded in Choris's images show the way that indigenous knowledge from Europe's periphery held a powerful influence at the metropole. Not just fellow travelers on a voyage, Kadu and Choris embarked on a journey of mutual discovery and knowledge production.

Gathering Intelligence and Indigenous Travelers

Individuals such as Kadu occupy a peripheral position in global maritime history. By tradition, maritime history focuses on European technologies that facilitated navigation, imperial designs often cloaked in voyages of discovery, market connections across vast oceanic spaces, and Western cartographic representations of terrestrial-aquatic relationships. Most maritime historians view indigenous people as tangential to these oceanic travels, flows of information, and historical currents. There are many problems with this established view, beginning with the relationship between movement and agency: the seagoing people of imperial polities moved across space, while natives and locals remained stationary and isolated. The fact that Kadu's ancestors—and Polynesian groups in general, to say nothing of other indigenous groups around the globe—were long-distance voyagers and "people from the sea" (*kakai mei tahi*) for millennia prior to European expansion is typically ignored or footnoted, placing natives in a remote and romanticized antiquity.[5]

Native individuals assumed a variety of roles on most European-sponsored exploratory and commercial voyages during the last half millennia. They served as pilots, cartographers, interpreters, navigators, negotiators, sailors, sexual consorts, and in many other positions—often, and perhaps most frequently, against their will. Famed explorers and common captains alike abducted indigenous people from their home communities and placed them in these vital roles that made possible what Thomas Bender considers the "real discovery" of Europe's imperial age: intelligence about the world's oceans.[6] However, some native individuals willingly signed on to ship manifests for wages and experience, even if the high mortality rates for indigenous crewmembers easily topped those of European sailors.[7] European voyages desperately needed such indigenous experience, and in many cases, native guides signed on for a price.

Going back more than 500 years, Vasco da Gama neglected to record the price charged by the Muslim guide he acquired in Malindi just north of Mombasa on the east African coast in 1498. Da Gama knew enough about the Atlantic coastline to find his way into the Indian Ocean, but once there he had to rely on native informants to reach his ultimate destination of Calicut, India. His Muslim guide possessed more than enough experience in the Indian Ocean to draw "a chart in the fashion of the Moors," and in less than a month his ship *São Gabriel* arrived at the famed pepper market of Calicut.[8] Vasco da Gama's pilot disappeared from the historical record once they reached India, but it may be safe to assume he found return passage to Malindi due to his familiarity with the trade system between India and East Africa.[9] European metropoles, it would seem, were not the only places with networks of information.

The prevalence of native-drawn maps or charts—such as the one produced by da Gama's guide—demonstrates both geographic and cartographic skills. Such was also the case almost three centuries later, when Philip Carteret's circumnavigation (1766–69) might have floundered without a valuable indigenous informant. Fortunately for Carteret, the Mapia Island "Indian" temporarily on board his ship knew the ocean's pathways to such a degree that he chalked a map of key Indonesian islands directly onto the ship's deck. According to Carteret, this indigenous navigator had joined the *Swallow*'s company so willingly that Carteret named him "Joseph Freewill."[10] He died within five months near the island of Celebes (now Sulawesi), due to either scurvy or the foreign microbes he encountered on the ship. European ships represented deadly contact zones for native guides like "Joseph Freewill."[11]

Tupaia, perhaps the most famous indigenous guide in the annals of global maritime history, joined James Cook's first Pacific voyage in Tahiti in 1769. This Ra'iatean navigator and *arioi* (priest) knew a great deal about most everything, according to Cook's onboard naturalist Joseph Banks: "[W]hat makes him more than any thing else desireable [*sic*] is his experience in the navigation of these people and knowledge of the Island in these seas; he has told us the names of above 70 [islands], the most of which he has himself been at."[12] Tupaia's "navigation of these people" referred to his ability to speak with (and translate for) a variety of Polynesian groups, whereas Cook confessed that his own grasp of native thoughts "might be quite erroneous."[13] Tupaia especially assisted Cook in his encounters with New Zealand's diverse Maori people; Tupaia did not particularly respect the Maori, who he thought were "given to lying" and generally untrustworthy.[14] "Tupaia had his biases," writes James Belich; "[h]e was inclined to see Maori as failed Tahitians" due to their practice of ceremonial cannibalism.[15] It should come as no surprise that indigenous guides like Tupaia possessed their own cultural baggage and prejudices, and to some extent Tupaia's biases may have shaped his translations of language and knowledge for both James Cook and the Maori.

Similar to Joseph Freewill, Tupaia had willingly joined Cook's voyage, and the list of known voluntary guides is an extensive one for this time period, including Comekala who sailed to China on the *Sea Otter*, Te Pahi who boarded the *Venus* bound for Australia, and Kualelo who circumnavigated the globe between 1788 and 1792 on British vessels. However, far larger numbers of indigenous people found themselves on foreign ships against their will, abducted from their home communities and forced to play a particular role or provide some key intelligence for a long-distance voyage. When in doubt—the great explorers believed—grab someone from shore who may be able to resolve that doubt.

European navigators regularly relied on the practice and strategy of captive-taking. The names of Native Americans stolen from the Atlantic coastline are mostly lost to history, barring a few notable individuals who seemed to transcend the boundaries of freedom and captivity, such as Manteo, Pocahontas, Epenow, and Squanto (who crossed the Atlantic five times).[16] Without the vital intelligence offered by or violently taken from Native Americans, Atlantic exploration might have ground to a halt. Christopher Columbus seized scores of West Indians for the purposes of navigation and local intelligence; according to Bartolomé de las Casas, Columbus captured natives "to get information of what to expect in these places."[17] Juan Rodriguez Cabrillo followed the same playbook for gathering intelligence on the Pacific coast of the Americas. Cruising the Pacific shoreline of Alta California on the *San Salvador* in 1542–43, Cabrillo temporarily abducted at least a dozen Indians in order to seek answers to pertinent questions: Where is your fresh water and food supply? Do you have any gold? Is there, by any chance, a Northwest Passage in the vicinity? Some points of information demanded better communication skills than others, and none of Cabrillo's sailors happened to speak a Chumash or Ohlone dialect. Therefore—and likely thinking about future trips to Alta California—Cabrillo's men "secured two boys [California Indians] to take to New Spain as interpreters."[18] We know nothing more about the two boys' fate, nor can we imagine the terror they felt as the *San Salvador* sailed off from their coastal homeland.

In many of these instances, indigenous people encountered oceanic explorers who were variously lost, directionless, unintelligible, hungry, violent, and understaffed. The locals taken on board may have offered assistance or just been in the wrong place at the wrong time. Kadu's situation was different: the Russian commander of the *Rurik* did not need his help nor did anyone urge this Caroline islander to join the voyage. He simply did.

Kadu, Choris, and Visual Representation from the *Rurik*'s Voyage

Kadu joined the *Rurik*'s small company of twenty-five sailors, naturalists, and officers in March 1817, and the exchange of information began immediately. The lack of a common language certainly made communication a drawn-out process, but Kadu would quickly acquire a passable fluency in German and Russian, while Choris and the naturalist Adelbert von Chamisso began compiling a vocabulary in Kadu's Caroline and Marshallese dialects. Chamisso, a French exile and notable author, developed an immediate attraction to Kadu as a traveling companion; years later he would describe Kadu as "one of the finest characters I have met in my life, one of the people I have loved the most."[19] With little prompting from Chamisso, Kadu offered his nautical knowledge for passing through the Ralik Chain of the Marshall Islands: he "confirmed" or "corrected" the ship's route "and every new path was diligently followed" by Captain Kotzebue.[20] Kadu's geographic knowledge—if only

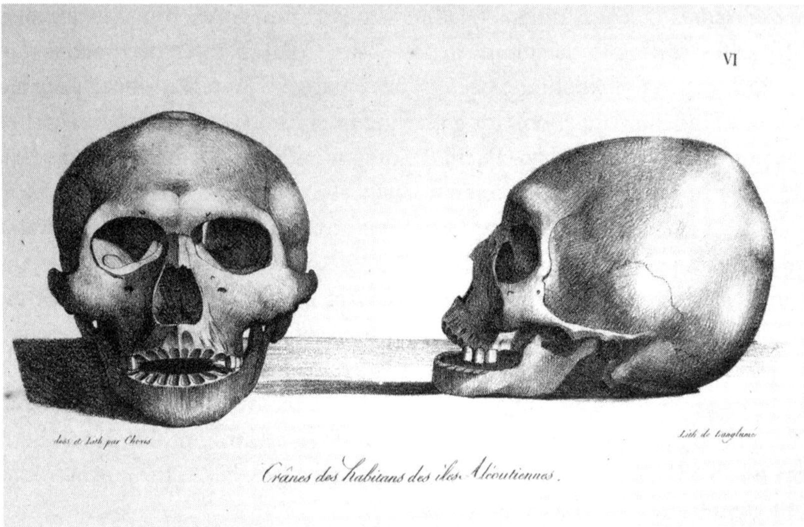

Figure 6.2. "Skulls of the Inhabitants of the Aleutian Islands," from Louis Choris, *Voyage pittoresque autour du monde* (Paris: Firmin Didot, 1822). Courtesy of Alaska State Archives.

specific to this one Pacific locality—would contribute to the maps included in Kotzebue's *A Voyage of Discovery* (1821), which soon circulated through European hands in German, Russian, and English.

But Choris, Chamisso, and the naturalist Johann Friedrich Eschscholtz also sought knowledge from Kadu well beyond the incidental or geographical. Only weeks into the northern voyage, these three curious men presented Kadu with a shocking exhibit: a small collection of human skulls that Chamisso admitted he had "ransacked" from a grave during the previous season of exploration in the North Pacific. "What is this?" Kadu exclaimed, as he scanned the expectant faces of Choris, Chamisso, and Eschscholtz. Chamisso claimed he "had no trouble at all in getting across to him that we were interested in comparing the skulls of the variously formed human races and peoples with each other," and yet skull-collecting and grave-robbing likely struck the islander as an incomprehensible way to learn anything about human difference.[21]

The men staged this macabre exhibit in an attempt to understand Kadu's instincts because they viewed him as a "pure" native with "uncorrupted customs," or so Chamisso claimed.[22] But what *were* his uncorrupted customs? What *was* a Pacific islander, they essentially asked by presenting Kadu with their exhibit of plundered skulls. These were questions about indigeneity, and Kadu's signs of indigeneity fascinated Choris—the many tattoos that adorned his body, the ease with which he sang songs about his home island, and the fact that he apparently had not one but two wives in the Marshall Islands.[23] The *Rurik*'s officers marveled at these outward cultural markers. But what other native habits did Kadu possess? Did he believe in multiple gods? Would he eat human flesh? Did he, by any chance, collect human skulls? This was the purpose of Chamisso's skull display: to test if Kadu might respond with savage instinct at the sight of the skulls. Kadu failed the test. Instead, he displayed fear for his safety and revulsion at the possible source of the skulls. And in failing this initial test, Kadu revealed to the enlightened observers that his instincts were not entirely dissimilar from their own, although his respect for human remains certainly set him apart from European scientists, many of whom collected skulls.

If not interested in the skulls, Kadu eagerly anticipated the radically different oceanic environments they witnessed as they passed into the North Pacific, by the Aleutian Islands, and sailed farther north toward the Bering Strait. The waterscape itself came alive with species that Kadu had never before seen. Choris was equally enthralled with the view: one morning, he wrote, "we saw the sea covered with walrus that were playing on the [ocean] surface; whales surrounded the ship and blew water into the air through their blowholes. It was a singular spectacle to see all these huge animals gathered together in a crowd in these unfrequented parts."[24] Choris hastily sketched these spectacles, only later reworking the images into the final lithographs produced with a well-known French lithographer, Joseph Langlumé. He focused great attention on the targets of the Russian fur hunt, such as seals, sea otters, and elephant seals—all species that Russian naturalists had warned were rapidly declining.[25] Choris drew a Bering seal with mottled fur, rich in detail down to the last whisker; he also sketched sea lions with their backs turned to the artist, they stare with amused curiosity at the ship *Rurik* in the distance. Kadu expressed amazement at the sea lions and ursine seals he studied from the ship's deck—almost a sense of what nineteenth-century naturalists called "the sublime," a mixture of awe and fear at the natural beauty of the scene.[26] Kadu also marveled at the sheer immensity of the Far North, such as the vast landscape depicted by Choris in "Gulf of Kotzebue," in which Choris placed himself in the foreground with Chamisso, a second officer, and Kadu off at a distance—all of them pondering this strange, boundless, and seemingly unoccupied terrain of the North Pacific.

Figure 6.3. "View of the Ice in the Gulf of Kotzebue," from Louis Choris, *Voyage pittoresque autour du monde* (Paris: Firmin Didot, 1822). Courtesy of Alaska State Archives.

Unoccupied it was not. A group of Aleut hunters and paddlers (two of whom would serve as translators for languages farther north) accompanied the *Rurik* for this portion of the springtime exploration into the Far North, and the Aleuts' presence represented the many other groups who had occupied the region for thousands of years. Kadu frequently interacted with these Aleut workers and he witnessed their "misery" as conscripted workers for the Russian-American Company—they were "squeezed like lemons," Choris noted in his journal.[27] Kadu knew the Aleuts possessed different skills than his own and they spoke an indecipherable language, revealing to Kadu new dimensions of human difference. At this stage in the expedition, the Aleuts' most important asset was their knowledge of the Far North. Captain Kotzebue hoped the Aleuts would help them resolve the "final question" regarding the existence of the long-sought Northeast Passage.[28] During the previous season of exploration in the Far North they had discovered no such passage, and Captain Kotzebue had repeatedly attempted to communicate his desire for information from native individuals he encountered.[29]

For his part, Kadu assisted Choris to artistically depict the indigenous people of the North as members of distinct cultural groups rather than simply

Figure 6.4. "Inhabitants of the Aleutian Islands," from Louis Choris, *Voyage pittoresque autour du monde* (Paris: Firmin Didot, 1822). Courtesy of Alaska State Archives.

"Alaskan" natives.[30] They had a variety of physiological features that Choris rendered: the Aleuts, the inhabitants of Kotzebue Sound, and the Chutkes. Choris sometimes depicted them in nuclear family units, which suggested long ancestral ties but may have also been an attempt to appeal to the domestic sympathies of his European audience.

Some of the artifacts sketched by Choris convey specific knowledge of their own. For instance, the Aleuts' *baidarka* canoe was constructed for ocean travel with great precision and symbolized a people who survived by the sea's resources and hunted by virtue of skills possessed by no European. Choris observed Aleuts hunting numerous times, and he especially valued the way they pursued the sea otter in formation, a choreographed display of indigenous knowledge. "When at sea," Choris wrote, Aleuts "place over their eyes a type of visor in order to protect them from the blows of the waves."[31] He sketched the visor with its detailed renderings of hunting sea creatures. The visor narrated an entire way of life for Aleuts: it showed the coordinated attack on sea otters, but also the diversity of the marine life that sustained the people—whales, fish, octopus, and seals. Kadu would have recognized the cultural and educational value of these native mimetic symbols, and surely he and Choris shared their thoughts about the possible meanings. Kadu would not have feigned special expertise in the matter of hunting sea creatures because he recognized the cultural specificity of the hunt, and this may in fact

Figure 6.5. "Chutkes and Their Homes," from Louis Choris, *Voyage pittoresque autour du monde* (Paris: Firmin Didot, 1822). Courtesy of Alaska State Archives.

represent the most significant ethnographic lesson he gradually conveyed to Choris and Chamisso—that the indigenous peoples of the Pacific represented a multiplicity of cultures. Today, this is a central theme for scholars who study Pacific history; as historian Matt Matsuda argues, the Pacific is best understood as a "multilocal" space rather than a single ocean world.[32] Kadu intuitively grasped this concept as many islanders did: from their travel to other islands and villages as well as from their oral traditions.

Many of the lithographs later published by Choris suggest conflicting notions about indigenous communities and the power of colonialism. Nowhere is this better displayed than in his images of coastal California and its native inhabitants.[33] California Indians—especially those attached to the Franciscan missions—received little but scorn from European visitors during this period; these natives, according to most foreign observers, were indolent in their natural state and further degraded by Spanish colonization. Gaspard Duché de Vancy, the artist attached to the French expedition in California in 1786, refused to even give visible features to the Indians of

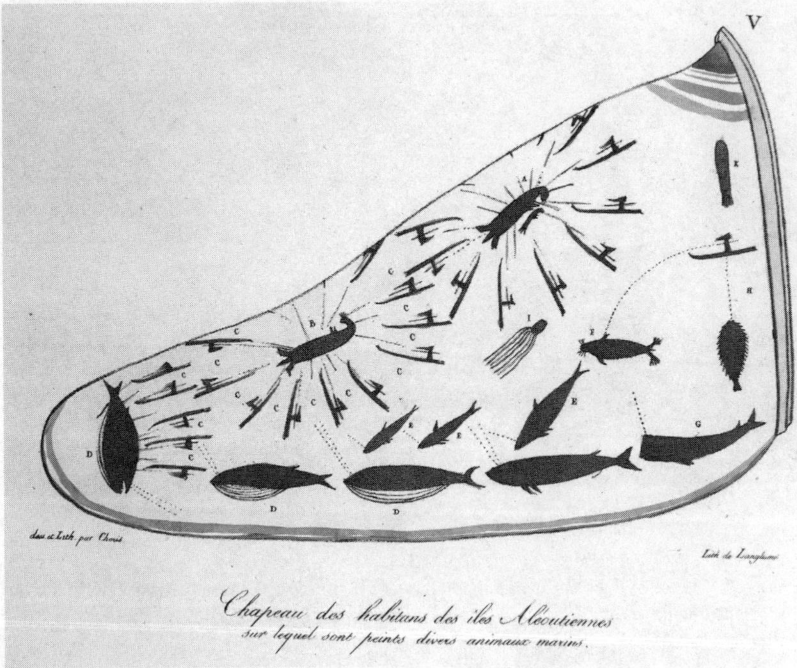

Figure 6.6. "Hat of the Inhabitants of the Aleutian Islands," from Louis Choris, *Voyage pittoresque autour du monde* (Paris: Firmin Didot, 1822). Courtesy of Alaska State Archives.

Mission San Carlos; they appear as one anonymous mass. Jose Cardero, a Spanish illustrator who worked from de Vancy's sketches, provided slightly more detail, but the overall effect remains equally horrid, suggesting prisoners in an eighteenth-century concentration camp. If this metaphor seems a bit extreme, one needs only to consult the disastrous trajectory of California Indian depopulation during the mission period.[34]

Choris, however, rendered the indigenous people of California with much greater nuance, in the process creating a visual "vocabulary" that subsequent narrators would utilize in the coming decades.[35] He depicted people with various countenances and expressions; people who relished and displayed their ceremonial accoutrements because they connected them with the very cultural traditions that the Spanish missions struggled to extinguish. Choris's images sought to document their real lives and communities: they maintained extended families, they nurtured children, respected ancestors, and they played games of skill and chance. Choris did not arrive at this understanding

Figure 6.7. "Dance of the California Inhabitants of Mission San Francisco," from Louis Choris, *Voyage pittoresque autour du monde* (Paris: Firmin Didot, 1822). Courtesy of Alaska State Archives.

on his own; Chamisso's progressive views certainly influenced him, as did Kadu's perceptions of indigenous cultures. Unfortunately, the sheer diversity of indigenous Californians was something Choris would not see or record—Alta California had a precontact population of more than 300,000 people who possessed a multiplicity of lifeways. Choris witnessed only a small slice of this diversity because the majority of the native population lived beyond the reach of the Spanish missions.

Alongside the confinement, forced labor, and demoralization promulgated by the California missions, Choris recognized and depicted the spark of resistance. Choris captured that element of resistance in one of his most stunning and widely reproduced lithographs, "Dance of the California Inhabitants of Mission San Francisco." The *Rurik*'s officers witnessed this event on October 9, the day of the Catholic festival for St. Francis, and Choris portrayed Indians engaged in many activities: dancing, chanting, and clapping, while others sat on the ground striking percussion instruments. Two Franciscan priests stand in the entrance to the mission church, an imposing structure built with the forced labor of those now demonstrating before it. The priests are potentially defenseless against the gathered celebrants. Choris's "Dance of the Inhabitants" shows not a subjugated native population, but instead a large

Figure 6.8. "View of Presidio San Francisco," from Louis Choris, *Voyage pittoresque autour du monde* (Paris: Firmin Didot, 1822). Courtesy of Alaska State Archives.

community that maintained many elements of its culture and also possessed the capacity for violent rebellion—a capacity they actualized at numerous missions during the early 1800s.

However, the agency and resistance suggested in this image seemingly contradicts its companion sketch, "The Presidio of San Francisco." Choris depicts mounted Spanish soldiers driving forward at least two groups of Indians. The neophytes carry bundles on their backs as they hurry in tight formation in front of the mounted soldiers. The Indians appear enslaved, or at best, they function as unfree laborers for the Spanish presidio that looms in the background. Rather than contradictory depictions, the knowledge drawn from these two images conveys the tragic tension at the heart of Spanish rule during this period: Mission Indians could only enact their freedom in certain defined spaces, while soldiers and priests governed their everyday lives through the force of violence.

Colonialism and a Hawaiian Kingdom

These contrasting images raise the vital issue of colonialism, not only in Alta California, but elsewhere around the Pacific during the early nineteenth century. Choris shared the opinion of his companion Chamisso, who wrote extensively and critically about Russian and Spanish colonial efforts. Both empires, he remarked, represented reactionary powers far out of step with his

Figure 6.9. "Port of Honolulu," from Louis Choris, *Voyage pittoresque autour du monde* (Paris: Firmin Didot, 1822). Courtesy of Alaska State Archives.

own brand of Enlightenment thinking. He feared the impact of Europeans everywhere in the Pacific. Chamisso addressed Kadu specifically and the Marshall Islands more generally when he pleaded: "May [God] keep Europeans away for a while from your bleak reefs, which offer them no temptations."[36]

Choris did not tend to focus on colonialism in his visual documentation, and yet certain symbols of European empires appear repeatedly. The artist included these symbols in the European clothing and the cross worn by a couple from the Mariana Islands; also the colonial symbol of the Russian Orthodox Church in a coastal view of Unalaska. Choris's depiction of Honolulu also displays elements of empire: the masts of the European ships provide the backdrop and symbolize maritime power, while imported domesticated livestock (a common symbol of colonial presence) highlight the left foreground. But here Choris's representational technique is at odds with most previous Pacific artists, who drew or painted coastlines as a backdrop to the real subject matter: the imposing imperial ships in the foreground. Choris inverts this traditional view and visually prioritizes the Hawaiian landscape and indigenous dwellings.

The Hawaiian Islands fascinated these fellow travelers. Historian Harry Liebersohn remarks that Choris depicted a "cleaned-up Hawaii . . . plenty of folklore, titillating hints of beauty . . . and above all, a monarch [Kamehameha] firmly in charge."[37] This may be partially true, and yet Choris's work also attempted to honor and visually translate the cultural traditions and even cosmology of native Hawaiians. The Hawaiian idols almost come alive in Choris's lithographs, while his rendering of Hawaiian temples (with a mother and child in the foreground) verify that the beliefs of ancient Hawaiians are not dead but vibrant and living, very much a part of everyday family life. The traditions of dance also remain vital, even if Choris tended to eroticize the dancers—both male and female—for the wealthy patrons who might purchase his expensive volume of lithographs. For every erotic image, however, the artist produced far more pictures that showed Hawaiians as people from the sea whose watercraft was equal parts technology and artistry. Why did the artist sketch indigenous seacraft, not only in Hawai'i, but everywhere visited by the *Rurik*? The answer is that Kadu possessed great knowledge of navigation and he talked constantly about his experiences. Kadu spoke of seacraft leaving his home island in the Carolines for trade and of other groups visiting the Carolines; he talked about his previous voyage all the way from Woleai to Palau, and he discussed the information gathered about far-off places and people—information that arrived via indigenous seacraft.[38] Finally, Kadu narrated his own voyage that took him and three companions almost 2,000 miles east from his home island of Woleai to the Marshall Islands, where he made his new home. Choris

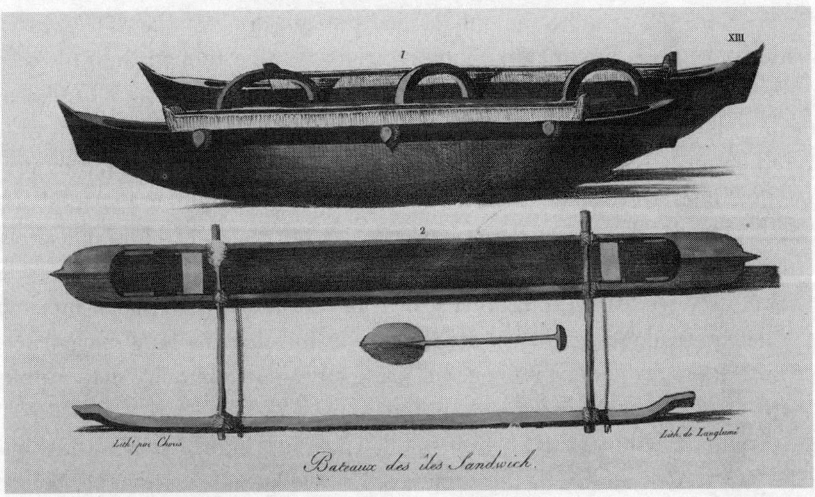

Figure 6.10. "Boat of the Hawaiian Islanders," from Louis Choris, *Voyage pittoresque autour du monde* (Paris: Firmin Didot, 1822). Courtesy of Alaska State Archives.

learned from all these stories and through them he began to understand the centrality of indigenous voyaging to all life in the Pacific.

The *Rurik* spent a few weeks in the Hawaiian Islands and the experience produced different impressions and reports from those aboard the ship. Chamisso, the naturalist, expressed dismay at the corruption of the people—namely the prostitution and other "adulterous customs"—for which he blamed European and American influences. Kadu, on the other hand, seemed to enjoy himself from the get-go. He communicated easily with the Hawaiians—at least Chamisso says so—and he "disappeared among the natives" almost as soon as the *Rurik* dropped anchor at Honolulu Bay.[39] By this time in his life, Kadu knew how to ingratiate himself with people who were different from him, and certainly the native Hawaiians offered Kadu a welcomed break from the stifling companionship of his fellow travelers on the *Rurik*. He offered no critique of Hawaiian behaviors or sexual mores, as Chamisso had done, and Kadu likely felt that this chiefly state and its people deserved his admiration. Kadu's respect for Hawaiian commoners as well as King Kamehameha rubbed off on Choris, who produced many images of ordinary Hawaiians, but only two portraits of the islands' supreme ruler, King Kamehameha I.[40]

The island ruler consented to sit for this portrait on November 24, 1817, but he did so only after considerable persuasion by the Russian captain, Otto von Kotzebue, who explained the king did not cherish the idea of being "transferred to paper."[41] There are two important stories attached to this likeness. First, this may be the only skilled portrait done of Hawai'i's greatest ruler during his lifetime. The king clearly put some thought into his self-presentation, changing out of the simple robe he wore for the outfit of a European sailor, which is known as his "red vest" portrait. He made the change of clothing because Captain Kotzebue implied that his likeness would be presented to Czar Alexander I, although Choris disagreed with this request and desired to sketch him in "native costume."[42] Choris sketched him quickly in this outfit and the king seemed pleased with the results. Choris, however, was not pleased with the results because he wanted to depict this island monarch in native dress. So he did: in a different version that the king did not see, Choris literally disrobed Kamehameha and represented him in a native tunic, which leads to a second story about the portrait.

Some variation of this portrait circulated almost immediately throughout the Pacific, demonstrating the circuits of knowledge in maritime spaces. The officers of the *Rurik* certainly showed it to the inhabitants of the Marshall and Marianas Islands, and copies of it soon materialized throughout Oceania,

Figure 6.11. "Kamehameha, King of the Sandwich Islands," from Louis Choris, *Voyage pittoresque autour du monde* (Paris: Firmin Didot, 1822). Courtesy of Alaska State Archives.

where many people had heard of the Hawaiian king. Chamisso reported viewing a copy of it the following year in Manila, where American merchants planned to bring it to Canton for reproduction in Chinese painting factories.[43] All of the publications that came from the *Rurik*'s expedition included some variant of Choris's portrait of Kamehameha, and it was reproduced in dozens of books in the coming decades. The version that Choris included in the volume *Voyage pittoresque* is compelling: Kamehameha's visage is serious, almost forlorn, as he peers just beyond the viewer. But the image also possesses an ethereal quality partially due to the backdrop: Choris situates him in front of a coastline almost as if he hovers above the water, far off from the land he rules. He is an islander, the artist suggests, and he may in fact be the king of all islanders. Choris would never meet another ruling monarch, and Kamehameha was not long for this world. He died three years later.

As the *Rurik* departed from Hawai'i en route to the Marshall Islands, Chamisso could not help but offer his perspective on the state of native Hawaiians. Within only two generations of European contact, he wrote, "We have grafted greed and avarice onto [them] and stripped the bark of shame off of them."[44] European diseases had raged across the islands since the first landing of Captain James Cook in 1778, and by the time of the *Rurik*'s visit the indigenous population was in a sharp decline. If Kadu shared this knowledge, he did not comment on it to Chamisso or Choris. He likely circulated a different view of Hawai'i to his friends once back in the Marshall Islands. He could not help being impressed by Kamehameha, the one man whom the *Rurik*'s officers identified as "more powerful than ourselves." Chamisso remarked that the king "showed [Kadu] some attention and had [Kadu] tell him" about their voyage. And further, that "this mighty [ruler] was a man of [Kadu's] race and his color"—although one can only guess the extent to which Kadu shared this understanding of racial markers and physiognomy.[45] One thing is certainly true about Kadu's reaction to the Hawaiian population: at this island chain Kadu was surrounded by more people than he had ever seen in his life; far more people than lived in his home island in the Carolines or his adopted home in the Marshall Islands, and again, more people than he had witnessed anywhere in his travels on the *Rurik*. Despite their population decline, the native Hawaiians who gathered around him in Honolulu outnumbered the inhabitants of any village he had ever visited, and to some extent, Kadu must have been awestruck by the island civilization produced by the Hawaiians. Most certainly he brought this information back home, and in some ways it may have been the most vital intelligence he provided from his voyage.

The Voyage Ends: What Became Known

Kadu arrived back in the Marshall Islands in late 1817. The *Rurik*'s voyage would continue for another eight months before its final destination: Count Nikolai Romanzov's estate on the Neva River, St. Petersburg. The crew unloaded crate upon crate of artifacts and scientific specimens, while the naturalists safeguarded their journals for the successful careers they hoped would materialize.[46] Choris carefully packaged his sketches, watercolors, notes, and diary. He set his sights on Paris—an artistic stopover—en route to the Humboldt-inspired land expedition through South America he began a few years later. Choris would only make it as far as Mexico's interior before he was killed on the road. Adelbert von Chamisso and Johann Friedrich Eschscholtz each published dozens of scientific reports in the years to come, circulating knowledge drawn from their journey on the *Rurik* and in part based on information gained from local inhabitants. But what happened to Kadu and the knowledge he brought to the Marshall Islands? And what visual knowledge did Choris produce about Kadu's adopted home? Both men returned with mental archives of the places and people they saw. As Harold J. Cook argues about information gathering in general, their archives provided "material details of the world as perceived by the senses [that] became the foundation for a new approach to knowledge."[47]

The only written account of Kadu's life after the *Rurik*'s voyage derives from Captain Otto von Kotzebue, who briefly returned to the Marshall Islands on a subsequent expedition in 1824. He did not actually see Kadu on this visit, but all the islanders he met spoke of Kadu's previous voyage on the *Rurik* as well as his new stature among Marshall Islanders. The inhabitants of Otdia (where Kadu had disembarked in 1817) initially displayed fear at the appearance of Kotzebue's ship; they seemed more impoverished than before, and Kotzebue learned from two elders named Rarik and Lagediak that many things had changed in the intervening years. According to Kotzebue, the villagers recounted how Kadu had joined a fighting force organized by Lamari from the island of Aur to carry out hostilities against Lavadok on the island of Odia or Wotho. Kotzebue expressed surprise that Kadu had taken with him the weaponry left behind by the *Rurik*, and Kadu had also absconded with the various animals, plants, and an inscribed copper plate left behind by Kotzebue. Nonetheless, Kotzebue proudly conveyed a report—again, offered by his informants—of Kadu charging into battle under Lamari, dressed in European clothes, "armed with a saber and lance." Kadu, the informants recounted, "had been raised to the dignity of a Tamon-ellip, or great commander, by Lamari."[48] Kotzebue reported all this with great relish because it seemed to indicate Kadu's adoption of European ways. Chamisso, upon reading Kotzebue's report and the informants' account of Kadu's new life, simply noted: "So the friends said."[49]

Some things appear certain regarding Kadu's homecoming. For instance, he brought home souvenirs, specimens, various "products of nature," and items produced by Hawaiians, Aleuts, and others.[50] Kadu had amassed many such items, including a depiction of a whale hunt etched into a walrus tusk. But he also brought home items with use-value, such as metal points or knives, discarded iron, and whetstones for sharpening tools; according to Chamisso, he presented these implements to friends and elders upon his arrival. Chamisso interpreted these gifts as examples of Kadu's untainted generosity, though Kadu's intentions surely had more to do with the traditional act of gifting: he displayed his wealth through kindness and distribution, and in the process, he bolstered his own status in the community hierarchy.

Yet material gifts alone would not account for Kadu's rise in stature reported by islanders to Kotzebue. Rather, his new status was likely due to his knowledge about the world far beyond the Marshall Islands and the way he circulated this knowledge among elders and commoners alike. Kadu certainly told stories—the primary means for transmitting and preserving important knowledge—about the many places he visited and the different climates he encountered on the long voyage; in some instances his discoveries would require new words, such as *jiNo* for snow. He would have also informed his people about the different types of expertise he witnessed, such as the hunting skill of Aleuts, the metallurgy of the *Rurik*'s blacksmith, and the political leadership of King Kamehameha, who ruled over an unfathomable number of Hawaiians. Kadu's new knowledge would have certain practical applications. He reportedly assumed the role of safeguarding the new plants (yams, breadfruit) brought from Hawai'i and the domesticated animals (goats, swine) that now flourished on the island of Aur. Finally, as the first person from the Marshall Islands to cohabitate with Europeans for almost a year, Kadu surely would have commented extensively on the beliefs and foreign behaviors of the men with whom he sailed. But of this we know nothing certain.

What visual knowledge of the Marshall Islands did Choris present to those wealthy sponsors who purchased *Voyage pittoresque autour du monde*? Choris portrayed these islanders as exceptionally healthy, strong, attractive, and to borrow Chamisso's word, "uncontaminated" by Western influence. They adorned themselves carefully and had physiques that projected desire and sensuality. Choris carefully depicted their products of nature: for instance, exotic and nourishing fruit, fit for a people who lived in an imaginary island paradise. And he also depicted their products of culture—seacraft, for instance, that sailed true while displaying the artistry of the craftsmen. Above all, he showed the people of the Marshall Islands as members of families and local cultures with no signs of social conflict. The children play, the adults work, and somewhat stereotypically, the people all dance in the warm island air.

Figure 6.12. "Interior of a House of the Radak Islands," from Louis Choris, *Voyage pittoresque autour du monde* (Paris: Firmin Didot, 1822). Courtesy of Alaska State Archives.

Choris's visual ethnography is certainly complicated and even contradictory at times. He had rendered other Pacific groups in a respectful manner, but he also provided visual knowledge of how colonial influences circumscribed their lives, such as the domineering presence of Spanish missions and presidios, or the strained visages of Aleut hunters whose lives were highly restricted by Russian colonization. These symbols and influences were rooted in a particular historical moment; yet they also symbolize the longer historical process of colonialism in the nineteenth century. By contrast, Choris depicts something different in the Marshall Islands: in this place that very few Europeans knew about, he displays communities almost bordered off from the outside world, almost static in time. True, only a handful of Europeans had even sighted Kadu's island chain of Ratak, but far more ships had visited elsewhere in the Marshall Islands since the 1500s. These islanders knew something about Europeans and what they had to offer—and most of it was not particularly good.

Part III

Thresholds

Chapter 7

Maritime Marronage in Colonial Borderlands

Jeppe Mulich

On the second of August 1798, a notice appeared in the Caribbean newspaper the *Antigua Gazette*, paid for by one Campbell Brown. The notice alerted readers that a "stout young Creole Negro Man named Alexis, well known at the Privateers-Men's haunts" had fled captivity as a slave at the estate of Thomas Montgomery. Alexis had, according to Brown, boarded a privateering vessel "as a free man" and ostensibly attempted to join the crew of the American ship. The notice ended with a stern warning: "All Masters, in particular of Privateers and armed Vessels, are therefore caution'd against employing him as they will be prosecuted with rigour if detected."[1] The notice appeared several more times in the paper over the course of August and September, with no indication that Alexis had been caught or returned to the plantation. The young man's fate is unknown, but it is likely that he was successful in leaving the island as a crew member on one of the many vessels passing through the harbor of St. John's, despite Mr. Brown's printed plea to captains and masters. If he did escape in such a manner, Alexis would be one of many maroons who took freedom into their own hands and fled across the sea in the turn-of-the-century Caribbean.

Marronage was a common practice throughout slave societies, from the beginning of European colonization of the Americas to the end of the nineteenth century. The act of fleeing the bonds of slavery, marronage is typically divided into two categories: petit marronage and grand marronage. The first of these refers to shorter periods of flight, as enslaved groups or individuals escaped captivity on plantations only to be brought back or to return within a span of days or weeks. The second involved a more permanent escape, either to other legal jurisdictions or to maroon communities existing more or less outside the bounds of colonial or national states. The escape routes employed by maroons could cross land as well as sea and inevitably looked different depending on their specific geographical and social contexts. While some types of marronage, particularly overland escape from larger plantations, have been given considerable attention in the historical scholarship on both North and South America, *maritime* marronage has been comparatively understudied.[2] This is a thus an area ripe for historical research given the preponderance of the practice not just in the Caribbean Sea, a region defined in no small part by the waterborne pathways connecting individual island colonies, but also in other maritime slave societies across the globe.

This chapter seeks to examine the practice of maritime marronage across colonial boundaries and the legal and political countermeasures taken by colonial elites in response. Drawing on historical examples from the late eighteenth- and early nineteenth-century Lesser Antilles in the Caribbean, and in particular the archipelago of the Leeward Islands, I show that marronage was a key strategy for subverting the existing social order of the region's colonial slave societies. This strategy in turn led to closer intercolonial integration among white elites, especially in the realms of law and security. In order to prevent slaves from throwing off their shackles of their own accord, colonial elites cooperated to a certain extent in the pursuit of runaway slaves and the eradication of independent maroon societies. Such cooperation was not constant, however, and in times of interimperial conflict and competition maroons often succeeded in using the political and economic rivalry between colonies to their own advantage, escaping from one jurisdiction to another in pursuit of greater freedom and autonomy.

The study of maritime marronage provides an illuminating example of the wider global phenomena of interimperial boundary crossing and the resulting cooperation between colonial elites. More specifically, it illustrates how enslaved people's movements across maritime space helped to stimulate specific patterns of intercolonial cooperation extending to legal reforms and coordinated colonial violence. It also shows the limits of such cooperation, especially in times of imperial rivalry and warfare, when escaped slaves became a potential resource for local administrators to exploit.

Marronage as a Practice of Resistance

The turn of the nineteenth century saw a steady growth in the number of free people of color in the Atlantic world.[3] Some of these individuals were born into freedom, while others were brought out of bondage through manumission or by purchasing their own freedom.[4] Not all freedom was granted, however, and a great many enslaved people forged a life for themselves outside the confines of bondage entirely through their own efforts. They did so by throwing off their shackles and escaping the institution of slavery altogether. The very act of escape was an assault against the social order of slave societies because it undermined their most fundamental power dynamic—the relationship between master and slave. By *taking* freedom, rather than having it bestowed on them or purchasing it through sanctioned transactions, maroons challenged the very underpinnings of the colonial world and all those social, legal, and economic institutions within it that relied on unfree labor. In the Caribbean and beyond, colonial society was built upon a foundation of slavery.

Maroon communities could be found in the Atlantic world since the earliest decades of institutionalized chattel slavery. Native Americans and newly arrived Africans fled the bonds of captivity in sixteenth-century New Spain, taking to the hills and forests of Central America and the Caribbean Islands to form new communities in defiance of European colonial rule. Often such communities were pragmatic in their approach to outsiders, working together with one European power in order to stave off the likely encroachments of another. This was certainly the case in that most famous of examples, the Panama Cimmarons, who worked with Francis Drake in the 1570s to undermine Spanish hegemony in the region and capture significant amounts of gold and silver. In other cases of this period maroons themselves became pirates, serving one imperial power or another, or in some cases none but themselves, by raiding colonial settlements and lone ships traversing the Caribbean Sea. A few of these maritime maroons also became slave traders, participating as active agents in that odious trade from which they themselves had broken free.[5]

The seventeenth century was similarly rife with both maritime marronage and maritime maroon communities, especially along the Caribbean coast of Central America and further south, along the coasts of Venezuela and Brazil. The latter colony was particularly prone to marronage, given the extent of Brazilian sugar production and associated slavery already in the seventeenth century. Here maroon villages, called *quilombos*, could grow to a startling size and while the colonial state was generally quick to strike them down, many continued to spring up in places like Bahia. One in particular, the so-called "Black Republic" of Palmares, became an almost mythical example of organized black resistance to slavery.[6] These communities were not restricted to the continental

Americas but could be found in great numbers on Caribbean islands, including in Cuba, Jamaica, and the colonial borderlands of Hispaniola.[7]

Historians and others have recently begun to shine a light on marronage as an act of resistance. Political theorist Neil Roberts has written of marronage as a key phenomenon influencing the development of modern philosophical notions of freedom in the Western world; his work has ignited a fascinating reexamination of marronage within the wider history of political ideas.[8] As welcome and productive as these discussions are, many questions still remain unanswered when it comes to marronage as a historical phenomenon and the official and unofficial responses to this particular act of defiance. Such responses have been especially understudied, but they are crucial when attempting to understand the impact marronage had on colonial societies. The range of strategies employed to combat marronage, from integration of maroon communities to all-out warfare, is indicative of the variety of colonial social patterns and state practices found throughout the world of early modern and modern slavery.

A common theme in the literature on marronage has been the relationship between colonial societies and liminal maroon communities. A traditional inside/outside distinction is not easy to maintain when it comes to the role played by maroons in the colonial order given the sheer extent of marronage and the way in which local colonial administrations were forced to deal with the phenomenon. While officials did their best to prevent slaves from seizing their own freedom in the first place, one of the solutions adopted by officials in response to successful acts of marronage was to coopt and even integrate maroon communities if and when their destruction was impossible or impractical. This strategy might include forcing maroons to undergo military service or perform other services for the colonial state, including hunting down other fugitive slaves.[9] At other times such communities were willfully ignored, either because of a lack of resources to deal with them or because their existence was seen as little more than a nuisance. Despite these exceptions, the colonial order could not simply allow marronage to grow, and officials did their best to prevent and combat it, often cooperating across imperial borders in the process. Not only was the inside/outside distinction thus blurred when it came to the place of maroon communities within colonies, but the boundary between one colony and another was similarly ambiguous at times. Maroon communities cannot be said to have existed wholly outside the wider colonial order, but rather they continued to occupy an uneasy and shifting position at the margins of this order—sometimes seen by officials as direct threats to social stability and sometimes as necessary evils to be contained rather than eradicated. The questions of when and why such views changed and what kinds of specific institutional configurations arose in response to border-crossing maritime marronage remain open.

A different set of questions relate to the practical and logistical aspects of the maroon's journey. The maritime component of so many Caribbean acts of marronage is particularly important here. In many ways the sea granted greater mobility than overland travel, but it was a peculiar sort of mobility requiring very specific tools. The Caribbean Sea was at once a barrier and an escape route, turning its island colonies into maritime prisons with brittle defenses, traversable by way of ship, boat, or even driftwood. For those in possession of such tools, escaping across the waves avoided some of the dangers of overland flight, including being tracked for long distances by men and beasts. Slave catchers and slave patrols, although employed on several islands, were a much more widespread phenomenon in the continental Americas, as were their terrifying canine companions, the so-called negro dogs.[10] But while some dangers were thus lessened by seaborne flight, different challenges faced the potential maritime maroon, including the fickle and dangerous weather of the Caribbean, the ravenous sharks below the surface, and the treacherous waters of the sea itself.[11]

Maritime marronage was often undertaken in groups, as enslaved individuals banded together to build, procure, or sometimes capture vessels on which to make their escape. This was the case on St. Vincent in 1819, when a group of eight slaves originally from St. Thomas reportedly took control of the schooner *Waterloo* in order to make their way to freedom, much to the chagrin of the vessel's owner.[12] Maroons sometimes enlisted the help of outsiders in their escapes across the water, but such relationships could be complicated. In 1785 a family of five were apprehended by Spanish authorities on Puerto Rico, suspected of being maroons. They were onboard a small vessel operated by two white men, who claimed they had stolen the slaves from a Tortolan captain after he refused to pay them for a job. The family alleged that the white men had promised to help them escape bondage on the British colony by transporting them to Spanish territory, only to make it clear that their intentions were less noble while out on the water, at one point drowning their youngest child to avoid authorities noticing the crying infant. Eventually an official from Tortola arrived to reclaim the enslaved family, confirming their story to the Spanish governor, Juan de Dabán—who was at the time faced with a host of similar cases and claims of extradition.[13]

Maritime marronage was an act of resistance to be sure, but it was also one of many other transgressive practices that exploited the fact that maritime Atlantic colonies often found it challenging to police their borders. These practices included smuggling, piracy, and—especially in the nineteenth century—the illegal interisland transportation of slaves, more often for the purpose of bondage than freedom. That colonial officials often saw these varied activities as belonging to the same broad category of illicit border-crossing traffic says more about the view from the governor's mansion than it does about the lived experience of enslaved individuals. For captives and maroons, the sea represented unique dangers and opportunities.

A Maritime Borderland

The northwestern part of the Lesser Antilles is particularly dense, with many of the islands being within just a few miles of each other, including the Virgin Islands and the western islands of Vieques and Culebra off the coast of Puerto Rico. This geographical proximity of islands made it comparatively easy, if still dangerous, for escaped slaves to traverse the sea and travel from one island to another with the use of very simple crafts or rafts, crossing imperial borders in the process and sometimes escaping the reach of vengeful masters and colonial jurisdictions. Maritime marronage was thus a remarkably widespread practice in the region. According to early nineteenth-century reports from the island of St. Croix, marronage was the single most common violation of the slave law in the Danish colony, making up fully one-third of total registered crimes committed by slaves on the island.[14] Maritime hubs such as Charlotte Amalie on St. Thomas and Oranjestad on St. Eustatius were particularly attractive destinations for maroons, since the islands' transient populations and heavy traffic of small craft made it relatively easy for fugitives to slip between the cracks and eventually escape into the wider world of Atlantic crossings.[15]

While the anonymity of these relatively small Caribbean ports can be overstated, they were nonetheless welcome havens of concealment for maroons fleeing the ordered regiment of plantation slavery.[16] As implied in Campbell Brown's notice quoted earlier, the inns and taverns of port towns—the "Privateers-Men's haunts"—not only provided places to lie low but also functioned as nodes in transimperial networks of merchants and mariners, which were extremely useful for maroons looking for off-island passage.[17] The heavily trafficked ports of the region provided many options of vessels to board for maroons, and few captains in need of new crewmembers were willing to ask difficult questions of potential recruits. This went double for privateering vessels, which were often in search of new hands when they were in port to offload prizes and stock up on provisions. For this reason, periods of interimperial warfare proved particularly beneficial to maroons, whose opportunities to join the crew of a passing vessel greatly increased their chances of escape from an island. Many nonmaroons, whether free or enslaved, also joined the crews of these vessels, as shipboard life often provided greater degrees of autonomy and mobility than most other positions in the Caribbean.[18]

None of this is to say that the port towns of the Lesser Antilles were safe harbors for black Caribbeans. In fact, overzealous officials attempting to catch escaped slaves often mistook for maroons the free people of color passing through these maritime hubs. Jan Simons, a free man from Curaçao, was thus apprehended in Christiansted on St. Croix in September 1805 while visiting a local tavern.[19] The sheriff questioned him repeatedly, suspecting him of being a maroon looking for passage aboard one of the many vessels passing through the port, despite Simons's repeated claims of being a free person already employed as a crewmember on the brig of one Captain Groth. After two days of questioning Groth finally appeared, forcing the sheriff to reluctantly release Simons.[20] This was far from a unique case, as free people of color traveling through the region frequently had to endure the suspicion and hostility of local officers of colonial law.

British, Danish, Dutch, French, Spanish, and Swedish colonies in the Leeward Islands coexisted in a sometimes uneasy tension between competition and cooperation. Colonial elites often had strong personal and economic ties to one another, and they shared a strong interest in keeping the colonial social order in place, founded as it was on the assumption of white masters positioned above their enslaved black and brown subjects. Shared concerns over the threat of black uprisings or the destabilization of the region's slave economy, combined with frequent border-crossings between colonies, led to the emergence of transimperial legal regimes.[21] Shared norms and practices, however, existed alongside continued intercolonial competition over sparse resources, including the labor force of slaves and freedmen.

Another runaway notice, this one posted in the *Saint Thomas Gazette* in 1810, illustrates some of the key factors driving marronage in the Leeward Islands. According to slaveowner George Martin of Tortola, three enslaved men from his estate going by the names of Jack Spot, London, and Atrix had "run away from Tortola in a small boat," arriving recently in St. Thomas. Between them the three men spoke "very good English, Spanish well . . . Creole and a little French" and the youngest, London, was trained as a cooper. Martin promised a significant reward of $120 "to any person or persons who will apprehend and lodge in the Fort of this Island the said three Negroes."[22] The fate of the three men is again unknown, but their actions are indicative of a wider pattern. The escape by boat from Tortola to St. Thomas was an exceedingly common route taken by maroons, and the impressive linguistic skills of this group, reflecting the polyglot nature of the microregion itself, would have facilitated transition to almost any other colony in the region. Much as with Alexis mentioned above, it is doubtful that St. Thomas was the captives' final destination, and once out of the Danish port it would have been very difficult indeed to track them down.

The Leeward Islands represent a prime example of a common phenomenon in global history: maritime borderlands composed of multiple imperial polities. These microregional zones of interpolity interaction were composed of colonies from several empires placed in close proximity to one another. Generally characterized by porous borders and often relatively weak state control, these microregions facilitated frequent cross-colonial movement among the inhabitants and strong transimperial networks in many different sectors of society; most border-crossings took place via maritime passageways.[23] Here and elsewhere, the waters around and between insular territories were integral to social and political processes of change, rather than composing discrete maritime spaces.[24]

While many maritime maroons settled down in foreign ports and cities across the region in order to forge new destinies for themselves, others chose a life further outside the sphere of imperial rule. They banded together in small villages that were largely self-sustaining, typically located on remote islands, in dense jungles, or on isolated mountainsides. Such maroon societies could be found across the rim of the western Atlantic throughout the eighteenth and early nineteenth centuries, and many of them have been well documented in the historical literature.[25] They represented a different aspect of maroon life, explicitly seeking the security and safety of a community existing at the margins of colonial society and shaped by the shared experience of enslavement and escape.

The Leeward Islands were hosts to several maroon communities. While the smaller islands of the western Leewards had fewer remote places for such communities to settle without drawing unwanted attention from officials, some of the small and otherwise uninhabited islands in the archipelago became hosts to a diverse group of inhabitants living on the edges of colonial societies. Salt Island, just five miles off the coast of Tortola, was one example of this type of maroon society. The small island, just one mile long and one mile wide, was uninhabited for most of the eighteenth century, but at some point in the second half of the century it became home to a small community of former slaves, either escapees from regional plantations or survivors of a wrecked slave ship. Very few records of this community remain, but there seem to have been few if any attempts to evict the inhabitants or bring any of them back into slavery. In late 1813 the British government was reminded of the island's existence through reports from naval officers patrolling the area, and in an effort to determine the territorial rights and production potential of the land they sent a request for information to John Julius, commander in chief of the British Leeward Islands.[26] Responding to the inquiry, the president of the Virgin Islands Assembly, Richard Hetherington, informed his superiors that Salt Island was an altogether inhospitable piece of land, being both "small and poor in soil," with "4 or 5 white poor people living on it, and some poor free people who endeavor to support themselves by fishing, and by such things as they plant being subject to dry weather, and they get their water from Tortola."[27]

Whether the Salt Island inhabitants in 1814 were indeed free people of color having relocated there from Tortola or the remnants of the earlier maroon community living there is unknown, but it is clear that authorities in Road Town had very little interest in the island or its inhabitants. Officials in London did not like the idea of a salt-producing community existing outside the reach of imperial authority, and through Commander Julius they sent Tortola magistrates scrambling to dig up an old declaration that officially acknowledged Salt Island as part of the British Virgin Islands, divided the land and salt ponds on the island between the existing inhabitants, and proclaimed a tax on the production of salt and cotton.[28] This declaration certified that no other empire could claim the patch of land for itself, but by the very act of delivering the document to London the local government had accepted a certain level of responsibility for actually policing this particular frontier outpost. Although local magistrates in the region cared relatively little for monitoring the outer bounds of their territories when such duties held little or no possibility of profit, the view from imperial capitals was quite different. The existence of spaces beyond colonial control was repugnant to the very idea of imperial order.

The example of the Salt Island village points to an important aspect of Caribbean maroon communities: While they were forged from an explicit desire to reject imperial rule, they were often unable to fully escape the reach of the colonial state. Such encounters might lead to partial integration into economic and legal systems or they might lead to outright eradication.[29] While the policing of territorial frontiers was not necessarily a core concern for most local administrators, territorial challenges posed by other imperial polities, as in the case of Salt Island, could cause the issue to be propelled to the top of the agenda of officials, as could increasing colonial anxieties caused by the growth of marronage and maroon communities. Both factors became increasingly prominent at the turn of the century, as the Revolutionary and Napoleonic Wars spurred on imperial rivalry over land and sea routes at the same time as the revolution on Saint Domingue intensified white fears of black mobility and freedom.

Colonial Countermeasures

Colonial countermeasures designed to combat marronage were common throughout the period, and they often involved a number of different actors and networks—both within and across the boundaries of individual colonies and empires. The problem of marronage was one shared by colonial elites despite their imperial allegiance, and the very act of maritime marronage almost always involved the crossing of official borders. Local measures, including the levying of heavy fines on those found to harbor or employ maroons, were often supplemented with intercolonial measures to varying degrees of success.[30]

The geography of the Lesser Antilles called for certain measures quite distinct from those in landlocked borderlands or larger insular territories. Borders and jurisdictions within insular microregions were far closer to one another, and existed in more complicated configurations, than in most other borderlands of the Atlantic world. The Lesser Antilles was truly a multipolity region, and a maritime one at that, requiring countermeasures that were both coordinated and cooperative and able to operate on the seas in order to be effective. While unilateral approaches to controlling the flow of interjurisdictional movements might be somewhat efficient in border zones such as those in North America, this was not the case in the archipelagoes of the Lesser Antilles, where even the concerted effort of a regional hegemon like the British Empire relied on the cooperation of other colonial powers to be successful.

The small size of the individual island colonies of the Lesser Antilles further contributed to an integrated and active response to intercolonial marronage. On larger islands like Jamaica, or along the sparsely populated coastlines of the continental Americas, maroon communities could sometimes exist as parallel societies with treaty-based relationships to the broader colonial order. But in the Lesser Antilles, where territory was scarce and competition over limited resources was fierce, few colonies could afford such an approach. When maroon communities did emerge, they were more likely to appear on small and otherwise uninhabited islands like Salt Island than on the fertile soil of already populated islands. What is more, the entanglement of intercolonial marronage with other forms of illegal trade and trafficking on the region's seas meant that measures to prevent the flight of slaves often went hand in hand with other measures to control the flow of goods and people, creating a decidedly maritime approach to colonial policing.

At the informal level, intercolonial cooperation in the Leeward Islands was fairly widespread. Many owners who lost slaves posted notices and promised monetary rewards for information leading to their capture in regional newspapers such as the *St. Christopher Gazette*, the *Antigua Gazette*, or the *St. Thomae Tidende*. These publications were integral parts of the burgeoning intercolonial public sphere of the Lesser Antilles, with news traveling across individual islands through word of mouth as well as via printed materials brought by regional traders.[31] While this informal cooperation seems to have worked to some extent, it often proved challenging to reclaim slaves once they had made their way to a different imperial jurisdiction, especially when the official layer of colonial administrations became involved. At times local officials proved willing to cooperate in bringing back maroons, as in 1825 when colonial authorities in the British Leeward Islands restituted a large number of slaves who had escaped plantations on Dutch St. Eustatius and Swedish St. Barthélemy.[32] This action only came about after substantial pressure from the neighboring islands, however, and it was followed by a subsequent British imperial order to end local policies of returning maroons to foreign jurisdictions.[33] That this official decree was not consistently followed by local authorities leading up to the emancipation of slaves in the British Empire illustrates that the gap between metropolitan and colonial interests was sometimes wide, especially when it came to dealing with practical issues, such as marronage, that crossed formal borders at the local level and at the same time threatened the integrity of imperial jurisdiction in the eyes of officials in London.[34]

If there was considerable collaboration in bringing back fugitive slaves between British, French, Dutch, and Scandinavian colonial elites in the region, Spanish authorities were generally more hesitant to engage in such intercolonial cooperation. This was certainly true in the case of Puerto Rico, a frequent destination for escaped slaves as local Spanish authorities proved reluctant to return maroons to neighboring colonies based on a long history of sanctuary decrees. Some of these decrees were specifically tied to conversion to Catholicism, essentially promising freedom at the cost of baptism, while others had little to say about religious faith.[35] A certain shift in the attitude toward foreign maroons took place during the middle decades of the eighteenth century, as the island's authorities realized the usefulness of the potential workforce arriving on their shores. According to magistrates on Tortola the maroons who fled to Puerto Rico were increasingly put to use as laborers there and were "essentially serviceable to the colonisation of a large and spacious island."[36] This result reflected the Spanish colony's comparatively small enslaved population at the turn of the century and the great need for labor in the island's agricultural production, which was undergoing a profound transition from a peasant economy to a plantation system in the early decades of the nineteenth century.[37]

Colonial countermeasures established to combat marronage fit within a broader pattern of efforts at controlling the maritime traffic in the region. Local administrators made frequent attempts to stem the tide of smuggling and other illicit crossings between territories at the turn of the nineteenth century, and although most of these measures were ultimately ineffective or half-heartedly enforced, they nonetheless point toward a desire for greater territorial and regulatory order, especially among British elites.[38] In the Leeward Islands such measures included the Amelioration Act of 1798, ostensibly an ordinance meant to improve the conditions of slaves in the British territories and curtail the excessive force used by planters, but equally serving as an attempt to stave off imperial intervention in local colonial governance amid growing abolitionist sentiment in London. Besides seeking to reduce the mistreatment of slaves, the act also stipulated the need to control the movement and actions of slaves, especially when it came to travel beyond the bounds of individual islands and plantations and engagement in commercial activities. Such movements and activities were not entirely banned, but they were subjected to increased monitoring, permissions, and permits.[39] The movement of slaves was thus meant to be controlled both by individual slave owners and by the institutions of the colonial state.

The staggered emancipation of slaves across different Atlantic empires in the middle decades of the nineteenth century was naturally a key factor in determining nineteenth-century patterns of intercolonial marronage, as well as an obstacle to regional cooperation between elites. Following emancipation in the British Empire in 1834, British colonies in the Lesser Antilles became favored destinations because of their close proximity to other empires and their at least partially free soil.[40] As an example, Tortola, just sixteen nautical miles from the Danish West Indies, saw a number of notable cases of grand marronage from the Danish colonies creating regional headlines amid a steady stream of individual escapes in the years leading up to the Danish emancipation in 1848.[41] In an 1841 report to Copenhagen, the governor of the Danish colonies, Peter von Scholten, explained that "the frequent flight of Negroes to Tortola" from the island of St. John "very much attracted my attention. It must be regarded as the highest necessity to expend the necessary resources to quell this rampant evil."[42] The frequent escapes from the Danish islands were sometimes blamed on overly lax slave owners who refused to apply the necessary force to keep their slaves under control. In a 1843 report, von Scholten complained that "yet another seven negroes are escaped from St. John to Tortola. As this however must be seen primarily as a consequence of the indifference of their owners, since they had shown the negroes an entirely too unrestricted trust and a foolhardy belief in their loyalty, ignoring the allure that complete freedom must inspire, I hope that this event of flight will have no greater consequences than that of the owners' financial loss."[43]

The foreign colonies neighboring British Caribbean islands imposed various countermeasures to prevent such flight, but few of them were very successful. Vessels would often be employed to patrol the maritime borders between colonies, in hopes of catching maroons crossing over into British territory—a task that proved nearly impossible in the Leeward Islands, given the great number of hidden coves and natural harbors on most islands in the region. One such patrolling vessel was the Danish brig *Mercurius*, which spent considerable time cruising the waters between the Danish West Indies and the British Virgin Islands. In 1840 sailors aboard the brig spotted a group of suspected maroons from St. Thomas on small Thatch Island and decided to open fire on them, killing a young woman. This act of violence caused some of the other maroons to turn themselves in, and the event was recorded as a great success—one of the few reported during the *Mercurius*'s patrols.[44]

The continuities in colonial practices before and after the abolition of slavery were remarkable. In the British Empire the institution of slavery was replaced with a new system of indentured servitude—the so-called apprentice system—requiring the continued labor and servitude of emancipated slaves for a period of four to six years, depending on the classification of their apprenticeship.[45] This situation of, at best, quasi-free labor did not lead to a cessation of marronage, but rather to a new wave of escapes in the mid-1830s, accompanied by renewed efforts toward capturing these "runaway apprentices." When escaped apprentices were apprehended, they were typically delivered back to their masters to serve out the remainder of their contract. However, if no notices had been posted or no claims had been made, they would instead be auctioned off to the highest bidder, in a process eerily similar to the slave auctions taking place in prior decades. In 1835 constables in Castries, Saint Lucia arrested a black man named Charlerie on suspicions of being a "runaway apprenticed laborer." The following week a public notice was posted in the *Saint Lucia Gazette*, declaring that "the apprenticeship of said Charlerie, will be sold at Auction to cover Gaol Fees, unless he be immediately claimed by his Employers, and those fees paid."[46]

There were several attempts made at enshrining marronage countermeasures into interpolity law, but relatively few of them proved to be of lasting consequence. One type of interpolity legal framework was created through treaties between colonial governments and maroon communities, as in the case of the Jamaican maroons. Such treaties were generally aimed at stabilizing the colonial legal order and preventing existing maroon communities from growing, and upholding such agreements relied as much if not more on political circumstances as on the letter of the law.[47] While they were acts of interpolity lawmaking in one sense, the agreements were simultaneously intracolonial affairs, enshrining what Michael Craton has called "the "ultimate suzerainty" of the "colonial regime."[48] At the other end of the spectrum, official treaties between different empires stipulating the reciprocal transfer of captured maroons were sometimes drawn up, especially in the larger borderlands of the Caribbean and Latin America. Even the more reluctant Spanish colonies participated in such treaty regimes, and local treaties stipulating the exchange of fugitive slaves were drawn up between Spain and Denmark in the 1750s, between Spain and Britain in 1767, and between Spain and France in 1776.[49] Most of these treaties, however, existed in a tangled mess of other, often contradictory, policies and decrees, giving local administrators significant flexibility in interpreting their specific obligations. As an example, Governor Dabán of Puerto Rico refused most claims of restitution he received in the 1780s in spite of the formal agreements with neighboring colonies drawn up by his predecessors.

Such treaties provided a slightly more robust legal framework than the informal cooperation between local elites, but the treaties were not necessarily more successful in combating the challenge of intercolonial marronage in practical terms, especially since they were often limited to a particular moment of exchange or were not consistently followed, even when they were written to be of a more permanent nature.[50] This was in part due to the continued competition between individual colonies over sparse resources, including the labor of Africans and Afro-Caribbeans—whether they were seen as slaves or fugitives. This creative tension between conflict and cooperation, competition and integration, both among empires and their constituent colonies, was a fundamental characteristic of the maritime borderlands of the Caribbean. It was also a central factor influencing the practice of marronage within the region, providing a space for escaped slaves to maneuver between jurisdictions while always facing the risk of a potential intercolonial response to their acts of resistance.

Maritime Marronage as a Global Phenomenon

This chapter has primarily focused on maritime marronage in the Lesser Antilles, but the practice was much more widespread. Indeed, the act of throwing off the shackles of slavery through seaborne flight was a common occurrence in any place where slavery existed near the sea. The Atlantic world was rife with border regions displaying patterns similar to those in the Leeward Islands. The area around Dutch Curaçao and the Spanish Main in the southern Caribbean was one such region, characterized, in the words of Linda Rupert, by the "extra-official exchanges" and "sociocultural intermixing" of intercolonial commerce and creolization.[51] This intermixing also involved widespread practices of maritime marronage, in both directions, between the Dutch island and the Spanish continental territories, as well as various official attempts at stemming the flow of crossings.[52]

Another Atlantic borderland was the coastal region of the Guianas in northeastern South America. Here the colonies of France, the Netherlands, Spain, and eventually Britain bordered one another and saw significant traffic in goods and people, both across land borders and along the coast. This traffic included a significant number of maroons moving between and across imperial spaces.[53] The region also saw its share of slave revolts that spilled across colonial borders, many of which involved the large maroon communities in places like Suriname and in turn led to more or less successful attempts at establishing new legal frameworks for dealing with this growing challenge to the intercolonial order.[54]

Beyond the Atlantic region, Mauritius and Seychelles are a prime example of an Indian Ocean slave economy that witnessed its own portion of maritime marronage and colonial countermeasures.[55] This too was a maritime colonial borderland, with relatively porous borders and frequent crossings between Mauritius and Seychelles, especially at the turn of the century when the French held the former colony and the British the latter.[56] The phenomenon of maritime marronage in this context, and indeed anywhere in the Indian Ocean, has been all but overlooked by those working on the Atlantic world, a remarkable historiographical absence showing the need for an approach that is not just regional but global in scope.

A common theme across these different maritime borderlands was the opportunities provided to otherwise liminal or disempowered actors to maneuver across and between competing jurisdictions in search of greater degrees of freedom. Only when a region's colonial elites displayed an especially high degree of coordination and cooperation, as was the case at certain times in the Leeward Islands, did they manage to create institutional frameworks for dealing with border-crossing maroons and other fugitives who used the density of jurisdictional claims to their own advantage. Incorporating both formal and informal modes of cooperation, such frameworks made it possible to exchange information about the movement of maroons, organize channels for exchanging captured fugitives, and police the primary nodal points of intercolonial traffic—if not maritime borders in general. These frameworks were not always successful, but they show how maritime marronage itself became a force for further intercolonial integration and a motivating factor in the development of new interpolity law. When such institutional frameworks failed to contain the movement of enslaved people, it was often because competing empires utilized the practice of intercolonial marronage to bolster their labor forces and build up their colonies at the cost of their neighbors. Colonial elites regarded fugitive slaves as resources with which to further expand their property, profits, and empires. Sometimes this competition benefited maroons, providing sanctuaries and free soil, but other times it merely created pathways to continued slavery. Captives broke free of their chains in one territory only to see them replaced by different chains in a territory across the sea.

Chapter 8

Sovereignty at the Water's Edge: Japan's Opening as Coastal Encounter

Catherine Phipps

Throughout the long nineteenth century, most of Japan's foreign encounters took place at the water's edge. After all, Japan's territorial boundaries are defined by water and engagement with the archipelago was predicated on maritime transport. The country's ports and coastline proved to be critical sites where unwelcome landings, external provocations, illegal dealings, and sanctioned foreign interactions took place. Despite having only minimal coastal defenses and no significant naval force for the majority of this period, Japan was able to keep foreigners at the periphery while adding a considerable length of coastline and a swath of connecting waterways to its official map.

This chapter is primarily concerned with the delineation of control at the country's outermost margins—along Japan's waterways and coastlines as well as in its harbors. Japan holds a unique position in world history in that it added to its territorial holdings (and became an imperial power) while its sovereignty was compromised through asymmetrical treaties with Western powers.[1] Following the 1868 Meiji Restoration, the state claimed Ezo (Hokkaido, 1869), the Kuril Islands (Chishima, by treaty with Russia, 1855 and 1875), the Bonin Islands (Ogasawara, 1862 and 1875), the Ryukyu Islands (1879), and the South Seas' Volcano Islands (Kazan Rettō, 1891), before taking Taiwan along with the Pescadores (Penghu) and the now highly disputed Senkaku Islands (Diaoyu, Diaoyutai, 1895) through the First Sino-Japanese War. Rather than focus on the specifics of territorial acquisition, this chapter is concerned with a parallel process to delineate control at the country's outermost margins. The Japanese not only expanded their territory while under informal imperialism, they also managed to keep foreigners out of the country's interior (except with explicit permission) until they regained sovereignty with the revision of unequal treaties in 1899.

Tracing practices and signs of sovereignty at the water's edge through a longer time frame reveals a graduated process of opening—from an early Russian effort to open Japan's trade in 1792 to the negotiated opening of its interior to foreigners with the end of the unequal treaties in 1899. This chapter argues that two things were crucial to the maintenance of territorial integrity and the country's expansion: the Japanese government's ongoing efforts to limit foreign encounters to the country's margins; and multinational cooperation, even as a kind of "cooperative imperialism," in the context of the vast and relatively remote nineteenth-century Pacific.[2] Although these conditions initially cost Japan its full sovereignty, they also enabled the country to participate in the process of defining maritime usage and territoriality in surrounding waters.

This chapter examines key moments during this century of encounters between foreigners and the Japanese to demonstrate the interplay between isolationism and accommodation along the extensive archipelagic coastline. The first section examines how Russian lieutenant Adam Laxman's arrival in the far north and his attempt to open trade relations with the Japanese led to reassessments of Japanese security within the system of Tokugawa foreign relations. The next section turns to the mid-nineteenth-century arrival of U.S. commodore Matthew Perry, showing how this encounter was part of a broader history of Japanese efforts to keep foreigners at bay. The third section considers two events—the Shimonoseki Campaign and the Japanese colonization of the Bonin Islands—that show how multinational cooperation aimed at maintaining shipping and trade rights could serve to hurt or help Japanese efforts to assert authority over its coastline (or, in the latter case, extend it by taking new territory). The fourth section details measures taken by the Meiji government to centralize national power and expand its domestic authority outward to the country's margins. The government expanded its modern administrative reach with the assistance of Western experts, an arrangement that worked to their mutual benefit even as it established conditions that ultimately enabled the Japanese to regain full sovereignty. The fifth section demonstrates that by the 1890s, the Japanese had gained the capacity to police the coastline from the water. Even if the foreign presence remained difficult to resolve, the domestic expectation was increasingly that the government should be able to exercise its authority in territorial waters. Over the course of the long nineteenth century, these encounters with both state and nonstate actors shaped Japan's ability to manage its territorial sovereignty, expand its borders, and keep foreigners restricted to the water's edge.

Tokugawa Security and the Northern Archipelagic Frontier

In October 1792, Russian lieutenant Adam Laxman sailed the *Ekaterina* from Okhotsk, a Russian port in the western Pacific, to Ezo (modern-day Hokkaido), the southern peninsula of which was under Japanese jurisdiction. Laxman's stated objective was to return castaways and open commercial relations with Japan, preferably through negotiations in the capital city of Edo (now Tokyo). For Japan, this arrival came at a time when the shogunate was adverse to forming state-to-state commercial ties. This was especially true for those who were not part of its carefully regulated system of trade and foreign relations. For Russia, Laxman's mission signaled the country's commercial aspirations as it expanded eastward as well as the growing relevance of the islands that lay along the waterways connecting Siberia and Alaska, including those with ambiguous territorial status just to Japan's north.

Adam Laxman's mission was the first serious attempt in decades to open commercial relations with Japan.[3] A memorial his father, Eric Laxman, wrote to convince Catherine the Great to back the expedition gives a sense of their perspective and aims: "For acquaintance and commercial relations with Japan no one has so much convenience as the Russian merchants, who trade on the Pacific Ocean, and what is more, our very proximity gives us the nearest right to it. No one has easier communication, no one can benefit from it more, than our merchants who for a long time already have been thinking of this acquaintance."[4] Beyond indicating a desire to trade with Japan, Laxman's message conveyed the distinct relevance of Japan's location in the northern Pacific to Russia's transoceanic activities. The message had its desired effect on the empress and she granted permission to make contact with the Japanese.

Adam Laxman landed at the port of Nemuro, located on Ezo's northeastern extremity just below the Kuril island chain, where there was a small Japanese settlement. Locals allowed the lieutenant and his crew to stay through the winter, partly out of courtesy for bringing the castaways home. Out of wariness over their true motives, though, they also contacted officials at the nearest castle town of Matsumae and at the capital for instructions on how to handle the intruders.[5] Senior councilor Matsudaira Sadanobu crafted Japan's response.

Shogunal officials arrived that spring to escort Laxman and his crew to Matsumae. Once there, two senior officials—who had come all the way from Edo with a considerable retinue of five hundred, and then were joined by an additional one hundred and fifty indigenous Ainu men—explained that Japanese foreign policy forbade their landing in Ezo. They gave Laxman a permit to go to Nagasaki, the only site in Tokugawa Japan authorized to receive foreign vessels. Without advance Russian permission to head south, Laxman instead turned toward home, followed by two Japanese vessels tasked with making sure he was really on his way.[6]

This late eighteenth-century situation at Japan's northern border shines light on the handling of foreign encounters within the Tokugawa system of foreign trade and diplomacy. This system reflected the principles of a world order in which authority, formulated in terms of civilization, spread concentrically outward from the center, becoming less civilized, or more barbarian (foreign), the farther away one went from the shogunate in Edo. This pattern was replicated in the centralization of power at Edo. Domains were in turn given a large degree of autonomy and land in exchange for declaring their loyalty to and performing specific services for the shogun. Some of these services were related to coastal defense. Wherever smuggling or shipwreck brought foreigners to the shore, local domains and their subjects were expected to serve as intermediaries and, when required, as the front line against incursions. At both state and domainal levels of governance, the Japanese worked to prevent illegal foreign landings through the monitoring and control of the coastline.

Tokugawa's domestic political system and its deliberate strategy of curtailing foreign trade and diplomacy resulted in the handling of foreign engagement at decentralized locations along the margins. The domain of Matsumae served as the northernmost of "four gates"—the other three were Satsuma, Nagasaki, and Tsushima—which the shogunate had authorized to handle regionally relevant foreign affairs and enabled trade at a more localized level (only Nagasaki, the sole international port, was directly administered by the shogunate).[7] The Matsumae domain served as an intermediary in the relationships between Japan and the peoples to the north.[8] Matsumae functionaries theoretically could have been left to handle Laxman on their own, but this episode rattled the shogunate.

Despite a resolution that was satisfactory to the Japanese, this encounter caused the shogunate to tighten its restrictions on foreigners. Laxman's arrival was a sign of the growing numbers of foreign vessels plying the waters around

Japan and the potential danger they represented, prompting the Japanese to harden their position against Westerners. In 1793, the shogunate ruled that no Westerners, except for the Dutch, would be allowed to enter Japan. What are known as Japan's "closed country" or *sakoku* policies, though predicated on earlier restrictions, came about during heightened concerns between 1792 and 1825 and the very term *sakoku* was, in fact, not coined until 1801.[9] These policies represent stringent defensive measures, but Japanese efforts did not end there for the shogunate also took more aggressive action.

By sending officials to Ezo as a response to Laxman's presence, the shogunate was, in effect, laying claim to the island.[10] Indeed, Tokugawa interests had been moving increasingly northward in what Tessa Morris-Suzuki has described as "a frontier zone between expanding Russian and Japanese mercantile power: the ragged edge of a tentative process of nation building."[11] For the Japanese, economic and security issues were both at stake. The shogun ordered an expedition in 1798 to Ezo, Sakhalin Island (Karafuto), and the Kurils before placing the island of Ezo under direct control in 1799.[12] After the threat was perceived to have receded (and officials had come to recognize the significant difficulties in establishing jurisdiction over this remote and rugged land), the shogunate returned the region back to Matsumae's oversight in 1821. Ezo's status would remain territorially ambiguous for the next half century until the newly formed Meiji government colonized it in 1869, sending samurai settlers to populate and develop the island, thus shifting the country's northern frontier to Sakhalin and the Kurils.[13]

The story of Adam Laxman's visit reveals that the long process of efforts to open Japan from the outside also involved a counter process of active domestic resistance to that opening. By the turn of the nineteenth century, Pacific waters, especially those flowing around Japan, encompassed newly popular whaling grounds, lucrative fisheries, and existing or envisioned transportation routes with global connections. Between Laxman's 1792 visit and U.S. commodore Matthew Perry's famed arrival in 1853, there were at least four other attempts to establish new ties with Japan from the Americans, British, and Russians as their economic interests began to converge on the archipelago from the north, east, and west.[14] Other planned ventures and proposals failed or never materialized. Outsiders made efforts to survey Japanese waters, trade illegally under the Dutch flag, and return or rescue castaways. A Danish ship even made an appearance in Uraga Bay in 1846. Beyond these encounters were numerous times when vessels were sighted along the extensive coastline and wrecked ships and distressed sailors turned up on shore.[15]

Decentralization and economic troubles got in the way of a comprehensive effort to strengthen coastal defenses, but the proliferation of unwanted attention heightened Japanese recognition of the country's vulnerability amid increasing maritime activity in East Asia.[16]

Keeping the Foreigners at Bay

The famed mid-century meeting between Japanese officials and U.S. commodore Matthew Perry needs to be viewed within this more extensive set of encounters for two main reasons. First, although it was Perry who secured a new relationship with Japan, his mission was unique more in fanfare and outcome than in its occurrence or the motivations behind it. Looking at this moment within the broader sweep of the century's encounters shows this moment was but one part of a broader convergence of Western interest in both Japan and its place in the Pacific world. Second, the encounter reveals the crucial importance of the littoral in Japan's strategic restrictions on foreign access to the country. When Perry arrived, the shogunate recognized the importance of protecting Japan's seaboard, even if it meant some opening to trade: "The national situation being what it is, if the Bakufu protects our coasts peacefully without bringing upon us permanent foreign difficulties, then even if that entails complete or partial change in the laws of our ancestors I do not believe such action could really be regarded as contrary to the wishes of those ancestors."[17] Indeed, Japanese officials and negotiators successfully managed to open trade and diplomatic relations at limited sites while severely restricting access to the interior.

As was the case with Laxman's visit, the timing of Perry's government-backed expedition of 1853–54 was related to broader calculations of commercial opportunity and diplomatic strategy. On the heels of the signing of unequal treaties in China in 1842, the Americans took California in 1848 and began viewing the Pacific Ocean as the next, watery frontier. Their neighbor on the Pacific's far side seemed within reach. Within just a few years, an expedition to Japan was ready to launch, and U.S. secretary of state Daniel Webster spoke of it in terms that echoed Eric Laxman's justifications more than half a century earlier. He extolled the importance of ocean crossing, of Japan's position within a maritime region that was strategically important, and of the advantages of becoming the first among competitors to gain access to Japanese ports.[18] In keeping with American ideas of manifest destiny, Webster's vision was even more grandiose: "The moment is near when the last link in the chain of oceanic steam navigation is to be formed. . . . It is the President's opinion steps should be taken at once to enable our enterprising merchants to supply the last link in that great chain which unites all nations of the world, by the early establishment of a line of steamers from California to China."[19] Webster understood the strategic significance of these waterways and the economic value of the archipelago in their midst.

Though establishing broader commercial relations with Japan was the U.S. government's ultimate goal, securing the safety of American whalers and access to Japan's coal were of greatest urgency. By the middle of the nineteenth century, hundreds of American whalers were annually plying the strong, sometimes treacherous ocean currents around Japan. They required some measure of support, especially when in distress. Rumors of Japanese brutality toward shipwrecked mariners fueled negative views of the Japanese and encouraged the idea that something needed to be done.[20] Moreover, the Americans wanted to establish coaling stations for their steamships, a chief consideration for anticipated Pacific crossings. It was within this environment that an expedition to Japan was discussed in U.S. government circles.[21]

In President Fillmore's letter to the emperor, which Perry delivered to shogunal officials, he clearly stated the expedition's objectives in asking for "friendship, commerce, a supply of coal and provisions, and protection for our shipwrecked people."[22] During his second visit in 1854, Perry and Japan's chief negotiator, Hayashi Akira, signed the Kanagawa Treaty, also known as a "wood and water" treaty, indicating that it provided for the essentials.[23] Perry did not insist on establishing commercial relations, expecting they would come later, and left satisfied that he had secured a relationship with the Japanese and key rights for American mariners.[24]

Although Perry did not realize it, the Japanese had long known that the Americans were coming. The Dutch had warned them about the impending mission and counseled them on how to handle the Americans' objectives.[25] Although the Japanese conceded to some American demands, they also successfully prevented greater encroachment on their territory. Not only did they keep all meetings with Perry and his landing party to the shores of the bay (Perry never saw Edo), they also kept the number of ports opened to a minimum. Perry originally wanted five or six ports, but Hayashi successfully brought him down to two and proposed using Shimoda (a fairly isolated port well to the south of Edo) and Hakodate (in Ezo), partly because he assumed these sites would be appropriate as weigh stations but not for commercial purposes.[26] Perry accepted those locations.

The next round of negotiations led to the signing of the 1858 Ansei, or "unequal," treaties, which set the terms for Japan's commercial relationships. These pacts—ratified with the Americans, followed by the British, Dutch, French, and Russians—opened five treaty ports, provided foreign concessions with rights of extraterritoriality, fixed tariff rates, and granted most favored nation status, none of which were reciprocated. Japanese negotiators, for their part, worked to minimize concessions and prioritized territorial security.[27] The treaties also served to define the country's position as subordinate to the treaty powers within the international order. Japan was legally becoming the country Westerners envisioned, one in a strategic location that was amenable to their needs while providing safe harbor and trade, and while becoming politically and diplomatically more in step with the countries of Europe and America.

Acceding to these imperatives rapidly led to a new level of Japan's engagement with the world, but even though the treaties were unequal, they also represented important limits on Western power. Mutual interest and competition in securing access to Japanese ports was codified in most favored nation treaty clauses, keeping any one power from taking control of Japan. Although this clause would be an impediment to later treaty revision, it helped reinforce the multinational nature of Western power, providing Japan space to negotiate and articulate its own position.

Significantly, the treaties did not open the country's interior to Westerners. Although colonization was never the goal, Japanese negotiators nevertheless successfully endeavored to push the foreign settlements away from major cities and keep them to locations they could better control.[28] After Japan had thus been "opened" to trade, access was still restricted as foreign settlers, merchants, and crews primarily remained in the treaty port settlements or on the vessels that carried them between the treaty ports. These arrangements legalized certain spatial patterns of contact—along the narrow band where land and water meet, and where zones of mixed or ambiguous jurisdiction existed, either in onshore enclaves with extraterritorial designation or on foreign ships in Japanese harbors and territorial waters.[29] As with contacts in the late 1700s and early 1800s, foreign encounters taking place in Japan under the late nineteenth-century treaty port system were concentrated at the water's edge.

Maritime Access Reconfigured

Tracing practices and signs of sovereignty at the water's edge helps illuminate the construction of the seas surrounding Japan as a multinational zone, even one undergirded by imperialist logic. Since a key goal of Western powers in the Pacific was to establish and maintain access to seaways and ports, Japan's cooperation was required. Hugo Grotius, in his 1609 treatise *Mare Liberum* (The Free Sea), argued that the seas are not owned in the same way as land. As Lauren Benton describes, Grotius "did not contemplate a sea space that was under the control of an international authority but rather one in which various sovereign nations operated 'in tension with one another' without interfering in each other's right to travel and trade freely."[30] In two cases—the Shimonoseki Campaign (1863–64) and the colonization of the Bonin Islands (1862–75)—nations operating "in tension" enabled active cooperation. In both cases, such tension ultimately allowed for Japan's active participation in determining its lines of sovereignty and the usage of maritime space, especially with regard to shipping rights.[31]

In the mid-1860s, the Shimonoseki Campaign was the result of a coastal encounter that became an international incident. It serves to emphasize first how unsettled Japan's new foreign trade remained and second how ideas of free seas and cooperative multinationalism were invoked. Turmoil at the domestic level in turn influenced the relationship between the shogunate and the treaty powers even after the treaties had been negotiated and trade had commenced. Ongoing questions over maritime access, trade, and sovereign rights continued to play out where they had the most immediate impact—along the coast.

The signing and implementation of the unequal treaties heightened existing tensions within Japan. Debates among those favoring a "closed country" foreign policy, those wanting international commerce, and those whose ideas fell in between persisted after the 1858 treaties had been signed. These camps fractured along domainal lines and would ultimately lead to the overthrow of the shogunate in the 1868 Meiji Restoration. In the interim, however, the decentralized nature of the Tokugawa polity fostered localized responses and actions, some of which ran counter to the central government's efforts.

In a sign of how unusual domestic politics had become, Emperor Kōmei made the surprising decision to intervene in governmental matters. Working against shogunal decision-making, the emperor issued a March 1863 order to disregard the treaties, close the ports, and expel the barbarians. The domain of Chōshū was the only one of some 250 domains to directly comply with the edict. One reason was its geographical location in relation to shipping corridors. The safest and most convenient route for vessels traveling from Nagasaki (or the China coast) to Yokohama was by way of the Seto Inland

Sea. Most foreign vessels, therefore, crossed through the very narrow Shimonoseki Straits to enter or exit the Inland Sea at its westernmost point. As a result, foreign vessels regularly skirted the domain of Chōshū (now Shimonoseki Prefecture), a stronghold for *sonnō jōi* (Revere the Emperor, Expel the Barbarian) advocates.

Quick to follow Kōmei's order, Chōshū samurai fired their cannon on American, French, and Dutch vessels passing their shore. Despite swift retaliatory shelling (which killed about forty Japanese and five Americans), the straits were closed to Western shipping for more than a year. Blocking passage through the straits did not end trade, but it did require vessels to take the longer and more exposed southerly course around Kyushu and along the Pacific shoreline in order to reach Yokohama. Theoretically, taking this route should have been acceptable since the Western powers had never claimed the legal right to travel through Japanese territorial waters.

The British had other ideas, however. British diplomat Sir Rutherford Alcock used the rationale that the treaties gave Western powers the right to maintain access to Japan's ports in orchestrating a joint attack (with the Dutch, French and Americans) on Chōshū—in effect asserting that the waterway was not territorial. After punishing the domain and destroying its shore batteries, Alcock demanded that the Japanese government either open Shimonoseki as a sixth treaty port or pay a stiff indemnity. Faced with a stark choice and against expectations, the shogunate opted to pay the $3,000,000 indemnity and began making installments on a penalty it could ill afford.[32] The Japanese understood that opening another treaty port and, therefore, providing foreigners access to a historically strategic chokepoint (in a rogue domain nonetheless) would be far more injurious to the nation.

The workings of international law in this region remained fragmented and open to interpretation.[33] Alcock's actions represented three inchoate positions. First, his response reflected fears about the potential risk posed to their access (and to the Westerners themselves) as domestic challengers imperiled the shogunate.[34] Second, he suggested that international law sanctioned their right to use the Inland Sea in reaching the treaty ports. Third, he relied on the mutual benefits gained by the treaties to create and assert a multinational, cooperative authority, one backed by force, over Japan and its waterways.

In the case of Japan's claim to the Bonin Islands (a small archipelago located approximately 600 miles south of Tokyo), multinational interest in maintaining free seas led to a very different result in enabling Japan to expand its territory even while under informal imperialism. The first Japanese had arrived on the Bonins in 1670 when a junk blown off course in a typhoon landed ashore, establishing what would be used as a baseline of possession but would not automatically lead to later Japanese control.[35] Over the next century and a half as travel slowly increased in the Pacific, more passing sailors discovered these islands and more castaways sheltered there. In 1827, the explorer Frederick William Beechey claimed the islands for the British during a three-year voyage that took him to the Bering Strait and across the Pacific. In the wake of Beechey's visit, a diverse group of Europeans, Americans (most notably Nathaniel Savoy), and Pacific Islanders established a small permanent settlement. They had been living at Port Lloyd (Futami) on the largest island of Chichijima for a couple of decades by the time Perry stopped there on his way to Edo during the 1853 Japan Expedition.[36]

Perry's intent to establish a coaling station and perhaps a naval base there helped reignite earlier Japanese interest in the islands. The idea of taking control of strategically located islands, especially ones that were naturally rich with flora and fauna and surrounded by abundant sea life, was not new. Japanese thinkers Hayashi Shihei (1738–1793) and Satō Nobuhiro (1769–1850), for example, had previously argued in favor of establishing a settler colony in the Bonins. An expedition to the islands was subsequently planned, but the growing presence of Russian vessels to the north prevented its realization.[37]

By the 1850s, the Japanese were well aware that the Bonins were at risk of colonization by one of the maritime powers. The shogunate decided to prevent this by sending Japanese settlers, led by foreign magistrate Mizuno Tadanori, to establish Japanese sovereignty over the islands.[38] Upon arriving on Chichijima in 1862 on a (recently acquired) Japanese steamboat laden with cannon, the group planted a Japanese flag on the summit of the highest mountain, issued harbor regulations, and replaced various English names of the islands with Japanese ones.[39] Although such gestures were not definitive markers of possession, they clarified Japanese intent and helped launch a "small-scale colonial experiment."[40] This attempt at colonization ended after only a year as political turmoil brewed on the home islands.

Nonetheless, after the shogunate was overthrown, the new Meiji government took up the issue of the Bonins in 1875, the same year they signed the Treaty of St. Petersburg establishing Japanese authority over the Kuril Islands and ceding their claims to Sakhalin to Russia. After renaming them the Ogasawara Islands, the government sent new settlers and officials, and established a branch of the Home Ministry there to oversee them. There was no accompanying military operation. As they had done in colonizing Hokkaido in 1869, the Meiji government populated the space with Japanese citizens as a way to demonstrate jurisdiction. In addition to sending settlers and civilian officials to the islands, the Japanese also worked to naturalize the existing foreign settlers as Japanese subjects.[41]

Japan's possession of these islands was not contested despite their lack of military power and their continuing subordination through the unequal treaties. America's Perry and Britain's Alcock had both previously indicated that as long as the islands and surrounding waterways "remained open to the shipping of all powers," they preferred allowing the Japanese to take possession over creating strife among the various polities with interests in the Pacific.[42]

The events in Shimonoseki and the taking of the Bonins demonstrate the significance of Japan's position in the Pacific, amid terraqueous zones that the maritime powers wanted to be able to access.[43] The same kind of "in tension" cooperation worked to ensure maritime access in the Shimonoseki case—to punish Chōshū so as to maintain the unequal treaties and passage through the Inland Sea—and in the colonization of the Bonins—to allow Japan to colonize remote islands sitting along important sea-lanes. Even when the balance of multiple national interests benefited Japan, however, the government was not complacent about its position. After the Meiji Restoration (1868), the new oligarchs (many of them hailing from the *sonnō jōi* domains of Chōshū and Satsuma) knew the country faced ongoing vulnerabilities, not least along its now expanding coastline, and that achieving sovereignty required gaining recognition as an equal member in the comity of nations.

Establishing Maritime Authority

After coming into power, the Meiji government endeavored to establish its authority, but doing so took time. Although the oligarchs delineated new national boundaries and settled recently claimed territories, they also had to consolidate and centralize national power through new initiatives in state-building. Although the Western treaty powers insisted Japan build up infrastructure that would facilitate their safe access to Japan's ports and waterways, this, in turn, bought the state some time to develop its commercial, administrative, and military reach. Japan could rely on the extensive network of foreign (especially British) shipping lines to carry their trade in East Asian waters, and since the country faced little Western opposition to its incorporation of nearby lands, developing its own commercial and naval fleets, especially in the face of pressing domestic issues, was less urgent than it might otherwise have been. Nonetheless, the government recognized that Japan would not be fully independent or truly possess sovereignty until it could exert greater authority over its territorial margins. They understood that being able to accommodate international trade and protect maritime borders in the modern age required surveying surrounding waters, placing navigational aids, creating a customs administration, establishing port facilities, and building naval and commercial fleets.

As part of broader efforts in state-building, the Japanese established the Kōbushō (Ministry of Industry) in 1871 to oversee the country's modernization in areas such as railroads, mining, and communications as well as shipbuilding, surveying, and coastal lighting.[44] These modernizing efforts did more than enable foreign trade, they also spread a new administrative and material infrastructure over the country's landscape. Doing so marked sites along the coast for navigation while also marking newly acquired territory as Japanese and bringing it under Japanese regulation.[45]

Hydrographic surveying, which involved taking soundings and creating maps, was a primary step in ensuring safe navigation in ports and along the coastline. The process also made these spaces "knowable" and claimable.[46] The early British and American expeditions to Japan conducted surveying as a matter of course in learning about waterways they were using or might use in the future.[47] Surveying was also used to gather information and to intimidate. Being able to survey another's shores in violation of the sanctity of territorial waters demonstrated a difference in power between those who could violate these norms and those who did not have the power to prevent it. The Japanese used surveying to the same effect in Korea in 1875 as they sought to open trade on the peninsula.

Surveying was not a treaty right. After the 1858 Ansei Treaties were signed, the British in particular worked with the Japanese to survey coastal waters in order to make Japan's waterways safe for international passage. Even though the Japanese had created some fairly accurate maps of the coastline and Japanese pilots were skilled at navigating it, foreign captains, especially those operating steamships, wanted up-to-date surveys and standardized navigational aids.[48] By 1872, though, Japan decided to conduct its own surveys, which W. G. Beasley argues "reflected aspirations to national sovereignty in an age of reform and hoped-for treaty revisions."[49] Conducting their own maritime surveys was evidence of Japan's modernity and its ability to assert authority.

In keeping with these initiatives, in 1871 the Meiji oligarchs also began implementing new port and harbor policies, which covered everything from harbor construction to the placement of lighthouses to the handling of cargo.[50] Some things, like the installation of navigational aides (lighthouses, buoys, beacons, etc.), were mandated by treaty. The 1866 Tariff Convention, signed with the British, French, Americans, and Dutch, specified in Article XI that Japan "will provide all the Ports open to Foreign trade with such lights, buoys or beacons as may be necessary to render secure navigation of the approaches to the said Ports."[51] The treaty powers believed it to be Japan's responsibility to provide (and pay for) the modern equipment deemed necessary for safe navigation in Japanese waters.

Here again, multinational cooperation, even if manifested as cooperative imperialism, was important to Japan's ability to continue defining its territory and exercising authority through modern infrastructural development. Sir Harry Parkes, the British minister to Japan, pushed for this to be handled without delay, especially given the frequency with which maritime accidents were occurring. The Japanese government hired Scottish engineer Richard Henry Brunton, one of many *oyatoi gaikokujin*, or foreign advisers to the government, to scout locations and begin the process of building lighthouses along the coast.[52]

Japan's trade advanced faster than navigational aids could be placed. Indeed, trade rapidly exceeded shipping capacity so that domestically owned ships only handled 10 percent of the country's overseas trade before 1894.[53] The rest was handled by foreign ships, some of which were chartered by the Japanese. While the availability of foreign vessels to manage much of Japan's trade with the West proved enormously helpful for a country trying to modernize in very short order, it also kept more foreign vessels in Japan's ports and territorial waters.

The Meiji government began to work more closely with local merchants and entrepreneurs to create a system that more effectively channeled foreign shippers to carry Japan's key exports from convenient ports without risking further loss of sovereign control. The central government opened twenty-two nontreaty ports—called Special Trading Ports (*tokubetsu yushutsunyūkō*)—to accommodate highly restricted trade under full Japanese jurisdiction. The Ministry of Finance, which oversaw the customs administration, established customs branches at these sites, increasing the number of locations conducting foreign trade (without new treaty ports or concessions) while significantly expanding the reach of the central government in another score of ports. These locations also handled the related functions of revenue collection and policing the country's maritime borders.[54]

Some of the ports, most notably those located in the country's more remote outposts, were opened with the specific purpose of curbing smuggling. Ports in Tsushima (Izuhara, Sasuna, and Shishimi), the Ryukyus (Naha), and Hokkaido (Muroran) had all served in more liminal capacities as part of the "gates" system during the Tokugawa era.[55] In the modern era, these outlying regions were sites of regional trade that was operating outside the state's dictates, and the authorities were able to start asserting a greater level of centralized authority there. By establishing Special Trading Ports, the Japanese authorities opted to oversee these locations by way of the same customs bureaucracy that handled the treaty ports.

The need for the Special Trading Ports to assist with law enforcement was partly borne of the fact that the development of Japan's navy had to wait until the state had the funds and the pro-navy faction had the political clout to enhance this branch of the military. Even though the Meiji emperor proclaimed the importance of a strong navy and the oligarchy had been purchasing naval vessels from the treaty powers, the reality of ongoing disturbances at home meant they soon gave fiscal and political preference to the army.[56] The development of the navy, and accompanying facilities like shipyards, would thus proceed very slowly.

After Japan's economy was on a more even keel following the Matsukata deflation in the mid-1880s, the oligarchs allocated more money to build their naval fleet while also giving new attention to coastal defense and the administration of foreign trade.[57] The government limned new naval districts, dividing jurisdiction across five *chinjufu*, or naval bases. Three new bases—Yokosuka, Kure and Sasebo—would open July 1, 1889, just two weeks before the Special Trading Ports were announced. These bases demonstrated the importance given to the creation of new trade venues and a need to protect them. Moreover, since these ports had to accommodate foreign vessels, the government wanted to ensure they had a greater capacity for regulating these sites themselves. In the wake of implementing changes in the navy, new districting for the customs administration quickly followed. In 1890, twelve provinces (*kuni*), representing places where heavy traffic, smuggling, or shipwrecks frequently occurred, were designated for coastal patrols.[58] These zones also covered some of the areas where traffic swelled due to the opening of Special Trading Ports, especially in northwestern Kyushu.

Another important development that enabled significant naval reforms was the opening of the first national assembly in 1890, which offered new opportunities for pro-navy advocates to present a strong case for naval reform.

The Meiji government still contained entrenched cliques based on domainal rivalries from the Tokugawa era, which had helped elevate the needs of the army (supported by those from Chōshū) over the navy (which was led by those from Satsuma). In 1891, a new display of power in Japan's waters turned the tide in the parliamentary debates over funding. This time the threat came from China, not the Western powers. This suggests not only that the balance of power in Asia was shifting but that the Japanese could no longer rely on the relatively safe status quo of the treaty port system under the Western powers.

In these late-century efforts, we see Japan moving away from largely unregulated coasts and reliance on what had often been a cooperative foreign presence—one that assisted modernization efforts and did not significantly challenge the expansion and consolidation of Japan's maritime borders—and toward new efforts at self-protection, territorial control, and the assertion of sovereignty.[59] Although far from complete, these improvements in oversight of Japan's coastlines indicate that it would become easier to envision one day opening the interior to foreigners when the unequal treaties were being revised in 1894.

The expansion of Japan's boundaries through territorial acquisition and new attempts to assert authority at the country's edges through surveying, patrolling, and lighting the coasts reflects both the advances in Japan's state-building capacities and a continued awareness of how important defining and maintaining territorial boundaries were. Indeed, in 1893, Kuroda Kiyotaka, former head of the Hokkaido Colonization Office and former prime minister, argued with regard to poaching in the Kurils: "Nothing could be more important for the maintenance of national dignity than to guard strongly the boundary lines of the Empire against the encroachments and trespassing of obscure foreigners."[60] The Japanese had undoubtedly learned the importance of protecting their coastal boundaries during the previous one hundred years.

Establishing an ever-larger perimeter around the main islands, even before being able to create effective military and administrative oversight, is one strategy that worked for the Japanese. By the 1890s, the country finally had the capacity to begin more fully protecting its boundaries with naval force, if necessary. The growing feasibility of cracking down on the significant problem of poachers and smugglers in Japanese waters demonstrates a growing, but still incomplete, capacity to gain control over coastal areas. Although the interest in curbing these transgressions was primarily driven by economic rationales, providing better offshore policing further served to claim and protect Japan's perimeter.

Exercising Maritime Authority as a Measure of Japan's Sovereignty

In February 1892, Japan's finance minister, Matsukata Masayoshi, issued a directive to the country's prefectures stating that if foreign ships were found entering unopened ports, or engaging in smuggling or poaching in Japan's coastal waters, local authorities were to consult with the custom house holding jurisdiction in their area. Just two years before that, these customs districts had been newly drawn in an effort to expand domestic authority over the country's seaboard. The parts of the extensive coastline that lay at a distance from the custom houses had until then been essentially unregulated, with jurisdictions effectively stopping at the ports with custom houses and leaving much of the coastline "in darkness."[61]

The directive continued to lay out proper procedures, declaring that once the customs officials received the location of a ship suspected of illicit activity, they were to notify an imperial warship to approach the vessel. In such a situation, the final word over whether a ship was to be confiscated rested with the minister of the navy.[62] In addition to providing instructions to those who would confront offenders, this legislation established a clear hierarchy of power—one that placed the military (namely, the navy) ahead of the civilian bureaucracy (namely, the Ministry of Finance), which held responsibility for the nation's customs administration. It also sanctioned national over local command while assuming that local officials would still likely be the first line of defense against maritime transgressions.

The year after the directive was issued, a poaching incident prompted such cooperation between local officials and naval officers. In the early morning of September 17, 1893, five Japanese warships sat at anchor in eastern Hokkaido's Nemuro port, which sits well over 200 nautical miles from the nearest custom house at Hakodate.[63] One of them, the *Takao*, weighed anchor in pursuit of a foreign vessel, later identified as the British *Arctic*, which they suspected of illegally hunting seals. The *Takao* headed toward the island of Shikotan's main bay in the Southern Kurils where its officers disembarked and headed directly to the village office. They happened upon a Japanese sailor who said he had fled the *Arctic* and asked for their protection. Taking the sailor with them, they cruised to the port of Anama where they found and boarded the *Arctic*, returned the sailor to his employer, and went back to Nemuro. After conferring with the other naval vessels there, they concurred that the *Takao* should return to Anama to observe the *Arctic*. Three days later it was joined by the *Naniwa*, another warship from the fleet, with the Nemuro police chief on board. Together the Japanese naval officers and local authorities approached the foreign ship, demanded they return all four Japanese sailors on board, and told them to leave the port immediately. After extended discussions, they allowed the vessel and its full crew to stay the night at port, but it slipped out before dawn. A small steamer sent in pursuit managed to chase it down and recover the four Japanese sailors before allowing it to continue on its way.[64]

This example reveals a convoluted attempt to curb illegal activity in territorial seas.[65] The presence of multiple naval vessels notwithstanding, it seems the *Takao*'s officers were loath to cause friction with the Western powers by capturing the *Arctic* even when exercising their legal perogatives. Such reluctance perhaps also explains why they initially returned the Japanese sailor to the *Arctic*. In the immediate circumstances, it made sense for Japan to forgo the assertion of its rights in deference to longer-term interests in regaining full sovereignty.

In July 1890, the English-language expatriate newspaper, the *Japan Weekly Mail*, published an article that stated: "It is a perfectly open secret that for years foreign vessels have been in the habit of poaching in Japanese waters, and that, in pursuance of this illegal business, they constantly violate the treaties by entering ports to which access is not given."[66] Another article appearing in the same newspaper on December 30, 1893, points out that "the right to engage in fishing has not been given to foreigners under the existing treaties." Even without such rights, however, foreigners regularly entered the treaty port of Yokohama to sell and export their catches, trade off the coasts, and occasionally enter unopened ports, but "the Local Authorities are afraid of meddling with them, lest some trouble may result, and so these vessels are suffered to come and go unmolested."[67] In other words, the problem was not just poaching, but that Japan, as a nation with compromised sovereignty, was not yet really in charge of its waterways.

That same year the problem was addressed by Speaker of the House Hoshi Tōru, previously the chief of the Yokohama Customs Office, who tied his concern over the loss of revenue with revision of the unequal treaties. He argued before the Diet that the government needs to "enforce proper regulations in the interests of the Japanese people." Failure to "enact and enforce such regulations" has led to a significant loss of profits, which is "being monopolized by foreign ships. The loss incurred by Japan in consequence of the present Treaties being so manifold" demonstrated that they needed to be revised.[68] Hoshi faulted the Japanese government for not sufficiently protecting the country.

Questions of maritime authority were ongoing even when Japan was on the verge of two major changes in its status: signing treaty revisions in 1894 and the Sino-Japanese War of 1894–1895. The signing of revised treaties demonstrated that the Meiji government had, in fact, achieved much greater levels of modern domestic authority (in effect a prerequisite for revision) and going to war revealed its increased capacity to assert its power outward. The Japanese victory over China, which included the naval Battle of Yalu (a model for British naval reforms), resulted in the acquisition of Taiwan, its first formal colony.

When the treaty revisions went into effect in July 1899, Japan had managed for more than a century to keep the foreigners at the margins even as domestic and foreign pressures pushed—in fits and starts—for opening. This fuller opening became possible as the central government increased its reach outward to the country's outermost margins—through infrastructural, administrative, diplomatic, and eventually naval means. Even though not all coastal encounters had been (or could be) settled, by the end of the nineteenth century, the Japanese had something they did not have when Laxman showed up on the northern frontier more than one hundred years earlier—the ability to allow foreigners into the interior with the legal, administrative, and military capacity to manage their presence as a sovereign and equal nation with a centralized authority that reached all the way to the water's edge.

Chapter 9

Working Women Who Got Wet: A Global Survey of Women in Premodern and Early Modern Fisheries

Lisa Norling

Several years ago, I had the good fortune to visit the island of Zanzibar and snorkel in the gorgeous waters of the Indian Ocean. The snorkeling was fine, but I was actually more interested in what I saw en route from the beach across the lagoon to the edge of the coral reef: several small groups of fully dressed women, up to their waists in the seawater, tending tidy rows of seaweed growing in the sandy lagoon bottom. On the far side of the lagoon, a few young men walked on the shallowest part of the barrier reef, occasionally crouching and poking sticks into the water, pulling something up that they deposited into bags tied around their waists. The two local fishermen who brought us out to the reef in a *ngalawa* (log canoe with double outriggers and a single sail) explained that the women were farming seaweed to be shipped overseas.[1] The young men were fishing on the reef itself for small octopi, likely destined for a more local market. After we were done snorkeling, the *ngalawa* captain said, he and his young deckhand would drop us off on the beach and then head out to fish in deeper water beyond the reef.

What I witnessed in Zanzibar that morning seemed a perfect example of a traditional gender division of subsistence labor in a small littoral community. The women farmed in the intertidal shallows of the lagoon; the men went farther out to the reef and beyond to fish. Women cultivating; men hunting. But, as it turns out, what I saw isn't really that simple nor is it traditional. According to a recent BBC report, Zanzibar women formerly gleaned both the intertidal zone and the reef, gathering shells, wild seaweed, octopi, and other small marine biota. In 1989, local entrepreneurs organized a couple of companies to promote commercial seaweed cultivation in the island's lagoons. The two competing firms bought the produce from small independent growers, almost entirely women, to ship to distant markets in Asia, Europe, and North America. The industry was an immediate success: by the end of the century, some 23,000 people—90 percent of whom were female—were employed in what had become the second largest sector of the island's economy, just behind tourism. Meanwhile, the diminishing number of local fishers, all men, sought their prey in deeper waters and also now on the reef itself, their catch and their economic contribution more locally oriented and small in scale. They supplemented their meager fishing earnings with boat hires to tourists like me.[2]

Women, Men, and Fishing

Almost forty years ago, the Canadian historians Rosemary Ommer and Gerald Panting suggested that sailors and fishermen were simply "working men who got wet."[3] As I saw in that Zanzibar lagoon, women work and get wet, too.[4] In fact, in virtually all coastal communities that have subsisted wholly or in part on marine resources, women have been involved in harvesting and processing them, it seems from time immemorial. On foot, stilt, or small boat, women ventured into water, beach, rocky strand, tidal pool, estuary, salt marsh, lagoon, reef. They collected by hand, stick, or rake various kinds of seaweed and marine algae, the eggs of seabirds, and salt- and freshwater shellfish; they netted, trapped, and caught with hook and line many other varieties of aquatic fauna. They gathered marine resources primarily for their nutritional value, but also shells, coral, and pearls to trade or use for currency, decoration, ritual observance, dye, or building material. This should not be surprising. Lots of evidence documents that women could be as comfortable in water as men, swimming and diving and surfing, and that they could handle at least small boats and navigate. In fact, there is nothing inherently gendered in the skill set required for fishing or seafaring more generally except possibly for the physical strength required to sail very large vessels before technological advances made such strength obsolete.[5]

Both popular and scholarly accounts, however, still tend to view historical (and contemporary) fisheries through a starkly binary gendered framework, rigidly associating men with the sea and women with the land.[6] It does appear that virtually all maritime cultures, past and present, have organized their marine resource utilization in part around a basic binary gender division of labor. Even in cultures that recognized more than two genders, there was work generally assigned to persons who identified as men and work generally assigned to persons who identified as women.[7] In spatial terms, however, this division rarely corresponded to a simple dry/wet, land/water separation. The simple equation of Sea and Male in opposition to Land and Female does not accurately describe, and even obscures, great variations in the location and content of women's work in premodern and early modern fisheries, as well as the meaning and value that their labor contributed to fisher families and communities.

In subsistence fisheries as far back in time as there is evidence, women seem to have been primarily gatherers, harvesting marine resources on shore and in shallower waters, whereas men have been hunters, venturing farther into deeper waters to pursue larger fish and marine mammals. But local practice varied considerably, locating in many different places the geographic/ecological zone beyond which women rarely went, gendered boundaries enforced by custom, taboo, law, diplomacy, and enemy threat. Understanding how fishing labor has been and is gendered, and how and why this has changed over time, requires what Paul Thompson proposed in 1985: detailed local studies contextualized historically within a broad comparative framework.[8] Thompson's preliminary review of "women in the fishing" focused on the nineteenth and twentieth centuries. This essay draws upon a wide range of detailed local studies—historical, anthropological, and archaeological—to identify broad trends in gender dynamics in the "Age of the Ocean," roughly 1500–1800, when, as W. Jeffrey Bolster has reminded us, "people not only crossed oceans and used them to stitch together empires of commerce and meaning, but also relied on ocean products and services as never before."[9]

Three general propositions emerge from this global comparative view.[10] First, to locate and assess women's historical involvement in fisheries, we need to foreground the foreshore in our analysis, scrutinizing the complex and fluid interpenetration of land and water that comprises the littoral zone.[11] This zone is, almost universally, where women in fishing communities have performed their work.

Second, when we broaden our view of fisheries beyond the ocean itself and beyond piscine prey to include the littoral margins and a wider variety of marine biota, we can discern a basic pattern amid all the local particularities: the persistent differentiation between women's work and men's work in subsistence fishing communities appears not simply binary but instead a matter of scale. The farther from land, the deeper the water, the greater the risk, and the larger and more pelagic the prey, the more exclusively the fishing becomes male-dominated.[12]

Third, dramatic changes in the scope and scale of many fisheries worldwide in the late medieval and early modern eras appear to have radically transformed the gender organization of fishing labor. Bolster points out that "Western Europeans' adaptation to the late medieval and early modern commercial revolution included searches for distant sources of whale oil and merchantable fish."[13] Indeed, Europeans' exploitation of North Atlantic whale, herring, and cod stocks comprised a significant part of that "commercial revolution." Parallel commercialization and intensification in fishing occurred contemporaneously in other oceans, notably in the seas of Southeast Asia, China, and Japan.[14] A broad comparative perspective suggests that rapid and far-reaching growth in the harvesting and international trade of marine commodities depleted local marine resources and disrupted local subsistence fisheries around the world—and dramatically transformed maritime gender roles as well.

Gender Dynamics and the Littoral in Premodern Fisheries

Feminist social scientists have identified two basic characteristics of women's work common to just about all human society: the malleability and quotidian regularity of women's labor and its circumscribed geographic scope relative to that of men. Both characteristics, it has been suggested, likely derive from women's primary reproductive responsibilities for childbearing and sustaining their families. A great many local studies establish that these characteristics are pervasive in the organization of labor in subsistence fisheries, past and present, from the indigenous Americas to East, South, and Southeast Asia, both West and East Africa, around the Mediterranean, and throughout Europe.[15]

In a comprehensive review of nearly a century of ethnological studies of subsistence fishing communities in Oceania (spanning Micronesia, Melanesia, and Polynesia), the anthropologist Margaret Chapman finds that all of the communities demonstrated gender differentiation in fishing practices. Throughout the vast oceanic region, "women contribute[d] significantly to marine food yields" primarily through inshore "reef gleaning," which involved "walking along the reefs probing with a stick, or simply with the bare hands, for octopus, shellfish, echinoderms, crabs, and other invertebrates." Performed all year long and in all sorts of weather, these activities were easily combined with childcare and other domestic tasks. In contrast, men typically undertook higher risk, lower yield fishing, venturing greater distances into deeper water to seek larger prey when season and weather permitted. Chapman argues that "the highly regular nature of women's fishing [made] women more reliable, and therefore more effective than men, as suppliers of protein for subsistence."[16]

Chapman constructed a typology of the Oceanian women's involvement in their communities' fisheries to examine the range of variation in the gender division of labor. In all thirty-five societies covered in her review, she found that reef gleaning constituted a core part of women's work. In six communities, women did "apparently no fishing" other than reef gleaning; in eight other locations, women did "minimal fishing." In the largest number of villages (seventeen), in addition to gleaning, women pursued "some types of fishing on reef" using traps, nets, and hook and line. In only three places, women did "general fishing including off reef [i.e., in deeper waters beyond the reef] except bonito, tuna, and turtle" which species were explicitly restricted to male fishers. In only one place, the Marianas, Chapman found "no restrictions upon techniques, zone, or species which women may fish."[17]

A broader perspective on subsistence fisheries in the premodern past reveals the same great range of Oceanian gendered practices writ worldwide: from cultures in which women's marine activities were restricted solely to the intertidal zones to cultures in which women and men worked side by side at sea. Representative of one end of the gendered labor spectrum were Arctic peoples such as the Yupik of St. Lawrence Island, in the Bering Strait between the Siberian and Alaskan mainlands.[18] According to the earliest outsider accounts from the sixteenth and seventeenth centuries, the St. Lawrence Yupik lived in small villages strategically situated to see the annual migrations of the whales and walrus that formed their primary sustenance and center of their spiritual and social worlds.[19] The gender division of labor in Yupik families and communities reflected their strongly patriarchal and patrilocal organization. Women and children foraged on beaches and tundra for supplemental foodstuffs including crabs and, from the island's limited vegetation, berries, rose roots, willow leaves, and other spring greens; young men made the dangerous climb up rugged cliffs to harvest birds' eggs. But it was strictly just men who ventured out into deeper waters and ice to hunt the highly valued large marine mammals. Women processed and preserved the catch after it was landed, turning the whale and walrus carcasses into the community's major sources of nutrition, clothing, shelter, heat, light, tools, and utensils, including preparing the skins used for the versatile and seaworthy craft, the *umiak*. Successful hunters might have multiple wives to handle the shoreside work. Yupik women did get wet: they too traveled by boat and might even paddle the large *umiaks* used for transport (later European observers occasionally termed these "women's boats"). But women never fished or hunted from boats.[20]

In a very different latitude—straddling the equator—and toward the other end of the gender division spectrum were "the boat-dwelling 'sea peoples'" of maritime Southeast Asia. One of the most distinctive groups of "Sea Nomads," the Bajau Laut, migrated into the "Sulu Zone," the Sulu and Celebes Seas, between the large islands of Mindanao, Borneo, and Sulawesi, as early as the tenth century CE. The Bajau Laut lived entirely afloat in loosely organized bands of generally nuclear families on single-masted wooden boats (*lepa*), 25–40 feet in length and 5–6 feet beam. While they spent long stretches of the year at sea on fishing and trading voyages, the Bajau Laut were not really nomadic: they regularly returned to anchorages near their band's ancestral burying grounds on shore, for fresh water, to barter dried fish and other sea products for rice and other foodstuffs and goods (including boats) only available on land, and to bury and honor their dead. Only scant evidence, brief mentions in travelers' accounts, hint at how the early Bajau Laut defined gender roles or organized their lives at sea. In 1675, for example, a Dutch colonial official, Robert Padtbrugge, visited the coast of Sulawesi and admired the Bajau Laut women he saw who, he claimed, navigated deeper waters "as well as the men, moving like heroines of the ocean among the reefs."[21]

Nineteenth- and twentieth-century observations and ethnographic studies document that among the Bajau Laut both women and men were accustomed to boat handling and navigation, fishing with lines and drift nets, and diving for sea cucumber (*tripang* or *bêche de mer*) and mother of pearl. Still, the family *lepa* were generally passed down from father to son, or parents would provide a new boat to their son upon his marriage. And space onboard was loosely defined by gender. The adaptable midsection, with its removable cover, served as a general living, working, and sleeping area for the whole family. The stern, where food, water, and cooking utensils were stored and meals prepared, generally by women, was coded female. The bow, the area aft of the single mast, was principally (though not exclusively) a male space, used for poling in shallow waters and handling sails at sea, and storing and deploying fishing equipment.[22]

Elsewhere in the premodern world, coastal peoples pursued more diversified lifeways based "upon one green foot and one blue foot," combining farming and fishing in seasonal cycles.[23] In the North Atlantic, the confluence of nutrient-rich polar currents flowing south with the warmer waters of the Gulf Stream flowing north produced a remarkably rich ecosystem and one of the world's richest fishing grounds.[24] Women in subsistence societies on both sides of that ocean—Native American women on its western shores and European women to the east (including the North and Baltic Seas)—actively participated in extracting marine resources from the sea and thereby contributed a substantial portion of their families' sustenance directly and indirectly.[25] And, on both sides of the North Atlantic, gender differentiation in a wide range of fisheries resembled that in Oceania, similarly assigning longer distances, deeper water, larger prey, and technologies of spear and harpoon to men.

In the region later known as southern New England, the ethnohistorian Kathleen J. Bragdon describes how distinctive estuarine ecosystems shaped settlement strategies and collective labor patterns of the indigenous peoples long before European contact. The estuaries, semi-enclosed bodies of water connected to the open sea, where fresh, brackish, and salt waters mixed, were characterized by a "remarkable biotic diversity" that supported "a mixture of shellfish-based subsistence and settlement cultures, and a mixed diet of intertidal and harbor-dwelling flora and fauna, nearly half (43%) of which derived from shellfish, centuries before maize horticulture became important" around 1000 CE.[26] Archaeological investigations of coastal sites created by ancestors of the Ninnimissinuok (the collective name of the Algonkian-speaking peoples who lived there when European newcomers arrived) suggest seasonal rotations between larger three-season settlements near the heads of estuaries and, for shorter periods, smaller single- or extended-family seasonal camps at special resource locations such as rivers where anadromous fish—shad, sturgeon, smelt, salmon—returned from sea to spawn in fresh water.

Coastal women worked in and near the domestic sphere, which extended from homesteads to the fields they cultivated and the "tidal pools, clam banks, and shallow ponds" where they collected shellfish and other marine resources. Clams were winter food, dug out of banks exposed at low tide. In summers, women gathered scallops with handheld nets from boats in shallow water; they also dove for quahogs and for lobsters that men used for bait.[27] They carried their male kin's catch from the boat, cleaned it, prepared it for immediate consumption, or preserved it by drying or smoking.

Much of men's work occurred at some distance from places of settlement; they specialized in "deep-sea fishing, hunting, the manufacture of tools, trade and warfare." Men were responsible for boat building, constructing larger dugout canoes as well as smaller, lighter birchbark canoes; they also generally made nets of woven hemp and other fishing tools including harpoons and spears. Both men and women fished from shore, in shallow water, and on ice in winter, with lines and hooks, weirs and nets and traps. But, although both men and women were strong swimmers, manipulated tools, and were accustomed to collaborative work, men alone fished in deeper waters farther from shore and hunted in distant forests. The further the distance and greater the risk, the "closer to the deep and mysterious places where only other-than-humans dwelt," the more exclusively male the activity.[28]

On the other side of the Atlantic altogether, some 3500 miles to the east, on the shores of prehistoric Scandinavia, the archaeologists Sophia Perdikaris and Thomas McGovern have found evidence of a similar utilization of a wide range of marine biota, including marine mammals, fish, sea birds and their eggs, and shellfish. Over the centuries, littoral Scandinavian society also developed on "one green foot and one blue foot" as men and women combined farming and fishing in seasonal cycles. Both men and women were adept at handling small boats for local transportation, and younger unmarried women might occasionally join their fathers and brothers on shore or close to it, fishing with traps, nets, and hook and line for baitfish, eels, and even close-by runs of cod, salmon, and herring. However, most often just men took to deeper water to fish, sailing considerable distances to follow annual fish migrations, while women generally remained behind to tend farms, children, and livestock. Again it was a matter of scale: women got wet too, but closer to home, in shallower waters, and in quotidian rounds of domestic (and often arduous) tasks. Not surprisingly, that work included much of the processing and preserving of the men's catch. Indeed, preserving cod by air-drying it in the steady, cool winds and low humidity of coastal Scandinavia yielded a highly nutritious and portable source of protein that could be stored up to seven years without salt or refrigeration. Historians agree that Viking expansion southward along Europe's coasts and rivers and eastward island-hopping across the North Atlantic was fueled in part by this air-dried cod.[29]

The Transformation of Gender Dynamics in Early Modern Fisheries

Littoral peoples around the world continued to harvest marine resources for subsistence and trade throughout the transformations marking the emergence of what historians term the early modern era. Many of these peoples were, of course, firsthand witnesses and participants in the vast expansion and intensification of the ocean-based interactions that increasingly brought distant parts of the globe together in unprecedented ways. International trade in the ocean's products comprised a significant share of those global interactions, radically altering littoral and pelagic ecosystems and the communities that depended upon them. As fisheries changed, so too did maritime gender roles.

The early modern transformations in the European fisheries that would eventually reorganize their gender dynamics appear to have begun, at least in England, in the late medieval period. Based on an analysis of ancient fishbones, the maritime archaeologists James Barrett, Alison Locker, and Callum Roberts argue that, between 950 and 1050 CE, there was a "revolutionary expansion" in the reliance on marine resources, a relatively sudden and comprehensive shift from freshwater fish to marine fish consumption, in England. Viking newcomers may have introduced a taste for seafood, and the spread of Christian ritual abstinence from meat markedly increased the consumption of fish. But more fundamental factors profoundly altered the relationship of coastal communities to marine resources: population growth, urbanization, and intensified agricultural production exhausted or spoiled sources of fresh water, increased pollution in rivers and lakes, obstructed streams with mill dams, and depleted stocks of freshwater species through uncontrolled overfishing.[30] English and Scottish fishers were forced to turn to the sea.

Fishbones do not, in and of themselves, reveal much about the gender organization of the humans who discarded them. For a glimpse of gendered work roles, we must turn to the scant medieval documentary record. Maryanne Kowaleski examined a series of thirteenth- and fourteenth-century wills in English port cities and uncovered a distinctive inheritance strategy that suggested "a shared identity and common investment in the maritime enterprise." She found that more than a third of fishers' wills bequeathed fishing nets and hooks to female family members, a "considerably higher" percentage than "the bequests of work-related equipment in wills of those [men] who did not go to sea." Parsing additional primary evidence, Kowaleski concludes that while English women remained on shore, they participated in the fisheries by "gathering seaweed, repairing nets, baiting hooks, and gutting and curing fish" primarily on a small-scale familial basis, working in partnership with their fisher men.[31] At least initially, the shift from freshwater to marine fish did not appear to alter gender roles in England's maritime communities.

On the Scandinavian shores of the North and Baltic Seas, the gender division of labor within the fisheries took a different trajectory as the premodern mixed farming-fishing economy described by Perdikaris and McGovern gradually evolved into the much larger and commercialized "Scanian" herring fishery that flourished from about the 1100s to the 1300s. Most of the fishers were still farmers who turned to the sea on a seasonal basis to augment their families' food stores and income, generally using their own equipment. But now they fished more intensively and exclusively for one particular species, herring, and they produced a much larger yield that they sold to merchants. The fishers congregated at particular locations in the autumn, when large schools of migrating herring appeared; they put out in small open boats to catch the herring with nets and landed the catch daily. There may have been a few women still working on the boats at this time, as implied by a German law of 1587 requiring that captains hire male crew members rather than relying on their wives or any other women. But by far the largest number of women worked in the fisheries on shore, in new circumstances that presaged future developments.

The freshly landed fish was auctioned off to (male) merchants right on the beach, then carted behind the seawalls to temporary workplaces, huts where one group of women specialized in gutting the herring and a second group of women specialized in packing the cleaned fish into barrels and covering it with brine. At its peak in the fourteenth century, an estimated 25,000 fishers, carters, merchants, fish processers, and victualers set up camp and worked in the Scanian fishery from midsummer to late September. The barrels of preserved herring they produced, which remained edible for up to two years, became an essential and lasting component of long-distance trade throughout Europe "from Lemberg/Lvov in the east to Wales in the west, from northern Norway to Italy and Spain in the south," and, over time, attracted further investment by merchant capitalists who increasingly owned the boats and employed the fishers.[32]

Innovations in shipbuilding, such as the fifteenth-century introduction of the distinctive, larger keel-built vessel known as the herring *buss*, also promoted intensification of the fishing. The *buss* featured a flat deck that made it possible to gut, salt, and pack the fish onboard while at sea, obviating the need to return to land daily; its rounded hull made the ship more seaworthy and its hold more capacious, simultaneously facilitating the exploitation of a wider catching area and the storage of a large volume of processed fish. As inshore stocks were depleted, fishers were forced to extend their hunt farther and farther from their home coast and pursue other species. From the sixteenth century onward, European commercial fishers—now exclusively male—ranged as far as Newfoundland and shifted their focus primarily to cod, which they processed in seasonal camps on the North American shore before shipping to markets developing around the North Atlantic world.[33]

Significantly, the well-known European exploitation of Newfoundland's enormous wealth of marine resources in the "Age of the Ocean" included the increasing concentration of women's work in subsidiary roles performed entirely on dry land. Over time, small numbers of European women migrated to Newfoundland, in part encouraged and subsidized by merchant capitalists and colonial promoters (one Captain Francis Wheler commented of the fishermen in 1684, "Soe long as their comes noe women, they are not fixed").[34] The women's role in the fishery remained for the most part indirect: they rarely worked directly with the landed cod in the way women had with herring back in the Scanian heyday. Rather, boys and young men, fishers in training, processed the catch on shore while women provided domestic services and contributed a measure of stability to the new settlements.

Over the course of the seventeenth and eighteenth centuries, the unprecedented commercialization, intensification, and sheer scale of the European and colonial fisheries had so thoroughly depleted the North Atlantic's marketable fish stocks that the littoral and pelagic ecosystems on the American side of the Atlantic became as disrupted and diminished as those on the European side. Competition and conflict between indigenous peoples and colonists over the reduced marine resources increasingly limited Native access to the shore along the Northeast coast. Centuries-old indigenous fisheries collapsed and Native economic strategies transformed along with social organization and gender roles along the coast from the Bay of Fundy to Cape Cod. Mi'kmaqs, Malecites, Abenakis, Ninnimissinuok, and many others, both women and men, continued to harvest what shellfish and seaweed they could for their own subsistence and to sell to colonial neighbors. But more Native men began to pursue deep-water fishing and whaling not in their own boats but instead on European and colonial vessels, shipping out for months at a time and leaving their families behind.[35]

Back in Scandinavia, specialized fishing villages began to appear along the coasts of Denmark in the seventeenth and eighteenth centuries, from where men went fishing for cod in the winter, plaice in the summer, and herring in the autumn. Many families still relied on their small farms for supplemental sustenance and income, but agricultural production was increasingly women's responsibility. Women and children also prepared the lines and baited hooks on shore before men set out to fish and, when the boats returned, they cleaned and preserved the catch. With further intensification of the Nordic fisheries in the nineteenth century (when "fisherman" was officially recognized as its own occupational category in Sweden for the first time), maritime men and some women—generally young, unmarried, and without family responsibilities—moved seasonally to temporary camps on shore close to the fishing grounds, where "between 100 and 200 girls baited the hooks and took care of the catch." The preserved fish was either consumed locally or transported by the fishermen to larger ports where they sold it to merchants.[36]

In early modern Amsterdam, the large and lucrative commerce in preserved and fresh fish was concentrated in eight specialized fish markets; many of the fishmongers working in the market stalls were female. Dutch women's participation in the fish trade ranged from lowly street vendors and delivery girls to the "wives of skippers" assisting their husbands to sell their catch and even to well-established independent female stall holders. The specialized and lucrative eel market was dominated by matrilineal family networks, although only the male members of the families could join the fish sellers' guild. Danielle van den Heuvel's study of seventeenth- and eighteenth-century Dutch "fishwives" documents their visibility, activity, and even a measure of empowerment. According to some of her sources, "fishwives were among the most important instigators in the many food and tax riots that took place in the province of Holland" in the 1600s and 1700s.[37]

Women had been hawking fish on streets and from market stalls not just in Amsterdam but in cities and towns across Europe for centuries. Darlene Abreu-Ferreira's work on the female fishmongers and financiers in early modern Portugal suggests an Iberian dynamic that differed in a few important ways from the North European experience. Abreu-Ferreira found a similarly sharp division of labor by gender in the coastal fishing communities she investigated, where "men fished and women sold the fish," but she also found evidence that the early modern Portuguese women operated on an unusually large scale, handling wholesale as well as retail merchandising of fish, locally and regionally. A number of women were also involved to a surprising degree in ship ownership and investment (although archival gaps and ambiguities prevent an exact assessment of the full extent). Abreu-Ferreira attributes these distinctive features to sixteenth-century changes in Portuguese property and inheritance law that, unlike in other European countries, allowed women, even married women, to enter into financial contracts, buy and sell, obtain credit, incur debt, and inherit property separately from their husbands or other male kin. A local aphorism, "men control the seas, but women rule the land," accurately summarized the gendered power dynamics in these Portuguese fishing communities.[38]

Abreu-Ferreira explains that in mid-sixteenth-century Lisbon, a more urban and occupationally specialized port, it was sometimes male *lavapexes* (fish washers) who transported the cargo of fish from ship to shore and cleaned it. These men then handed it over to the fishers' wives and other women who were responsible for marketing the catch locally and regionally. In many of the smaller fishing communities, though, women took care of both the cleaning and the marketing of their men's catch; they also made and mended the fishing nets. Their work also included gathering shellfish for food and seaweed for fertilizer for their own families or to be sold locally; they collected firewood and maintained vegetable gardens, and they cared for dependent family members. A familiar proverb summed up the local division of labor: "whether he brings fish or not, at the end of the voyage the fisher's job is done; now it is the woman's turn" to look after the catch, or deal with the lack of it.[39]

The concurrent expansion of the European and Euro-American whale and seal fisheries in the seventeenth and eighteenth centuries was predicated on an even more nearly complete separation of men's and women's work. Christina Folke Ax describes how family, household, and community life on the island of Rømø, just off the west coast of Denmark in the Wadden Sea, adapted to the increasing labor demand of the early modern Arctic whaling industry. Farming was marginal on the relatively barren island. By the eighteenth century, most of the male population migrated on an annual basis to Hamburg, Amsterdam, and elsewhere, seeking berths as masters or crew on ships heading for a summer-long season of whaling and sealing in the far northern seas from Spitsbergen to the Davis Strait. This kind of fishing was strictly men's work from start to finish, from wielding the harpoon to marketing the finished product. The women and children of Rømø remained at home, performing all the farm labor with the occasional assistance of a few male field hands hired from the mainland during the short harvest period.[40]

Women's responsibility for the family farms on Rømø was so complete, Ax reports, that fully two thirds of land transfers by inheritance over the course of the century went to daughters and sons-in-law rather than to sons. The land transfers were frequently combined with written agreements to take care of aging parents. Ax finds that while "the majority of families on Rømø depended on the man's income from the sea," the family farms "became the stable element in the household economy. Even if families could not subsist for long on farming alone, it could keep them going for a while if income from the sea failed." Here again we see the familiar maritime gender patterns: women's production was local, low risk, reliable yield, while men's was more distant, potentially higher yield but also higher risk. Now, however, the gender division of labor more closely aligned with a basic binary geographic division between sea and land. In fact, according to Ax, the women of Rømø rarely left the island at all.[41]

There are clear indications of the impact of European-style intensified exploitation of marine resources on gendered labor across the globe. In the sixteenth-century Caribbean, Spanish colonizers co-opted the indigenous pearl fishery on the Venezuelan coast in much the same way that they seized control of the production of American gold and silver.[42] Columbus himself reported on the lavish pearls worn by the peoples he encountered there. It is not clear how the Guayquerí inhabitants of the "Pearl Coast" organized their harvesting of the extraordinarily rich beds of oysters for meat and pearls before contact with Europeans, although both men and women were reputedly adept at swimming and diving. The Spaniards soon exhausted the supply of pearls available to them through trade, which problem they resolved by taking over production directly. They forced the Guayquerí to dive for the oysters and extract the pearls in a labor regime so relentless, brutal, and perilous that Bartolomé de las Casas exclaimed that "there is no life as infernal and desperate in this century that can be compared with it."[43]

When the Guayquerí population plummeted from the effects of disease, violence, and accidents related to pearl diving, the Spaniards imported Lucayans, Arawaks, and Caribs from elsewhere around the Caribbean basin to work the oyster beds. When their numbers dwindled too, the Spaniards turned to enslaved Africans to fill their pearling crews. Based on fragments and ambiguities in the Spanish colonial documentary record, the historian Molly Warsh surmises but cannot state definitively that enslaved men handled the boats and did the diving, while a much smaller number of female "servant slaves" remained on shore and provided support and domestic services. Kevin Dawson, historian of the African diaspora, concurs. He has found abundant evidence demonstrating the considerable aquatic prowess of diverse West African men and women on, in, and under the water up and down the Atlantic coast. Both men and women dove for oysters off the Sierra Leone shore, for instance, and on the Kongo Kingdom's Luanda Island, it was primarily women who dove for the cowry shells used for currency and export commodities. Dawson suggests that Dutch and Portuguese travelers' accounts alerted the

Spanish Pearl Coast slaveholders to the particular diving abilities of the Gold Coast Africans; in the 1590s, Dutch merchant-adventurer Pieter de Marees wrote that "'[b]ecause they are so good at swimming and diving, they are specially kept for that purpose . . . and employed in this capacity where there is a need for them, such as the Island of St. Margaret in the West Indies, where Pearls are found.'" Dawson adds that "[e]ven though many African-descended women were expert divers, European claims that maritime labor was a male occupation precluded the exploitation of the women, at least in the water."[44]

On the other side of the world, a dramatic expansion of international commerce and maritime trade in Asian waters similarly marked the beginning of the early modern era at the turn of the fifteenth century. Spices, textiles, and sandalwood are the most well-known of the many commodities circulating, of course, but there was also substantial regional trade in marine products such as shark fins, sea cucumber, abalone, dried fish, turtle eggs, tortoise shell, coral, mother-of-pearl, and edible seaweeds. Many East and Southeast Asian fishing communities responded to the rapidly growing demand in part with expanded and intensified harvesting much like that occurring contemporaneously in the North Atlantic.[45] Yet, while the changing scale and scope of production similarly depleted Asian marine resources and altered local subsistence fisheries, transformations in the gendered organization of fishing labor seem more varied, more localized, and in many areas more gradual than in other parts of the early modern world.

The Bajau Laut of the Sulu Zone, for example, participated in the expanding production and trade of marine commodities throughout the early modern period with apparently little impact on their traditional way of life, including its gender practices. As in previous centuries, they continued to trade with the land-dwellers, exchanging dried fish for rice and other agricultural and forest-derived goods. In the fifteenth and sixteenth centuries the Bajau Laut also became deeply involved in the lucrative trade in sea cucumbers, a luxury item much in demand in China. The Sulu sultanate, which emerged in the early 1400s as the dominant power in the Sulu Archipelago, extended control over the regional trade networks extending from China to Borneo. The sultanate established authority over the Bajau Laut in a kind of patron-client relationship, offering a measure of protection and a ready market in exchange for their allegiance and labor. As long as they supplied sufficient quantities of sea cucumbers and other lucrative products of the sea, the sultan did not interfere with the Bajau Laut. Indeed, their distinctive seaborne way of life and gender roles persisted through multiple threats and disruptions in the seventeenth and eighteenth centuries, including maritime marauding and slave raiding by neighboring groups and incursions by competing European powers.[46]

The case was quite different for the *ama*, the famed female divers of Japan. Traditional Japanese fishing practices had been rigidly gendered since antiquity: fishing of almost all kinds was strictly a male occupation. Women were restricted to gathering marine resources in the littoral zone, with just one notable exception: in certain fishing villages, while men still handled the boats, it was predominantly women who dove into deeper waters for shellfish and seaweed. Those villages were generally uxorilocal (residence with wives' kin), and diving skills were passed down from mother to daughter. Underwater for a minute or more at a time, the *ama* harvested the shellfish using just a knife to pry them from the rocks on which they clustered. Abalone was the most prized yield, a delicacy enjoyed by the wealthy and sent as tribute to imperial and shogunal courts. By the seventeenth century, abalone became increasingly important as a luxury good exported to China. After the Tokugawa Shogunate rose to power in 1603, it established more centralized control over Japan and its economy with new policies including annual village quotas of abalone, shark fins, and other marine commodities. Fishing intensified, fish stocks were depleted, and male fishers began to poach the abalone in female divers' territories, wielding spears from boats to harvest the shellfish in a more ecologically destructive way. The Tokugawa authorities also tried to impose comprehensive social conformity, including virilocal residence patterns (living with husbands' kin), which disrupted the traditional organization of the female divers' families and villages. By the end of the eighteenth century, the numbers of female divers, along with the abalone, had dwindled precipitously.[47]

Concluding Thoughts

This comparative review suggests that, at least in the past millennium, nearly all societies based on the extraction of marine resources have organized work in part around a basic binary gender division of labor. This division of labor has been located and practiced in different ways, varying considerably across time and place in localized patterns that—before the modern era—rarely corresponded to a simple geographic bifurcation between land and water. Rather, the variations seem to have arrayed along a gendered spectrum based on scale: generally, the larger, deeper, farther, more technologically complex, more intermittent in effort, more focused, higher risk and more uncertain yield of the work, the more firmly it was coded male; the smaller, shallower, nearer, less technologically complex, more regular or continuous in effort, more multitasked, lower risk and more reliable yield of the work, the more firmly it was coded female.

In the early modern "Age of the Ocean," however, the dramatic geographic expansion, commercialization, and intensification of marine resource extraction produced not only enormous quantities of preserved fish but also a significant shift in the gender dynamics in fishing labor and communities. Particularly in European and European-dominated colonial fisheries, over time the labor of harvesting the sea became more strictly the domain of men while women were relegated more exclusively to support roles on shore. Women continued to form a significant part of the fishery workforce, but fewer and fewer of them were actually getting wet. The spectrum along which the division of labor was gendered in subsistence fisheries, where the intertidal had often been intergender, evolved into a more simplistic, even reductionist gender dichotomy. In short, the myth was made material. Contemporaneously, on the other side of the world, parallel processes of expansion, commercialization, and intensification in many Asian fisheries also produced transformations in the gendered division of labor, although these changes did not necessarily correspond to a similarly simplistic sea/land, wet/dry, male/female binary. Yet, though local forms may have differed, over all worldwide changes in the scale and scope of commercial fisheries appear to have effected a newly sharpened spatial differentiation in fishing labor practices in one place after another.

A more recent fundamental reorganization of the world's fisheries has occurred in the modern era and continues to the present, with exploding demand for marine resources driving unprecedented technological innovations, industrialization, and new forms of globalization in the sector. But the more simplistic gender binary that emerged in the early modern period appears perniciously persistent. Drawing on her field research in twentieth-century fishing communities on the U.S. North Atlantic coast, the sociologist Carrie Yodanis explains that "gender in fishing villages is defined in relation to fishing. 'Man' is defined as one who fishes and 'woman' is defined in opposition to that which is a fisherman. To be a woman is to not be a fisher(man). . . . The result is a strong, unequal, and persistent gender division of labor in fishing communities."[48] Valerie Burton adds insightfully: "technology no more sophisticated than a small open wooden boat is [all that is] needed to establish a discursive framework for male supremacy. But with more capitalization comes greater obstacles to women's participation as investors in maritime trades, and the idea that the material world can be modernized with technology augments men's claims to mastery."[49]

Men's claims to mastery of the fisheries, however, are now under assault by much larger forces—as are women's contributions to maritime economies. Attempts by nation-states to regulate the take and technologies of fishing and to protect the ocean's resources have proven largely futile as demand soars, fish migrate, and ocean waters elude territorial control. Global fisheries have decimated entire populations of numerous species of fish and harmed ocean environments, and mining the ocean's other resources has inflicted equally catastrophic damage. Most threatening of all, of course, is seemingly inexorable climate change. The seas are warming faster than its flora and fauna can adapt, and water levels are rising everywhere.

On Zanzibar, the seaweed industry is showing the dire effects of global warming. Higher water temperatures, more intense sunlight, and more extreme tides weaken the seaweed and increase its susceptibility to bacterial disease. Marine scientists have recommended moving the seaweed cultivation to deeper, cooler water, but few of the farmers have done so. It turns out that most of these island women, who are used to working in lagoon waters, cannot swim.[50]

Afterword

Land-Sea Regimes in World History

Lauren Benton and Nathan Perl-Rosenthal

Few scholars doubt that maritime history ought to move into the mainstream of world historical research. The question is how to make that happen. One option is to continue to pursue the promise of Braudelian ocean "worlds" as objects of analysis, deepening accounts of Mediterranean, Atlantic, Pacific, and Indian Ocean regions and expanding the approach to encompass smaller seas. Another option is to position maritime trends at the heart of the history of globalization—for example, by identifying changes in sea trade or communications as turning points in world history. Still another possibility is to build on the analysis of shipboard political cultures to examine global processes such as militarization, waves of violence or revolt, or large-scale patterns of labor coercion. These and other existing approaches have already moved maritime history forward.[1] Yet these trends have not yet produced an analytical framework with wide application, capable of reframing broad narratives in world history.

Given this state of the field, scholars may be tempted to turn for help to theoretical approaches from outside maritime history. The field has a long history of pursuing such a strategy, for example by embracing class conflict and borderlands frameworks, or by mining critical geography for theoretical insights. Today, one of the most seductive possibilities seems to be a turn to the work of Carl Schmitt. In *Land and Sea*, first published in 1942, Schmitt develops a distinction between so-called land and sea peoples, with superior land peoples epitomized by Germans and inferior sea peoples represented by the English—and also by Jews.[2] In spite of its fascist origins and barely concealed anti-Semitism, Schmitt's work will surely appeal to some scholars searching for ways to make maritime history analytically more sophisticated and truly global. Appearing to offer lessons for world history, Schmitt defines spatial orders and revolutions as "planetary" in scope.[3] He tags each age as corresponding to a particular "spatial order" and associates the transition from one age to another with a global "spatial revolution."[4]

For all its seeming usefulness as a framework for global maritime history, *Land and Sea* would lead us down an intellectual blind alley. The trouble with the book goes beyond Schmitt's disturbing ideological bent. His representation of land and sea as opposed juridical and social spaces poses deep analytical problems. Schmitt uncritically accepts the historical existence of a broad consensus that the sea is free, and consistently and fundamentally different from the land. Indeed, for Schmitt that dichotomy is a settled premise of the modern global order, providing the very logic by which he can imagine various maritime engagements resolving into spatial revolutions centered on efforts to "appropriate" the seas.[5]

Dynamic land, inert seas: Schmitt's analysis is built on false claims about the inherent differences between land and sea. He relies, at bottom, on a superficial understanding of maritime legal history in which actual capacities of enforcement on the seas and accompanying rationales for extending imperial control over ocean spaces counted for less than the force of a single celebrated tract by Hugo Grotius.[6] Schmitt's vision reproduces, too, a tendency in European thought to represent the land as a "fully historicized" space standing in opposition to an "atemporal, 'ahistorical' sea."[7] Further, while highlighting spatial phenomena considered "planetary" in scope, Schmitt characterizes regional orders as the products of the actions of great powers. An insistent focus on European power as the engine of global change corresponds to Schmitt's utter neglect of indigenous and non-European political projects and the polyglot production of geographical knowledge of local, regional, and global spaces.[8]

Schmitt is not alone in his reification of the land-sea divide. Michel Foucault's influential essay "Of Other Spaces" is another important transmitter of this same damaging dichotomy—albeit from the other end of the political spectrum. Foucault memorably concludes his essay with a strikingly romanticized rendering of ships and the sea in which the ship appears as "closed in on itself"—a world apart—declared by Foucault to be the "heterotopia par excellence." These special qualities, he argues, have made ships into the "greatest reserve of the imagination" in world civilization.[9] A similar opposition continues to structure the popular imagination of the maritime world, from work on what one author has called the "outlaw sea" to cinematic depictions of mariners as radical outsiders.[10]

Against such views, recent historical research, exemplified by the chapters in this volume, works to fundamentally challenge the notion of terrestrial and maritime spaces as opposed and disconnected spheres. The findings build on other recent scholarship that highlights shared and cross-cutting processes: the production of partial and divided sovereignty on land and sea; the fitful thrust of landed legal authority onto the seas; interwoven practices of violence and protection; and social and cultural representations of vast, uneven, and connected terrestrial and maritime geographies.[11] As historians' findings point toward a *longue durée* in which land and sea composed deeply interpenetrating zones, we reveal the need for ways of describing such land-sea processes and the formations they generated.

Drawing on the essays in this volume, this afterword proposes "land-sea regimes" as a concept useful for naming globally distributed sociospatial formations that emerged from maritime and terrestrial processes crossing the land-sea divide. We envision land-sea regimes as a concept useful in the creation of a global maritime history that is not reductionist (à la Schmitt) and that also moves beyond the Braudelian "ocean worlds" methodology. We begin by rejecting narratives that oppose settled territorial sovereignty to the "lawless" ocean.[12] Instead, historians can focus on the processes that crossed the land-sea divide and inquire about their regulatory effects. The word "regimes," we hope, points to the interpolitical and multicultural dimensions of such crossings and their incorporation of multiple processes, including those highlighted in this volume: the production and dissemination of knowledge on and about the seas and the distribution and imprint of imperial practices related to labor, captivity, flows of trade and finance, and legal conflicts. In illuminating such processes and the broader shifts they helped to propel, the chapters place land-sea regimes at the center of global history.[13]

Perhaps not surprisingly, the emphasis on land-sea connections comes into especially sharp focus in the study of shorelines and proximate seas. As Phipps shows in her chapter on Japan's efforts to assert control over its coastline and harbors, demonstrations of command over coasts and nearby waters held enormous symbolic significance as markers of sovereignty, as well as great pragmatic force in enabling states to tap trade for revenue. At the water's edge, prevailing notions of where jurisdictional lines divided territorial waters from the open sea might seem to have evolved in straightforward ways. But across several centuries there was nothing clear-cut about jurisdiction in such spaces. Even jurists who argued for definite doctrines about the law of the sea found themselves altering their positions in the context of specific conflicts.[14] Estuaries, beaches, harbors, lagoons, channels, straits, and other bodies of water—some as large and geopolitically important as the Malacca Strait or the English Channel, others as small and seemingly insignificant as a rough stretch of French coast prone to shipwrecks or a harbor in Taiwan frequented by ships from China and Japan—seemed to offer opportunities for definite control over water but in fact also developed as pluri-political and multijurisdictional zones.[15]

The imbrication of land and sea did not stop at the shoreline. The high seas, though featured in some juridical tracts as legally distinctive spaces, emerge as a sphere of ambiguous claims and confused regulatory order, even when patrolled by powerful navies. As the chapters by Schotte and Perl-Rosenthal in this volume show, the unevenness of regulatory regimes on the high seas resulted only in part from distance and the difficulties of communications. Interpolitical conflicts and the rhythms of maritime voyaging caused news of events on the seas to reach metropolitan centers in staccato bursts rather than steady streams. Perl-Rosenthal shows in his chapter that intercepted letters disrupted and supplemented routine flows of correspondence by shore communities engaged in long-distance trade, and the information the letters held mattered deeply to the conduct and outcomes of maritime violence. In parallel fashion, as Schotte describes, scientific knowledge advanced fitfully around particular navigational challenges. The high seas, in these essays, appear much more like crowded near shores and enclosed seas than empty or purely natural realms corresponding to a "mythical view of the sea" as trackless and unchanging.[16]

As we gain a clearer sense of the diversity and complexity of sea spaces, the Braudelian framework of ocean basin worlds begins to appear increasingly limited. Each ocean region clearly encompasses multiple zones. In the Atlantic world, trade flows of varied intensity and involving different mixes of commodities combined with diverse environmental conditions to produce many Atlantics.[17] For similar reasons in the Indian Ocean, as one scholar has argued, it makes much more sense to refer to that ocean world as an "interregional arena" than to regard it as a unified entity. Nor were "ocean worlds" ever self-contained. The navigational practices examined by Schotte, like the epistolary and juridical practices at the center of Perl-Rosenthal's essay, stretched beyond a single ocean. They also connected land with sea, and sea with land again, also moving across fluid, pluri-political zones.

Although no polity could own the sea, maritime-land configurations featured efforts of a wide variety of political communities, from microstates to empires to loose confederations, to exercise a degree of control over ocean spaces. We also discover that cross-cultural and cross-religious practices of communication and exchange could generate long-lasting institutional effects. The essay by Clulow and Hang in this volume traces the way interimperial politics, including the threat of war, guided the trade in deerskins in Asian waters. In their account, maritime trade emerges as a phenomenon with tentacles deep inside land-based polities. And as Mulich shows in his chapter, interimperial relations developed not just in metropoles but also in and across colonial landscapes and seascapes. When French, British, and Danish authorities in the Leeward Islands appealed to officials on adjacent islands for aid in repressing slave rebellions, they composed an "interimperial microregion" with powerful regulatory effects.

Curiously, some interpolity land-sea regimes only come into clear view when we probe land-sea processes within a single empire or state. In her chapter examining the shifting Spanish imperial policies around maritime labor, Phillips reveals a complex network of conduits for moving mariners from land to ships and back again. Infamous coercive processes, such as condemning men to the galleys, worked alongside less visible incentives that also straddled the land-sea divide, from antivagrancy legislation to the lure of petty trade. Phillips's essay reminds us that large-scale, coercive labor practices knitted together empires even as they helped to compose interpolity regions.[18]

Using the land-sea regime as a framework for maritime history allows us to respond to Schmitt's call for a plantetary approach to spatial change without making Europeans appear to be the sole agents of global transformations. Schmitt's absurd and racist rendering of "sea" and "land" peoples falls in the face of pervasive evidence that indigenous communities everywhere recombined the resources of lands and their proximate seas. Nonelite actors and vulnerable subjects—from enslaved mariners to impoverished port workers to female laborers in fisheries and on farms—structured the interface between land and sea. Several essays in this volume continue the ongoing project of recovering their voices and practices. As Igler shows in his chapter, individuals from very different societies confronted the challenges of transposing experience into knowledge about the seas, and they entered maritime worlds with incentives to acquire information, prestige, and wealth from voyages. Familiar goals produced analoguous or (in the case of Kadu and Choris) connected forms of communication that converted travel narratives into cultural capital. Vernacular knowledge merged with official reporting conventions to shape perceptions of oceans and their resources.

Going still further, we argue that the contributions in this volume call attention to several mechanisms linking land-sea regimes to global orders. Some land-sea regimes, such as the pluri-political microregion described in Mulich's chapter or the interimperial trade regime explored by Clulow and Hang in their chapter, represent widely recurring patterns that act as modular components of global ordering.[19] Norling's essay in this volume analyzes a related but different type of widely recurring pattern: similar practices produced by structural features shared across regions. Her chapter on the gendered division of labor at the land-sea junction shows that culturally and politically very different enclaves were positioned to change in step as economic integration intensified in the long eighteenth and nineteenth centuries.

Not all land-sea regimes were modular in the way that insular regions and fisheries were. Another kind of land-sea regime sprang from the power of a single empire or the deep influence of changes in one or more regulatory processes. Consider as an example the Anglo-American Atlantic at the turn of the nineteenth century. The period from the 1780s through the early nineteenth century featured both revolutionary and reactionary projects to refashion Atlantic empires. Some British thinkers responded to the loss of American colonies by imagining the Atlantic as "a space organized by commercial relations," while others sought to devise an Atlantic legal order comprising a constitutionally unified colonial sphere alongside messy interpolitical spaces.[20] The resurgence of U.S. shipping after the American Revolution and the successful resistance of the United States to British naval aggression gave rise to an Anglo-American regulatory order in the North Atlantic, albeit one still in tension with multiple political communities. Even a staunch loyalist such as Thomas Pownall recognized that the "empire" of the United States was becoming "a new primary planet in the system of the world." This vision of a "great marine Atlantic alliance" was unevenly and imperfectly realized, generating at best a patchy oceanic regime studded with microregional spaces.[21]

Of course, the Atlantic is not the only region where we can find land-sea regimes of vast scale and influence, as studies of Indian Ocean and Pacific orders show.[22] The challenge in profiling such regional land-sea regimes is not to reproduce the "ocean world" perspective in a different form. Several chapters in this volume illustrate one way to avoid this pitfall, by studying the local variants and global reach of regulatory processes. Imperial maritime labor policies (Phillips), the circulation of maritime law (Raffety), and the documentation of nationality (Perl-Rosenthal) stand as examples. It then becomes possible to ask how patterned practices aligned with global shifts. Janice Thomson's classic account of global prohibition regimes against piracy and other forms of nonstate violence remains useful as a model for tracing the outsized influence of specific regulatory projects.[23] We can also improve on Thomson's approach by beginning with processes and asking open-ended questions about their regional variations and global imprint.[24]

Land-sea regimes, it must be stressed—and this is one of the strengths of the essays in this volume—did more than simply extend land-based institutions and practices into marine environments. Striking similarities in forms of raiding, jurisdictional jockeying, and coercive labor practices crossed land and sea environments, creating more continuities than discontinuities. On land and sea, sovereignty was still imagined and structured as divisible and layered, and the same qualities that produced fluid, interpolitical zones of surprising durability operated across these spaces. The arrow of influence did not necessarily point from land to sea. As Raffaele Laudani has noted, conflicts over sovereignty at sea could be "reterritorialized" through various legal and economic processes.[25] In the long nineteenth century, for example, maritime-centered conflicts influenced emerging definitions of citizenship and forged routines for inventing borders and developing foreign relations policies.[26]

As these points and the chapters in this volume suggest, a powerful conceptual framework for maritime world history is within reach. A focus on land-sea regimes shaped by practices that straddled the line between the aqueous and terrestrial realms makes it possible to globalize maritime history without relying on a self-sealing "ocean world" methodology, and without recourse to Schmitt's crude generalizations. It is possible, we have argued, to recognize the deep influence of European seafaring on changes within vast imperial and interimperial formations while also doing justice to the autonomy and influence of non-European societies. It is possible, too, to study consequential institutional shifts encompassing maritime worlds while tracing the generative effects of vernacular knowledge created on and about the seas. As politically and legally plural compositions, land-sea regimes represent key elements of global ordering. Their study promises to enhance global maritime history and engender robust comparative analysis across time and space—placing maritime practices at the center of world history.

Notes

Introduction

1. In spite of some efforts to argue for the centrality of the maritime world, such as Jerry Bentley, "Sea and Ocean Basins as Frameworks of Historical Analysis," *Geographical Review* 89, no. 2 (1999), 215–24, major studies continue to treat maritime affairs as marginal. See, for instance, the very brief discussion of the maritime world in Jürgen Osterhammel, *The Transformation of the World* (Princeton, NJ: Princeton University Press, 2014), 96–100, 275–83. The "acquacentric" world history perspective celebrated by Rainer Buschmann in "Oceans of World History: Delineating Aquacentric Notions in the Global Past," *History Compass* 2 (2004): 1–10, remains more aspiration than reality.

2. Our approach to land-sea regimes has some similarities to Alison Bashford's call for the study of "terraqueous histories." On the differences, and for a fuller discussion of land-sea regimes, see the afterword in this volume. Alison Bashford, "Terraqueous Histories," *Historical Journal* 60, no. 2 (June 2017): 253–72.

3. The most influential of these amateur projects was A. T. Mahan's *The Influence of Sea Power upon History* (Boston: Little, Brown, 1890). Of the publication projects, see, e.g., *Official Records of the Union and Confederate Navies in the War of the Rebellion*, 30 vols. (Washington, DC: U.S. Government Printing Office, 1894–1922). These projects in the United States expanded significantly in the 1920s and 1930s, with series of *Naval Documents Related to the United States Wars with the Barbary Powers* (6 vols.) and *Naval Documents Related to the Quasi-War Between the United States and France* (7 vols.).

4. See Léon Guérin, *Histoire maritime de France* (Paris: Dufour, Mulat et Boulanger, 1851–56); Ch. Rouvier, *Histoire des marins français sous la République* (Paris: Bertrand, 1868); E. Chevalier, *Histoire de la marine française sous la première République* (Paris: Hachette, 1886); O. Havard, *Histoire de la Révolution dans les ports de guerre* (Paris: Nouvelle Librairie Nationale, 1911–13); Gardner Weld Allen, *A Naval History of the American Revolution* (Boston: Houghton Mifflin, 1913).

5. Samuel Eliot Morison's *Maritime History of Massachusetts Bay, 1783–1860* (Boston: Houghton Mifflin, 1921) was a transitional work between this amateur tradition and academic scholarship. On the amateur tradition, see, e.g., Samuel Roads, *The History and Traditions of Marblehead* (Boston: Houghton Osgood, 1880); D. H. Hurd, *History of Essex County, Massachusetts: With Biographical Sketches of Many of Its Pioneers and Prominent Men* (Philadelphia: Lewis, 1888).

6. See Charles R. Boxer, *The Portuguese Seaborne Empire, 1415–1825* (London: Hutchinson, 1969); J. P. Oliveira Martins, *Historia de Portugal*, vol. 1 (Lisbon: Bertrand, 1880); G. L. Beer, *The Old Colonial System, 1660–1754* (New York: Macmillan, 1912); Charles McLean Andrews, *The Colonial Period of American History*, 4 vols. (New Haven, CT: Yale University Press, 1934–1938); Arthur M. Schlesinger Sr., *The Colonial Merchants and the American Revolution, 1763–1776* (New York: Longmans, 1918).

7. Bernard Bailyn, *The New England Merchants in the Seventeenth* Century (Cambridge, MA: Harvard University Press, 1955); Richard Pares, *Yankees and Creoles: The Trade Between North America and the West Indies Before the American Revolution* (Cambridge, MA: Harvard University Press, 1956); Huguette Chaunu and Pierre Chaunu, *Séville et l'Atlantique, 1504–1650* (Paris: Colin, 1955); Holden Furber, *Rival Empires of Trade in the Orient, 1600–1800* (Minneapolis: University of Minnesota Press, 1976); K. N. Chaudhuri, *Trade and Civilisation in the Indian Ocean: An Economic History from the Rise of Islam to 1750* (Cambridge: Cambridge University Press, 1985). This scholarship reflected the delayed influence of some notable work of the immediate prewar period, esp. Richard Pares, *War and Trade in the West Indies, 1739–1763* (New York: Oxford University Press, 1936).

8. Early issues of *De West-Indische Gids* in 1919/1920, the first scholarly journal to focus on the West Indies, featured numerous articles about maritime commerce: e.g., R. Bijlsma, "Suriname's handelsbeweging 1683–1712," *De West-Indische Gids* 1, part 2 (1919/1920): 48–51.

9. Alain Cabantous, "Les populations maritimes du littoral français de la manche orientale et de la mer du nord du milieu du XVIIème siècle à 1793: Essai d'histoire sociale comparative" (PhD diss., Université de Lille III, 1987). After Jaap R. Bruijn and E. S. van Eyck van Helsinga, *58 miljoen Nederlanders en de zeevaart* (Amsterdam: Amsterdam Boek, 1977), a book for the general public, Bruijn edited or coauthored a number of books in social history, including J. R. Bruijn and Jan Lucassen, eds., *Op de schepen der Oost-Indische Compagnie* (Groningen: Wolters-Noordhoff, 1980); and J. R. Bruijn and E. S. van Eyck van Heslinga, eds., *Muiterij: Oproer en berechting op schepen van de VOC* (Haarlem: De Boer Maritiem, 1980). For a call for a similar shift in English maritime history, see Kenneth R. Andrews, "The Elizabethan Seaman," *Mariner's Mirror* 68, no. 3 (1982): 245–62; Ira Dye, "Early American Merchant Seafarers," *Proceedings of the American Philosophical Society* 120, no. 5 (1976): 331–60.

10. See also T. J. A. Le Goff, "Les origines sociales des gens de mer français au XVIIIe siècle," in *La France d'Ancien Régime: Etudes réunies en l'honneur de Pierre Goubert*, t.2 (Toulouse: Privat, 1984). Excellent early work on women and seafaring in the Atlantic appears in Margaret S. Creighton and Lisa Norling, eds., *Iron Men, Wooden Women: Gender and Seafaring in the Atlantic World, 1700–1920* (Baltimore, MD: Johns Hopkins University Press, 1996).

11. A long anthropological tradition of studying Pacific maritime cultures took a historical turn with Marshall Sahlins, *Islands of History* (Chicago: University of Chicago Press, 1987); Greg Dening, *Mr. Bligh's Bad Language: Passion, Power and Theatre on the Bounty* (Cambridge: Cambridge University Press, 1994); and James F. Warren, *The Sulu Zone: The Dynamics of External Trade, Slavery and Ethnicity in the Transformation of a Southeast Asian Maritime State, 1768–1898* (Singapore: National University of Singapore Press, 2007).

12. See Cabantous, "Les populations maritimes"; and Daniel Vickers, *Farmers and Fishermen: Two Centuries of Work in Essex County, Massachusetts, 1630–1850* (Chapel Hill: University of North Carolina Press for the Omohundro Institute of Early American History and

Culture, 1994); Marcus Rediker, *Between the Devil and the Deep Blue Sea: Merchant Seamen, Pirates, and the Anglo-American Maritime World, 1700–1750* (Cambridge: Cambridge University Press, 1987); Peter Linebaugh and Marcus Rediker, *The Many-Headed Hydra: Sailors, Slaves, Commoners, and the Hidden History of the Revolutionary Atlantic* (Boston: Beacon Press, 2013). Later work by Cabantous took a cultural turn and moved away from his initial focus on serial sources: see, e.g., Alain Cabantous, *Les citoyens du large: Les identités maritimes en France (XVIIe–XIXe siécles)* (Paris: Aubier, 1995).

13. Fernand Braudel, *The Mediterranean and the Mediterranean World in the Age of Philip II*, 2 vols. (New York: Harper & Row, 1972).

14. The literature on ocean-centered regions is too vast to summarize. Recent examples include Peregrine Horden and Nicholas Purcell, *The Corrupting Sea: A Study of Mediterranean History* (Malden, MA: Wiley-Blackwell, 2000); David Igler, *The Great Ocean: Pacific Worlds from Captain Cook to the Gold Rush* (Oxford: Oxford University Press, 2013); Sugata Bose, *A Hundred Horizons: The Indian Ocean in the Age of Global Empire* (Cambridge, MA: Harvard University Press, 2006); and numerous works in Atlantic history, together with studies of regional seas such as Rene Barendse, *The Arabian Seas: The Indian Ocean World of the Seventeenth Century* (London: Routledge, 2001); B. W. Higman, *A Concise History of the Caribbean* (New York: Cambridge University Press, 2011); and Warren, *The Sulu Zone*. For summaries of the literature on each ocean basin that include some reflections on the limitations of the approach, see David Armitage, Alison Bashford, and Sujit Sivasundaram, eds., *Oceanic Histories* (Cambridge: Cambridge University Press, 2017).

15. Warren, *The Sulu Zone*; Adam Clulow, *The Company and the Shogun: The Dutch Encounter with Tokugawa Japan* (New York: Columbia University Press, 2013); Tonio Andrade, *Lost Colony: The Untold Story of China's First Great Victory over the West* (Princeton, NJ: Princeton University Press, 2011); Giancarlo Casale, *The Ottoman Age of Exploration* (Oxford: Oxford University Press, 2010); Joshua L. Reid, *The Sea Is My Country: The Maritime World of the Makahs* (New Haven, CT: Yale University Press, 2015); Sebastian Prange, "A Trade of No Dishonor: Piracy, Commerce, and Community in the Western Indian Ocean, Twelfth to Sixteenth Century," *American Historical Review* 116, no. 5 (2011): 1269–93; Prange, *Monsoon Islam: Trade and Faith on the Medieval Malabar Coast* (Cambridge: Cambridge University Press, 2018).

16. Clare Anderson, *Convicts in the Indian Ocean: Transportation from South Asia to Mauritius, 1815–53* (New York: St. Martin's Press, 2000); Stephanie E. Smallwood, *Saltwater Slavery: A Middle Passage from Africa to American Diaspora* (Cambridge, MA: Harvard University Press, 2007); N. A. T. Hall, "Maritime Maroons: 'Grand Marronage' from the Danish West Indies," *William and Mary Quarterly* 42, no. 4 (1985): 476–98; David S. Cecelski, *The Waterman's Song: Slavery and Freedom in Maritime North Carolina* (Chapel Hill: University of North Carolina Press, 2001); Jeffrey Bolster, *Black Jacks: African American Seamen in the Age of Sail* (Cambridge, MA: Harvard University Press, 1998).

17. On commerce, see, e.g., David Hancock, *Oceans of Wine: Madeira and the Emergence of American Trade and Taste* (New Haven: Yale University Press, 2009); Pedro Machado, *Ocean of Trade: South Asian Merchants, Africa and the Indian Ocean, c. 1750–1850* (Cambridge: Cambridge University Press, 2014); and Fahad Ahmad Bishara, *A Sea of Debt: Law and Economic Life in the Western Indian Ocean, 1780–1950* (Cambridge: Cambridge University Press, 2017); on race, ethnicity, gender, and identification among mariners, see Lisa

Norling, *Captain Ahab Had a Wife: New England Women and the Whalefishery, 1720–1870* (Chapel Hill: University of North Carolina Press, 2000); Andrew Lipman, *The Saltwater Frontier: Indians and the Contest for the American Coast* (New Haven, CT: Yale University Press, 2015); Nancy Shoemaker, *Native American Whalemen and the World: Indigenous Encounters and the Contingency of Race* (Chapel Hill: University of North Carolina Press, 2015); Brian Rouleau, *With Sails Whitening Every Sea: Mariners and the Making of an American Maritime Empire* (Ithaca, NY: Cornell University Press, 2014). On culture, see Alain Cabantous, *Le ciel dans la mer: Christianisme et civilisation maritime, XVe–XIXe siècle* (Paris: Fayard, 1990); Paul A. Gilje, *To Swear Like a Sailor: Maritime Culture in America, 1750–1850* (Cambridge: Cambridge University Press, 2016).

18. Consider just a few examples: Philip Stern and Carl Wennerlind, eds., *Mercantilism Reimagined: Political Economy in Early Modern Britain and Its Empire* (New York: Oxford University Press, 2013); Kerry Ward, *Networks of Empire: Forced Migration in the Dutch East India Company* (New York: Cambridge University Press, 2008); W. Jeffrey Bolster, *The Mortal Sea: Fishing in the Atlantic in the Age of Sail* (Cambridge, MA: Harvard University Press, 2012).

19. For a view of the English production of knowledge about the New World, see Peter Mancall, *Haklyut's Promise: An Elizabethan's Obsession for an English America* (New Haven, CT: Yale University Press, 2019); on the Dutch, see Michiel van Groesen, *Amsterdam's Atlantic: Print Culture and the Making of Dutch Brazil* (Philadelphia: University of Pennsylvania Press, 2017); on "Atlantic creoles," see Jane Landers, *Atlantic Creoles in the Age of Revolutions* (Cambridge, MA: Harvard University Press, 2011); and on circulating news about revolution, Ada Ferrer, *Freedom's Mirror: Cuba and Haiti in the Age of Revolution* (New York: Cambridge University Press, 2014).

20. On "vectors of law" and sovereignty at sea, see Lauren A. Benton, *A Search for Sovereignty: Law and Geography in European Empires, 1400–1900* (Cambridge: Cambridge University Press, 2010), chap. 3, 112; see also Mark G. Hanna, *Pirate Nests and the Rise of the British Empire, 1570–1740* (Chapel Hill: University of North Carolina Press, 2015); Henry J. Bourguignon, *Sir William Scott, Lord Stowell, Judge of the High Court of Admiralty, 1798–1828* (Cambridge: Cambridge University Press, 1987); Philip C. Jessup et al., *Neutrality: Its History, Economics and Law* (New York: Columbia University Press, 1937); Nathan Perl-Rosenthal, *Citizen Sailors: Becoming American in the Age of Revolution* (Cambridge, MA: Belknap Press of Harvard University Press, 2015); Renaud Morieux, *The Channel: England, France and the Construction of a Maritime Border in the Eighteenth Century* (Cambridge: Cambridge University Press, 2016); Guillaume Calafat, "Une mer jalousée: Juridictions maritimes, ports francs et régulation du commerce en Méditerranée (1590–1740)" (PhD diss., Université Paris I, 2013); Lauren Benton and Lisa Ford, *Rage for Order: The British Empire and the Origins of International Law, 1800–1850* (Cambridge, MA: Harvard University Press, 2016), chap. 5; Nathan Perl-Rosenthal, "On Mobile Legal Spaces and Maritime Empires: The Pillage of the East Indiaman *Osterley* (1779)," *Itinerario* 42, no. 2 (August 2018): 183–201.

21. Niklas Frykman, "The Mutiny on the *Hermione*: Warfare, Revolution, and Treason in the Royal Navy," *Journal of Social History* 44, no. 1 (2010): 159–87; Alain Cabantous, *La vergue et les fers: Mutins et déserteurs dans la marine de l'ancienne France, XVIIe–XVIIIe s.* (Paris: Tallandier, 1984); Denver Brunsman, *The Evil Necessity: British Naval Impressment in the Eighteenth-Century Atlantic World* (Charlottesville: University of Virginia Press, 2013); Martine Acerra et al., *Les marines de guerre européennes: XVIIe–XVIIIe siècles* (Paris: Presses

de l'Université de Paris-Sorbonne, 1998); John S. Bromley, *Corsairs and Navies, 1660–1760* (London: Hambledon Press, 1987); Sarah Kinkel, *Disciplining the Empire: Politics, Governance, and the Rise of the British Navy* (Cambridge, MA: Harvard University Press, 2018); Jane Samson, *Imperial Benevolence: Making British Authority in the Pacific Islands* (Honolulu: University of Hawai'i Press, 1998).

22. For example, Peter Mancall and Carole Shammas, eds., *Governing the Sea in the Early Modern Era: Essays in Honor of Robert C. Ritchie* (San Marino, CA: Huntington Library, 2015); Tonio Andrade and Xing Hang, eds., *Sea Rovers, Silver, and Samurai: Maritime East Asia in Global History, 1550–1700* (Honolulu: University of Hawai'i Press, 2016); Emma Christopher, Cassandra Pybus, and Marcus Rediker, eds., *Many Middle Passages: Forced Migration and the Making of the Modern World* (Berkeley: University of California Press, 2007); and Stefan Amirell and Leos Müller, eds., *Persistent Piracy: Maritime Violence and State Formation in Global Historical Perspective* (London: Palgrave Macmillan, 2014). Edited volumes that explicitly embrace a global perspective include Mike Brown and Barbara Humberstone, eds., *Seascapes: Shaped by the Sea: Embodied Narratives and Fluid Geographies* (Farnham, Surrey: Ashgate, 2015); Maria Fusaro and Amélia Polónia, eds., *Maritime History as Global History* (St. John's, NL: International Maritime Economic History Association, 2010); Bernhard Klein and Gesa Mackenthun, eds., *Sea Changes: Historicizing the Ocean* (New York: Routledge, 2004); Clare Anderson, Niklas Frykman, Lex Heerma van Voss, and Rediker, eds., *Mutiny and Maritime Radicalism in the Age of Revolution* (Cambridge: Cambridge University Press, 2013).

23. For a more extended discussion of the land-sea divide, see the afterword in this volume. Historians have taken two virtually opposite approaches to interrogating the relationship between land and sea: a microscale mode and a super-macroscale mode. These literatures have rarely if ever been in dialogue. For examples of the former mode, see esp. Christophe Cérino, Aliette Geistdoerfer, Gérard Le Bouëdec, and François Ploux, eds., *Entre terre et mer: Sociétés littorales et pluriactivités (XVe–XXe siècle)* (Rennes: Presses Universitaires de Rennes, 2004); and Vickers, *Farmers and Fishermen*. For the latter mode, which has been powerfully influenced by historical geography, see esp. Martin W. Lewis and Kären Wigen, *The Myth of Continents: A Critique of Metageography* (Berkeley: University of California Press, 1997); and Philip E. Steinberg, *The Social Construction of the Ocean* (Cambridge: Cambridge University Press, 2001).

24. Cf. Lauren Benton and Richard Ross, *Legal Pluralism and Empires, 1500–1850* (New York: New York University Press, 2013); Saliha Belmessous, ed., *Native Claims: Indigenous Law Against Empire, 1500–1920* (New York: Oxford University Press, 2014); and especially Benton, *A Search for Sovereignty*, chap. 3. On British admiralty law and universalism, see Jennifer Pitts, "Empire and Legal Universalisms in the Eighteenth Century," *American Historical Review* 117, no. 1 (February 2012): 92–121; Benton and Ford, *Rage for Order*, chap. 5.

25. On vernacular knowledge on the seas, see supra note 20; and Gabriel Rocha, "Empire from the Commons: Making Colonial Archipelagos in the Early Iberian Atlantic" (PhD diss., New York University, 2016); Nile Green, "The Waves of Heterotopia: Toward a Vernacular Intellectual History of the Indian Ocean," *American Historical Review* 123, no. 3 (June 2018): 846–74.

26. For example, Kenneth J. Banks, *Chasing Empire Across the Sea: Communications and the State in the French Atlantic, 1713–1763* (Montreal: McGill-Queen's University Press, 2002). This is a theme in the work of James C. Scott (*Seeing Like a State: How Certain Schemes*

to Improve the Human Condition Have Failed [New Haven, CT: Yale University Press, 1998]). Other scholars have seen this weakness as equally characteristic of nineteenth-century empire; see Frederick Cooper, *Colonialism in Question: Theory, Knowledge, History* (Berkeley: University of California Press, 2005). For a discussion of this problem in the maritime context, see Perl-Rosenthal, "On Mobile Legal Spaces and Maritime Empires."

27. "Introduction: On the Threshold of the State," in Annabel S. Brett, *Changes of State: Nature and the Limits of the City in Early Modern Natural Law* (Princeton, NJ: Princeton University Press, 2011), 1–10.

28. An early exploration of the symbolism of such zones is Greg Dening, *Beach Crossings: Voyaging Across Times, Cultures, and Self* (Philadelphia: University of Pennsylvania Press, 2004). Michael Pearson recognized before many historians the importance of distinctive coastline and port political cultures: *Port Cities and Intruders: The Swahili Coast, India, and Portugal in the Early Modern Era* (Baltimore, MD: Johns Hopkins University Press, 1998). A recent surge in case studies of coastlines and proximate seas has expanded the possibilities for comparative analysis. See, e.g., Morieux, *The Channel*; Christopher L. Pastore, *Between Land and Sea: The Atlantic Coast and the Transformation of New England* (Cambridge, MA: Harvard University Press, 2014). And for further discussion of the historiography and its promise, see the afterword in this volume.

29. Adam M. McKeown, *Melancholy Order: Asian Migration and the Globalization of Borders* (New York: Columbia University Press, 2008); Peter Sahlins, *Boundaries: The Making of France and Spain in the Pyrenees* (Berkeley: University of California Press, 1989).

30. For examples, see Ernesto Bassi, *An Aqueous Territory: Sailor Geographies and New Granada's Transimperial Greater Caribbean World* (Durham, NC: Duke University Press, 2017); Benton and Ford, *Rage for Order*, chap. 6; David Wheat, *Atlantic Africa and the Spanish Caribbean, 1570–1640* (Chapel Hill: University of North Carolina Press, 2016); Rocha, "Empire from the Commons"; Jeppe Mulich, "In a Sea of Empires: Networks and Crossings in the Leeward Islands, 1783–1834" (PhD diss., New York University, 2015); Warren, *The Sulu Zone.*

Chapter 1

Note to epigraph: Richard Armstrong, *The Early Mariners* (New York: Praeger, 1968), 9.

1. Quoted in José Cervera Pery, "Marina Mercante y Armada: Análisis de una interrelación," *Cuadernos Monográficos del Instituto de Historia y Cultura Naval* 9 (1990): 25.

2. *Libros Generales de Galera,* Archivo del Museo Naval (AMN), Madrid. A long-term project aims to restore the twenty-five extant galley registers from the late seventeenth and early eighteenth centuries. See Carmen Torres López et al., *Restaurando el testimonio del pasado: Los libros generales de galeras* (Madrid: Órgano de Historia y Cultura Naval, 2010). Published work using these registers includes F. Javier Guillamón Álvarez and Jesús Pérez Hervás, "Los forzados de galeras en Cartagena durante el primer tercio del siglo XVIII," *Revista de Historia Naval* 5, no. 19 (1987): 63–76; and Manuel Martínez Martínez, *Los forzados de marina en la España del siglo XVIII, 1700–1775* (Almería: Universidad de Almería, 2011).

3. Paul van Royen, Jaap Bruijn, and Jan Lucassen, eds., *"Those Emblems of Hell"? European Sailors and the Maritime Labour Market, 1570–1870* (St. John's, NL: Memorial University of Newfoundland, 1997); hereafter, *"Those Emblems of Hell."*

4. Maria Fusaro, Bernard Allaire, Richard J. Blakemore, and Tijl Vanneste, eds., *Law, Labour, and Empire: Comparative Perspectives on Seafarers, c. 1500–1800* (London: Palgrave Macmillan, 2015); hereafter, *Law, Labour, and Empire.*

5. Scott Anderson, "Coercion," *Stanford Encyclopedia of Philosophy,* rev. ed. 2011, https://plato.stanford.edu/entries/coercion/. Anderson considers that coercion includes any means—positive or negative—to persuade someone to do something they might not otherwise do.

6. Amélia Polónia, "Portuguese Seafarers: Informal Agents of Empire-Building," in *Law, Labour, and Empire,* 218.

7. Daniel Vickers with Vince Walsh, *Young Men and the Sea: Yankee Seafarers in the Age of Sail* (New Haven: Yale University Press, 2005), 51–53, 58.

8. Gustav Sætra, "The International Labour Market for Seamen, 1600–1900: Norway and Norwegian Participation," in "*Those Emblems of Hell,*" 173.

9. Paul van Royen, "The 'National' Maritime Labour Market: Looking for Common Characteristics," in "*Those Emblems of Hell,*" 4.

10. J. Th. Thór, "Iceland," in "*Those Emblems of Hell,*" 163.

11. Royen, "'National' Maritime Labour Market," 4.

12. Vickers, *Young Men and the Sea,* 59–60.

13. Carla Rahn Phillips, "The Labour Market for Sailors in Spain, 1570–1870," in "*Those Emblems of Hell,*" 335. The figure is 0.74 percent. Unfortunately, the published version of the essay changed that to "seventy-four percent," which grossly overstates the maritime population.

14. Michael North, "German Sailors, 1650–1900," in "*Those Emblems of Hell,*" 253–58.

15. Anderson, "Coercion," 2.

16. Ibid., 1.

17. Carla Rahn Phillips, *The Struggle for the South Atlantic: Pedro de Rada's Account of the Armada of the Strait, 1581–84* (London: Hakluyt Society, 2016).

18. Polónia, "Portuguese Seafarers," 220–21.

19. Karel Davids, "Maritime Labour in the Netherlands, 1570–1870," in "*Those Emblems of Hell,*" 61–65.

20. Peter Earle, "English Sailors, 1570–1775," in "*Those Emblems of Hell,*" 80–82, 91–92.

21. Vickers, *Young Men and the Sea,* 177–78.

22. Bernard Allaire, "Between Oléron and Colbert: The Evolution of French Maritime Law until the Seventeenth Century," in *Law, Labour, and Empire,* 90–91, discusses various types of recruiting contracts in France.

23. Yrjö Kaukiainen, "Finnish Sailors, 1750–1870," in "*Those Emblems of Hell,*" 223–25.

24. Jelle van Lottum, *Across the North Sea: The Impact of the Dutch Republic on International Labour Migration, c. 1550–1850* (Amsterdam: Aksant Academic, 2007), 61–62.

25. Tijl Vanneste, "Sailing Through the Strait: Seamen's Professional Trajectories from a Segmented Labour Market in Holland to a Fragmented Mediterranean," in *Law, Labour, and Empire,* 125.

26. Roland Baetens, "Sailors in the Southern Netherlands and Belgium (16th–19th Centuries)," in "*Those Emblems of Hell,*" 283.

27. Matthias van Rossum, "Claiming Their Rights? Indian Sailors Under the Dutch East India Company," in *Law, Labour, and Empire,* 274.

28. Ibid., 278-79.

29. Yu Po-Ching, "Chinese Seamen in London and St. Helena in the Early Nineteenth Century," in *Law, Labour and Empire*, 289–90.

30. Richard J. Blakemore, "The Legal World of English Sailors, c. 1575–1729," in *Law, Labour, and Empire*, 104.

31. Lottum, *Across the North Sea*, 80–81.

32. Adam Clulow, "Determining the Law of the Sea: The Long History of the Breukelen Case, 1657–1662," in *Sea Rovers, Silver, and Samurai: Maritime East Asia in Global History, 1550–1700*, ed. Tonio Andrade and Xing Hang (Honolulu: University of Hawai'i Press, 2016), 182.

33. Vickers, *Young Men and the Sea*, 57–58.

34. Baetens, "Sailors in the Southern Netherlands and Belgium," 279.

35. Anderson, "Coercion," 12–14.

36. Baetens, "Sailors in the Southern Netherlands and Belgium," 273.

37. Earle, "English Sailors," 80–81.

38. Gordon Jackson, "Scottish Sailors," in "*Those Emblems of Hell*," 131–33.

39. Pierre Chaunu and Huguette Chaunu, *Séville et l'Atlantique, 1504–1650,* 8 vols. in 12 (Paris: S.E.V.P.E.N, 1955–60), 3: 295–96.

40. Carla Rahn Phillips, "'The Life Blood of the Navy': Recruiting Sailors in Eighteenth-Century Spain," *Mariner's Mirror* 87, no. 4 (November 2001): 420–45.

41. The 150 galleys ranged in size from 24 benches with 6 men per bench (3 per oar on each side of the ship), to 30 or more benches with 14 or more men per bench. The figure of 21,000 men is a minimum, based on 144 men for a 24-bench galley. Torres López et al., *Restaurando el testimonio del pasado*, 23.

42. The qualities desired in military officers featured in European treatises from ancient times onward. Niccoló Machiavelli, *Discourses on the First Ten Books of Livy* (c. 1517), Book III, discussed those qualities, as did numerous other authors. Current scholarship has shown a renewed interest in the topic, including the recent edition of Norbert Elias, *The Genesis of the Naval Profession*, ed. René Moelker and Stephen Mennell (Dublin: University College, 2007).

43. "Discurso de García de Toledo sobre los inconvenientes que tienen los cargos de galeras," in Juan Martínez de Burgos, Miscelánea literaria de los S. XV–S. XVI, fols. 100r–100v. Biblioteca Nacional de España, Madrid (BNE), MS 19164, fols. 100r–107v. The discourse is analyzed in Carla Rahn Phillips, "Spanish Noblemen as Galley Captains: A Problematical Social History," in *Strategy and the Sea: Essays in Honour of John B. Hattendorf*, ed. N. A. M. Rodger, J. Ross Dancy, Benjamin Darnell, and Evan Wilson (Woodbridge, Suffolk, UK: Boydell & Brewer, 2016), 9–18.

44. AMN, Colección Sanz Barutell, MS 389, fols. 164r, 186r–187r.

45. AMN, *Libros Generales, Gente de Cabo, 1654–88.*

46. In that period, the honorific "Don" was a reliable indication of noble status.

47. Although the register is labeled 1654–88, a few records date from the 1640s.

48. Elias, *Genesis of the Naval Profession*, 33–40.

49. Diego de Zúñiga to Philip II, September 24, 1584, AMN, Colección Sanz Barutell, MS 389, fol. 184r.

50. Officials in the House of Trade to Philip II, August 24, 1584, AMN, Colección Sanz Barutell, MS 389, fols. 158r–158v. The back pay amounted to more than 70,000 ducats.

51. Council of the Indies to Philip II, June 14, 1586, Archivo General de Indias (AGI), Seville, Patronato, leg. 33, N. 3, R. 65.

52. For example, the records for 142 men recruited for the Indies fleets in 1587. Karpeles Collection, Santa Barbara, CA; Medina Sidonia, Capitanía: Cuentas, vol. 10, fols. 3r–14v.

53. W. Jeffrey Bolster, *Black Jacks: African American Seamen in the Age of Sail* (Cambridge, MA: Harvard University Press, 1997), 22, 26, 28.

54. Ibid., 154–56, 159.

55. Vickers, *Young Men and the Sea*, 181–82, 184–85.

56. Bolster, *Black Jacks*, 188–89.

57. Polónia, "Portuguese Seafarers," 220–21.

58. Claire Anderson, *Subaltern Lives: Biographies of Colonialism in the Indian Ocean World, 1790–1920* (Cambridge: Cambridge University Press, 2012), 69.

59. T. J. A. Le Goff, "The Labour Market for Sailors in France," in "*Those Emblems of Hell*," 287–90. Le Goff describes the French system in general as conscription, but the men were conscripted only after their prior registration or inscription. Elsewhere, conscription in wartime required men to serve without prior inscription. See Allaire, "French Maritime Law," 87–91, for legal provisions regarding the French registration system and other aspects of naval reform.

60. Le Goff, "Labour Market for Sailors in France," 299–300.

61. Unless otherwise noted, the following discussion of the *matrícula* comes from Phillips, "'Life Blood of the Navy,'" 420–45. Earlier studies of the Spanish system include Francisco Javier de Salas, *Marina española. Discurso histórico. Reseña de la vida de mar y memoria* (Madrid: Fortanet, 1865); Salas, *Historia de la Matrícula de Mar y examen de varios sistemas de reclutamiento* (Madrid: Fortanet, 1870); and Rolf Mühlmann, *Die Reorganisation der Spanischen Kriegsmarine im 18. Jahrhundert* (Cologne-Vienna: Bohlau, 1975).

62. Carla Rahn Phillips, "Naval Recruitment and Basque Resistance in Early Modern Times," in *ITSAS Memoria: Revista de Estudios Marítimos del País Vasco* (San Sebastián, Spain, 2006), no. 5, 173–85.

63. Archivo General de Simancas (AGS), Simancas, Valladolid, Secretaría de Marina, leg. 276. See also AMN, Colección Vargas Ponce, 1a Ser., tomo XXII, docs. 21–24.

64. AGS, Guerra Antigua, legs. 3176–3178, 3886. Nonetheless, non-Catholic foreigners might be recruited for specific jobs such as gunners. Brice Gossart, "More Gunners for the Galleons of the King of Spain! Crews of Gunners, Skill Management and the Development of Spanish War Fleets in the Late Sixteenth Century," paper presented at the Annual Meeting of the Association for Spanish and Portuguese Historical Studies, San Diego, CA, March 7–20, 2016.

65. "[P]ara que la marinería sea tratada con dulzura y buen modo, y que hagan los más estrechos encargos a los capitanes, y oficiales mayores, para que zelen muy particularmente que los oficiales de mar depongan el rigor con que suelen tratar los marineros" [spelling and punctuation modernized], AGS, Secretaría de Marina, leg. 277.

66. Earle, "English Sailors," 89.

67. Hans Chr. Johansen, "Danish Sailors, 1570–1870," in "*Those Emblems of Hell*," 240, 249; North, "German Sailors," 260–61.

68. Polónia, "Portuguese Seafarers," 221, 234.

69. See, e.g., Baetens, "Sailors in the Southern Netherlands and Belgium," 283.

70. Blakemore, "Legal World of English Sailors," 104–5.

71. Ibid., 117–20. This was true in customary law long before punishments became fixed in written law with an act of Parliament in 1729.

72. Sarah Palmer and David M. Williams, "British Sailors, 1775–1870," in "*Those Emblems of Hell*," 104–5.

73. Earle, "English Sailors," 83–84.

74. Davids, "Maritime Labour in the Netherlands," 64.

75. Francisco Duarte to Antonio de Eraso, September 18, 1581, AMN, Colección Sanz Barutell, MS 388, fols. 192r–192v.

76. Frederic C. Lane, *Venice: A Maritime Republic* (Baltimore, MD: Johns Hopkins University Press, 1973), 45, 167–68, 176, 364–68.

77. Le Goff, "Labour Market for Sailors in France," 299.

78. AMN, *Libro General de Forzados, 1648–1660, 1708–1721.*

79. Ibid.

80. Paul Bamford, *Fighting Ships and Prisons: The Mediterranean Galleys of France in the Age of Louis XIV* (Minneapolis: University of Minnesota Press, 1973).

81. Bolster, *Black Jacks*, 71, makes this point as well.

Chapter 2

1. Rapport van Van Rijk aen haer Ed. tot Batavia overgelevert den 3 November 1662, Nationaal Archief, Den Haag, access number 1.04.02, Verenigde Oostindische Compagnie (VOC), hereafter: NL-HaNA, VOC, inventory 1240: 1489v. News of the fall of Fort Zeelandia reverberated across the region, and it is likely that rumors and reports had reached Ayutthaya prior to the arrival of the ambassador.

2. Rapport van Van Rijk, f. 1490.

3. The Zheng network had been established by the pirate turned admiral, Zheng Zhilong, in the last decades of Ming rule, when the court could no longer control the centrifugal forces along the littoral. The organization was subsequently expanded and strengthened by his son, Koxinga, who transformed it first into a center of pro-Ming military resistance against the Manchu Qing and then into an occupying force. Koxinga died shortly after displacing the Dutch from Taiwan. He was succeeded by his son, Zheng Jing, who established a state with a strong maritime orientation on the west coast of the island before intervening disastrously in continental politics in the 1670s.

4. There are too many to list in full here but some representative works by these scholars include: Tonio Andrade, "Beyond Guns, Germs, and Steel: European Expansion and Maritime Asia, 1400–1750," *Journal of Early Modern History* 14, no. 1–2 (2010): 165–86; Patrizia Carioti, "The Zhengs' Maritime Power in the International Context of the 17th Century Far Eastern Seas," *Ming-Qing Yanjiu* 5, no. 1 (1996): 29–68; Xing Hang, *Conflict and Commerce in Maritime East Asia: The Zheng Family and the Shaping of the Modern World, c. 1620–1720* (Cambridge: Cambridge University Press, 2016). Such work follows on from the pioneering scholarship of John E. Wills Jr. and Leonard Blussé.

5. See, for instance, Tonio Andrade, *Lost Colony: The Untold Story of China's First Great Victory over the West* (Princeton, NJ: Princeton University Press, 2011); Andrade, "The Company's Chinese Pirates: How the Dutch East India Company Tried to Lead a Coalition of Pirates to War Against China, 1621–1662," *Journal of World History* 15, no. 4 (December 2004): 415–44; John E. Wills Jr., "The Dutch Reoccupation of Chi-lung, 1664–1668," in *Around and About Formosa: Essays in Honor of Professor Ts'ao Yung-ho*, ed. Leonard Blussé (Taipei: SMC, 2003).

6. Wei-Chung Cheng, *War, Trade and Piracy in the China Seas, 1622–1683* (Leiden: Brill, 2013). Cheng shows a contest that went much further than Taiwan into the distant corners of Southeast Asia and much longer than 1662, when VOC forces surrendered on the island. While Cheng's work has productively expanded the parameters of the standard focus, his primary concern is with the two central actors, the Zheng network and the company. As a result, the wider ramifications of this contest and its impact on other parties remain largely unexplored. For important work on Siam that approaches the conflict from another angle, see Bhawan Ruangsilp, *Dutch East India Company Merchants at the Court of Ayutthaya: Dutch Perceptions of the Thai Kingdom, c. 1604–1765* (Leiden: Brill, 2007); Dhiravat Na Pombejra "The Dutch-Siamese Conflict of 1663–1664: A Reassessment," in *Around and About Formosa*, 291–306; Dhiravat na Pombejra, "A Political History of Siam Under the Prasatthong Dynasty, 1629–1688" (PhD diss., University of London, 1984).

7. Scholars focused on the Indian Ocean have long charted the ways in which territorial powers used such weapons to restrain European maritime enterprises. One prominent historian describes this balance between maritime might and power on land as a "balance of blackmail . . . between land and sea." Ashin Das Gupta, "Indian Merchants and the Western Indian Ocean: The Early Seventeenth Century," *Modern Asian Studies* 19, no. 3 (1985): 494.

8. Most work on the deerskin trade has focused on the role of the VOC. See Michael Laver, "Skins in the Game: The Dutch East India Company, Deerskins, and the Japan Trade," *World History Bulletin* 28, no. 2 (Fall 2012): 13–16; Hui-wen Koo, "Deer Hunting and Preserving the Commons in Dutch Colonial Taiwan," *Journal of Interdisciplinary History* 42, no. 2 (2011): 185–203; Pol Heyns (Han Jiabao), *Helan shidai de Taiwan jingji, tudi yu shuiwu* (Taipei: Appleseed Press, 2003); Thomas Höllmann, "Formosa and the Trade in Venison and Deerskins," in *Emporia, Commodities, and Entrepreneurs in Asian Maritime Trade, c. 1400–1750,* ed. Roderich Ptak and Dietmar Rothermund (Stuttgart: Steiner Verlag, 1991), 263–90. For a more Japan-focused analysis that considers deerskins shipped from northern Japan, see Brett Walker, *The Conquest of Ainu Lands: Ecology and Culture in Japanese Expansion, 1590–1800* (Berkeley and London: University of California Press, 2001).

9. The most reliable figures for the quantities of deerskins shipped from Taiwan to Japan come from two important articles: Koo, "Deer Hunting in Dutch Colonial Taiwan"; Weichung Cheng, "Emergence of Deerskin Exports from Taiwan Under VOC (1624–1642)," *Taiwan Historical Research* 24, no. 3 (2017): 1–48.

10. W. Coolhaas, "Een brief aan Jan Pietersz. Coen teruggevonden," *Bijdragen tot de Taal-, Land- en Volkenkunde* 112, no. 4 (1956): 407. For an analysis of the Japanese role in trade with Ayutthaya, see Nagazumi Yoko, "Ayutthaya and Japan: Embassies and Trade in the Seventeenth Century," in *From Japan to Arabia: Ayutthaya's Maritime Relations with Asia*, ed. Kennon Breazeale (Bangkok: Printing House of Thammasat University, 1999). Nagazumi reads the figure in this source as 500,000 rather than 50,000 but we see no evidence to support this interpretation. Sappanwood (*Biancaea sappan*) was a prized source for dye and formed another important export from Ayutthaya to Japan.

11. W. P. Coolhaas, ed., *Generale Missiven van Gouverneurs-generaal en Raden aan heren XVII der Verenigde Oostindische Compagnie*, 9 vols. (The Hague: M. Nijhof, 1960–), 1:136.

12. W. Coolhaas, "Een brief aan Jan Pietersz. Coen teruggevonden," 407.

13. Ruangsilp, *Dutch East India Company Merchants*, 20.

14. Dhiravat, "The Dutch-Siamese Conflict of 1663–1664," 292. The shifting nature of politics meant that there were multiple agreements between the VOC and Siam that were made, then abandoned, then confirmed again. For example, a reference in the *Batavia Dagregister* suggests that monopoly rights were first granted in 1633. J. A. van der Chijs, H. T. Colenbrander, and J. de Hullu, eds., *Dagh-register gehouden int Casteel Batavia vant passerende daer ter plaetse als over geheel Nederlandts-India*, 31 vols. (Batavia / The Hague: Landsdrukkerij / Martinus Nijhoff, 1887–1931), 1:301.

15. Jack Wills and Leonard Blussé have argued that by this time, Taiwan's value to the company had already diminished as the island lost its role first as an entrepôt in the intra–East Asian exchange of silk for silver, and then as a transit station for gold to India. This analysis is important, but the loss of Taiwan still came with very significant economic consequences. John E. Wills Jr., *Pepper, Guns, and Parleys: The Dutch East India Company and China, 1662–1681* (Cambridge, MA: Harvard University Press, 1974), 32; and Leonard Blussé, "No Boats to China: The Dutch East India Company and the Changing Pattern of the China Sea Trade, 1635–1690," *Modern Asian Studies* 30, no. 1 (February 1996): 67.

16. See Dahpon David Ho, "Sealords Live in Vain: Fujian and the Making of a Maritime Frontier in Seventeenth-Century China" (PhD diss., University of California, San Diego, 2011), esp. 200–297.

17. Tokugawa measures included encouraging the export of gold as an alternative to silver, manipulating the conversion rates between the two metals, and concentrating all foreign trade into the hands of a select cartel of wholesale merchants from Sakai and Osaka. Nakamura Tadashi, *Kinsei Nagasaki bōekishi no kenkyū* (Tokyo: Yoshikawa Kōbunkan, 1988), 282–83. For the VOC search for alternative sources of silk, see Anh Tuấn Hoàng, *Silk for Silver: Dutch-Vietnamese Relations, 1637–1700* (Leiden and Boston: Brill, 2007).

18. Blussé, "No Boats," 68–70.

19. For the rupture of the VOC relationship with Cambodia, see Alfons van der Kraan, *Murder and Mayhem in Seventeenth Century Cambodia* (Chiang Mai: Silkworm Books, 2009)

20. Cheng, *War, Trade and Piracy*, 218–19.

21. J. E. Heeres and F. W. Stapel, eds., *Corpus Diplomaticum Neerlando-Indicum*, 6 vols. (The Hague: 1907–1955), 2: 308.

22. Hang, *Conflict and Commerce*, 163–67.

23. For a discussion, see Adam Clulow, *The Company and the Shogun: The Dutch Encounter with Tokugawa Japan* (New York: Columbia University Press, 2014), chaps. 4 and 5.

24. Heeres and Stapel, *Corpus Diplomaticum*, 2:311. Although we should be careful of superimposing modern forms onto early modern practices, this designation can be viewed as the first iteration of Cambodian territorial waters. In negotiations, Cambodian officials suggested that such limits had first been laid down by the king's father, although they offered no evidence of this.

25. Rapport van den coopman Johan de Meijer wegens sijn verrichtingh in Cambodia, NL-HaNA, VOC 1252:118. Cheng, *War, Trade and Piracy in the China Seas*, 219.

26. Hendrik Muller, *De Oost-Indische compagnie in Cambodja en Laos; verzameling van bescheiden van 1636 tot 1670* ('s-Gravenhage: M. Nijhoff, 1917), 433.

27. August 8–10, 1667, Dagregister Daniel Six, Nationaal Archief, Den Haag, Nederlandse Factorij in Japan, access number 1.04.21 (hereafter NL-HaNA, NFJ), inventory number 80:73–4. Adam Clulow, "Distant Justice: Maritime Networks and Legal Forum Shopping," in

Robert Antony and Angela Schottenhammer, eds., *Beyond the Silk Roads: New Discourses on China's Role in East Asian Maritime History* (Wiesbaden: Harrassowitz Verlag, 2018).

28. Lin Taiwen and Li Gaokui, *Guangdong Wuchuan xianzhi* (1825), *juan* 10, 29.

29. Niu Junkai and Li Qingxin, "Chinese 'Political Pirates' in the Seventeenth-Century Gulf of Tongking," in *The Tongking Gulf Through History*, ed. Nola Cooke, Li Tana, and James A. Anderson (Philadelphia: University of Pennsylvania Press, 2011), 139.

30. Cheng, *War, Trade and Piracy in the China Seas*, 221. For more on the alliance between the Dutch and Tonkin, see Tuấn, *Silk for Silver.*

31. The best account of Piauwja's arrival is provided in: Rapport van den ondercoopman Jacob van Wijckersloot, gedaen aan den Ed. Daniel Sicx, coopman en opperhooft in Japan, omme in tijde en wijle Haere Eds. op Batavia bekent te maken de droevige toestant in 'sCompagnies voorgevallen saecke en ongehoorde proceduren in 't rijck van Cambodia, aldaer 'sCompagnies ministers door den Chinesen rover Piauwja aengedaen, alsmede het affloopen en verbranden der logie mitsgaders het droevigh vermoorden van 't Pieter Kettingh als 't gene andersints daer voorgevallen is. Geschr. int jacht Schelvis, August 19, 1667, NL-HaNA, VOC 1265. See also Cheng, *War, Trade and Piracy*, 220–22.

32. Rapport van den ondercoopman Jacob van Wijckersloot. See also Muller, *De Oost-Indische compagnie in Cambodja en Laos*, 447–49; Hang, *Conflict and Commerce in Maritime East Asia*, 173.

33. Mak Phoeun and Po Dharma, "La deuxième intervention militaire vietnamienne au Cambodge (1673–1679)," *Bulletin de l'Ecole française d'Extrême-Orient* 77 (1988): 233–35; and Phạm Khắc Trạch, ed., *Cao Man kỉ lược*, Institute of Hán-Nôm Studies A. 832, n.p.

34. August 8–10, 1667, Dagregister Daniel Six, NL-HaNA, NFJ 80.

35. August 19, 1667, Dagregister Daniel Six, NL-HaNA, NFJ 80.

36. Rapport van den ondercoopman Jacob van Wijckersloot.

37. *Batavia Dagregisters, Anno 1668–9*, 5.

38. They eventually reported their experience in: Verbael van drie Nederlanders uijt Cambodia gevangen te Macassar aengebraght, nopende haer wedervaren geduijrende haere gevanckenisse aldaer, NL-HaNA, VOC 1269.

39. Lin Taiwen and Li Gaokui, *Guangdong Wuchuan xianzhi* (1825), *juan* 10, 29.

40. Mak Phoeun, *Histoire du Cambodge: de la fin du XVIe siècle au début du XVIIIe* (Paris: Ecole française d'Extrême-Orient, 1995), 350–60.

41. Robert Antony, "Righteous Yang: Pirate, Rebel, and Hero on the Sino-Vietnamese Water Frontier, 1644–1684," *Cross-Currents: East Asian History and Culture Review* no. 11 (June 2014): 20; and Trạch, *Cao Man kỉ lược*, n.p.

42. VOC relations with Siam are superbly dealt with in: Ruangsilp, *Dutch East India Company Merchants*.

43. Cheng, *War, Trade and Piracy in the China Seas*, 200.

44. George Vinal Smith, *The Dutch in Seventeenth-Century Thailand* (DeKalb: Northern Illinois University, 1977), 36.

45. Rapport van Van Rijk aen haer Ed. tot Batavia overgelevert den 3 November 1662, NL-HaNA, VOC 1240, f. 1489. The report by Van Rijk describes "expeditions of the king's large armies."

46. Resolutie van gouverneur-general Joan Maesuijcker ende raden, Batavia, May 11, 1663, Kopie-resoluties van gouverneur-generaal en raden, NL-HaNA, VOC 678.

47. Resolutie van gouverneur-general Joan Maesuijcker ende raden, Batavia, May 11, 1663, NL-HaNA, VOC 678.

48. For an examination of the relationship between the king, the court and trade, see Dhiravat na Pombejra, "Crown Trade and Court Politics in Ayutthaya During the Reign of King Narai (1656–88)," in *The Southeast Asian Port and Polity*, ed. J. Kathirithamby-Wells and John Villiers (Singapore, 1990), 127–42. Such work charts the way in which successive kings competed directly with foreign merchants.

49. Commercial ties with the Tokugawa *bakufu* had been severed since 1630, when Prasat Thong usurped the throne from his rival, who had been supported by the Japanese community resident in Ayutthaya. In retaliation, the new king expelled the Japanese and burned down their settlement. Iwao Seiichi, who has completed the key study, lists a total of six embassies dispatched from Siam that either failed to reach Japan or were rejected by Tokugawa officials. Iwao Seiichi, "Reopening of the Diplomatic Relations between Japan and Siam During Tokugawa Days," *Acta Asiatica* 4 (1963): 1–31.

50. Resolutie van gouverneur-general Joan Maesuijcker ende raden, Batavia, May 11, 1663, NL-HaNA, VOC 678.

51. Cynthia Viallé and Leonard Blussé, eds., *The Deshima Dagregisters, Volume 13, 1660–1670* (Leiden: Intercontinenta No. 27, Universiteit Leiden, 2010), 21–22; Ruangsilp, *Dutch East India Company Merchants,* 20–21.

52. Iwao, "Reopening of Diplomatic Relations," 22. Iwao writes that the "voyage was made by the direct order of the king." Voyages like this do not appear in diplomatic compilations like *Tsukō ichiran*, which includes a section on Japan's relations with Siam. See Iwamoto Yoshitoru and Simon James Bytheway, "Japan's Official Relations with Shamuro (Siam), 1599–1745: As Revealed in the Diplomatic Records of the Tokugawa Shogunate," *Journal of the Siam Society* 99 (2011): 81–104.

53. Nagazumi, "Ayutthaya and Japan," 254; Ishii Yoneo, *The Junk Trade from Southeast Asia. Translations from the Tosen Fusetsu-gaki 1674–1723* (Singapore: ISEAS 1998), 2–3.

54. *Batavia Dagregister Anno 1664*, 248.

55. Resolutie van gouverneur-general Joan Maesuijcker ende raden, Batavia, May 11, 1663, NL-HaNA, VOC 678. Some VOC officials insisted the vessel was attacked because it was carrying a Portuguese flag. See George Vinal Smith, *The Dutch in Seventeenth-Century Thailand* (DeKalb: Center for Southeast Asian Studies, Northern Illinois University, 1974), 36; Dhiravat, "The Dutch-Siamese Conflict," 294. The exact nature of the Portuguese connection remains unclear but as discussed, most such junks were overwhelmingly crewed by Chinese mariners.

56. Smith argues that the apparent Portuguese identity was the key determinant. Smith, *The Dutch in Seventeenth-Century Thailand*, 36.

57. This response seems to have been orchestrated in part by a high-ranking Persian official, Oya Pieschijt or Abdu'r-Razzaq, operating in alliance with the head of the Chinese community. Ruangsilp, *Dutch East India Company Merchants*, 21; Rapport van Van Rijk, f. 1490.

58. *Batavia Dagregister Anno 1663*, 176; Cheng, *War, Trade and Piracy*, 217.

59. Rapport van Van Rijk, f. 1493v and 1493.

60. Rapport van Van Rijk, f. 1493.

61. Viallé and Blussé, eds., *The Deshima Dagregisters, Volume 13, 1660–1670*, 52.

62. Rapport door den Coopman Enoch Poolvet aen d' Ed. Hr. Joan Maetsuycker, March 31, 1663, NL-HaNA, VOC 1246, f. 353.

63. *Batavia Dagregister Anno 1664*, 247.

64. 12 June 1664, Archief van de gouverneur-generaal en raden van Indië (Hoge Regering) van de Verenigde Oostindische Compagnie en taakopvolgers, ANRI/HR/876, fol. 260.

65. *Batavia Dagregister Anno 1664,* 525–26.

66. The situation was the same, Ayutthayan officials insisted, as Batavia where VOC officials tolerated a sizable Chinese population even as they waged aggressive war against Koxinga.

67. *Batavia Dagregister Anno 1664*, 524; Dhiravat, "The Dutch-Siamese Conflict," 300.

68. *Batavia Dagregister Anno 1664*, 525.

69. *Batavia Dagregister Anno 1664*, 523.

70. *Batavia Dagregister Anno 1664*, 538.

71. *Batavia Dagregister Anno 1665*, 42; Dhiravat, "Political History of Siam," 305.

72. *Batavia Dagregister Anno 1665*, 81.

73. *Batavia Dagregister Anno 1665*, 384.

74. Hang, *Conflict and Commerce*, 173; Sarasin Viraphol, *Tribute and Profit: Sino-Siamese Trade, 1652–1853* (Cambridge, MA: Council on East Asian Studies, Harvard University, 1977), 45.

75. Hayashi Shunsai, *Ka'i hentai*, vol. I, 398.

76. Dhiravat, "Dutch-Siamese Conflict," 301.

77. See table in Cheng, *War, Trade and Piracy*, 236. For one example of the king's junks in Nagasaki, see Viallé and Blussé, eds., *The Deshima Dagregisters, Volume 13, 1660–1670*, 174.

Chapter 3

1. See Peter A. Coclanis, "Atlantic World or Atlantic/World?" *William and Mary Quarterly*, 3rd ser. 63, no. 4 (October 2006): 725–42; Lauren Benton, *A Search for Sovereignty: Law and Geography in European Empires, 1400–1900* (Cambridge: Cambridge University Press, 2009), chap. 3.

2. Nathan Perl-Rosenthal, *Citizen Sailors: Becoming American in the Age of Revolution* (Cambridge, MA: Belknap Press of Harvard University Press, 2015), 10–11, 50.

3. Jonathan Ziskind, "International Law and Ancient Sources: Grotius and Selden," *Review of Politics* 35, no. 4 (October 1973): 542.

4. *The Digests or Pandects of Justinian*, XVI §II.9.

5. Maria Fusaro, "The Invasion of Northern Litigants: English and Dutch Seamen in Mediterranean Courts of Law," in *Law, Labour, and Empire: Comparative Perspectives on Seafarers, c. 1500–1800*, ed. Maria Fusaro et al. (New York: Palgrave Macmillan, 2015): 21–42; Janet J. Ewald, "Crossers of the Sea: Slaves, Freedmen and Other Migrants in the Northwestern Indian Ocean, c. 1750–1914," *American Historical Review* 105, no. 1 (February 2000): 70; Michael Kempe, "'Even in the Remotest Corners of the World': Globalized Piracy and International Law, 1500–1900," *Journal of Global History* 5, no. 3 (November 2010): 354; Glen O'Hara, "The Sea Is Swinging into View: Modern British Maritime History in a Globalised World," *English Historical Review* 124, no. 510 (October 2009), 1111–12.

6. Kempe, "Remotest Corners," 354.

7. Louis B. Sohn and Kristen Gustafson, *The Law of the Sea* (St. Paul, MN: West, 1984), 13.

8. Fusaro, "Afterword," in *Law, Labour, and Empire*, 304.

9. Kempe, "Remotest Corners," 354; Fusaro, "Afterword," 306.

10. Edward E. Cohen, *Ancient Athenian Maritime Courts* (Princeton, NJ: Princeton University Press, 1973), 5.

11. Ziskind, "International Law," 541–42.

12. Robert D. Benedict, "The Historical Position of the Rhodian Law," *Yale Law Journal* 18, no. 4 (February 1909): 223–42; Wolfgang Graf Vitzhum, "From the Rhodean Sea Law to UNCLOS III," in *Marine Issues: From a Scientific, Political and Legal Perspective*, ed. Peter N. Ehlers et al. (New York: Kluwer Law International, 2002), 1–18. For the earliest surviving description of *Lex Rhodia*, see Julius Paulus, *Opinions of Julius Paulus, Addressed to His Son*, Book II, § 7.

13. Edda Frankot, *"Of Laws of Ships and Shipmen": Medieval Maritime Law and Its Practice in Urban Northern* Europe (Edinburgh: University of Edinburgh Press, 2012), 10.

14. Travers Triss, ed., *Monumenta Juridica: The Black Book of the Admiralty*, vol. I (London: Longman, 1871), xx–cxl.

15. Frankot, *Of Laws of Ships and Shipmen*, 26.

16. Grant Gilmore and Charles L. Black Jr., *The Law of Admiralty*, 2nd ed. (Mineola, NY: Foundation Press, 1974), § 1.2–1.4.

17. George F. Steckley, "Instance Cases at Admiralty in 1657: A Court 'Packed Up with Suitors,'" *Journal of Legal History* 7, no. 1 (May 1986): 68–83; Steckley, "Litigious Mariners: Wage Cases in the Seventeenth-Century Admiralty Court," *Historical Journal* 42, no. 2 (June 1999): 315–45; Howard M. McCormack, "Uniformity of Maritime Law: History, and Perspective from the U.S. Point of View," *Tulane Law Review* 73, no. 5/6 (June 1999): 1484.

18. António Manuel Hespahna, "Jurists as Gamekeepers," *Acta Historiae* 16, no. 4 (2008): 492.

19. Hespahna, "Jurists as Gamekeepers," 499. See also Sugata Bose, *A Hundred Horizons: The Indian Ocean in the Age of Global Empire* (Cambridge: Harvard University Press, 2006), 36–71.

20. Hespahna, "Jurists as Gamekeepers," 490.

21. Gerard de Malynes, *Consuentudo, vel, Lex Mercatoria, or, The Ancient Law-Merchant* (London: Adam Islip, 1629); G. Jacob, *Lex Mercatoria, Or, the Merchant's Companion* (E. Curll: London, 1718). On the development of commercial law from the medieval *Lex Mercatoria*, see Vito Piergiovanni, ed., *From Lex Mercatoria to Commercial Law* (Berlin: Dunker & Humboldt, 2005).

22. Bernarde Allaire, "Between Oléron and Colbert: The Evolution of French Maritime Law until the Seventeenth Century," in *Law, Labour, and Empire*, ed. Maria Fusaro et al., 82, supra 9. *Encyclopedia Britannica* has a more fulsome etymology, tracing the Arabic borrowing through Sicilian and Genoan sources before its arrival in French. "Admiralty," *Encyclopedia Britannica*, 11th ed. (New York: Cambridge University Press, 1910).

23. Allaire, "Between Oléron and Colbert," 89–91.

24. John Selden, *Mare Clausum: Of the Dominion, Or, Ownership of the Sea* (London: W. Du-Gard, 1652), trans. Marchamont Ledham (repr. Clark, NJ: Lawbook Exchange, 2004), I. On Selden's importance and interaction with continental legal ideas, see: Martha A. Ziskind, "John Selden: Criticism and Affirmation of the Common Law Tradition," *American Journal of Legal History* 19, no. 1 (January 1975): 22–39; Eric G. M. Fletcher, "John Selden (Author of Mare Clausum) and His Contribution to International Law," *Transactions of the Grotius Society* 19 (1933): 1–12; Paul Christianson, *Discourse on History, Law*

and Governance in the Public Career of John Selden, 1610–1635 (Toronto: University of Toronto Press, 1996).

25. Ziskind, "International Law," 541–43.

26. Richard Blakemore, "The Legal World of English Sailors, c. 1575–1729," in *Law, Labour, and Empire*, 100.

27. Blakemore, "English Sailors," 100; Matthew Taylor Raffety, *The Republic Afloat: Law, Honor and Citizenship in Maritime America* (Chicago: University of Chicago Press, 2013), 41.

28. David W. Robertson, *Admiralty and Federalism* (Mineola: Foundation Press, 1970), 18–27; Joseph Story, *Commentaries on the Constitution of the United States* (Boston: Hilliard, Grey, 1833), § 1666; Erastus C. Benedict, *The American Admiralty, Its Jurisdiction, and Practice* (New York: Banks, Gould, 1850).

29. Kempe, "Remotest Corners," 354.

30. Lauren Benton, "Toward a New Legal History of Piracy: Maritime Legalities and the Myth of Universal Jurisdiction," *International Journal of Maritime History* 23, no. 1 (June 2011): 225, 226, supra 2.

31. Alexander Tabarrok, "The Rise, Fall, and Rise Again of Privateers," *Independent Review* 11, no. 4 (Spring 2007): 567.

32. Donald A. Petrie, *The Prize Game: Lawful Looting on the High Seas in the Days of Fighting Sail* (Annapolis: Naval Institute Press, 1999), 5–6; William R. Castro, "The Origins of Federal Admiralty Jurisdiction in an Age of Privateers, Smugglers, and Pirates," *American Journal of Legal History* 3, no. 2 (April 1993): 127.

33. Tabarrok, "Privateers," 566; Petrie, *Prize Game*, 6.

34. Martine Julia Van Ittersum, "Introduction," in *Commentary on the Law of Prize and Booty*, Hugo Grotius (1603, repr. Indianapolis: Liberty Fund, 2006), xviii–xix.

35. Sarah Kinkel, *Disciplining the Empire* (Cambridge: Harvard University Press, 2018), 138–49.

36. *Constitution of the United States*, Art. I, § 8; Tabarrok, "Privateers," 566, Perl-Rosenthal, *Citizen Sailors*, 38–43.

37. U.S. v. Miranda, U.S. Circuit Court for the Southern District of NY 1806 (National Archives and Records Administration [New York], RG 21, #175).

38. Charles Gibbs, *Mutiny and Murder: Confession of Charles Gibbs* (Providence, RI: Israel Smith, 1836).

39. "Chronicle," *Niles Register*, July 22, 1820, p. 364.

40. Ibid.; see also U.S. v. George Mitchell, 1820, U.S. Circuit Court for the Southern District of NY 1806 (National Archives and Records Administration [New York], RG 21, #175); Matthew Mason, "Keeping Up with Appearances: The International Politics of Slave Trade Abolition in the Nineteenth-Century Atlantic World," *William and Mary Quarterly*, 3rd ser., 66, no. 4 (October 2009): 821–22.

41. Tyson Reeder, "'Sovereign Lords' and 'Dependent Administrators': Artigan Privateers, Atlantic Borderwaters, and State Building in the Early Nineteenth Century," *Journal of American History* 103, no. 2 (September 2016): 226, 324, 338, 344.

42. W. Winthrop, "The United States and the Declaration of Paris," *Yale Law Journal* 3, no. 4 (March 1894): 116–18; Faye M. Kent, *Privateering: Patriots and Profits in the War of 1812* (Baltimore: Johns Hopkins University Press, 2015); Lauren Benton and Lisa Ford, *Rage for Order: The British Empire and the Origins of International Law* (Cambridge, MA: Harvard University Press, 2016), 164–76.

43. Todd Emerson Hutchins, "Structuring a Sustainable Letters of Marque Regime: How Commissioning Privateers Can Defeat the Somali Pirates," *California Law Review* 99, no. 3 (June 2011): 819–84.

44. Benton and Ford, *Rage for Order,* 119. See also Jenny S. Martinez, *The Slave Trade and the Origins of International Human Rights* (New York: Oxford University Press, 2016).

45. Richard Blakemore, "Legal World of English Sailors," 100; Lauren Benton, "Legal Spaces of Empire: Piracy and the Origins of Ocean Regionalism," *Comparative Studies in Society and History* 47, no. 4 (October 2005): 700–24; Benton and Richard Ross, eds., *Legal Pluralism and Empires, 1500–1800* (New York: New York University Press, 2013); Benton, "Toward a New Legal History of Piracy," 1–15.

46. Brian Rouleau, *With Sails Whitening Every Sea: Mariners and the Making of an American Maritime Empire* (Ithaca: Cornell University Press, 2015).

47. *An act for the Punishment of Certain Crimes against the United States,* 1st Cong., Sess. II, Ch. 9, April 30, 1790, § 8–13; 16. Jonathan Thayer, "The Working Seafarer: Early Legislation," *Seaman's Church* Institute, March 29, 2011, accessed August 31, 2018, http://seamenschurch.org/article/working-seafarer-early-legislation.

48. Blakemore points out that in Roman usage, *lex* is written law, "custom" is the law of the community's tacit agreement, and "usage" is "mere repeat behavior." Both of the former are "law" in the sense of enforceable and compulsory. Blakemore, "English Sailors," 102. See also Emily Kadens, "The Myth of the Customary Law Merchant," *Texas Law Review* 90, no. 5 (April 2012): 1163–66.

49. Blakemore, "English Sailors," 106.

50. Marcus Rediker, *Between the Devil and the Deep Blue Sea: Merchant Seamen, Pirates and the Anglo-American Maritime World, 1700–1750* (New York: Cambridge University Press, 1989), 150; Blakemore, "English Sailors," 117; Leon Fink, *Sweatshops at Sea: Merchant Seamen in the World's First Globalized Industry, from 1812 to the Present* (Chapel Hill: University of North Carolina Press, 2011).

51. Raffety, *Republic Afloat,* 101–120; Nicholas Peter Isaacs, *Twenty Years Before the Mast, or Life in the Forecastle* (New York: K. P. Beckwith, 1845); Elbridge S. Brooks, *The Story of the American Sailor in Active Service on Merchant Vessel and in Man-of-War* (Boston: D. Lothrop 1888), 189–90.

52. Fusaro, "Northern Litigants," 33.

53. Deposition of Charles James (2nd Mate), Last v. Porter et al. (1847), Dana Case File #730, Box 1; Richard Henry Dana Collection, American Antiquarian Society, Worcester, MA.

54. Fusaro, "Northern Litigants," 23.

55. Joan Abela, "Sailors' Rights in a Mediterranean Hub: The Case of Malta," in *Law, Labour, and Empire,* 65.

56. Abela, "Sailors' Rights," 61–78; see also T. Freller, "'Adversus Infedeles': Some Notes on the Cavalier's Tour, the Fleet of the Order of St. John and the Maltese Corsairs," *Journal of Early Modern History* 4, no. 3/4 (January 2000): 405–430.

57. On the notion of maritime law as a site of the definition of citizenship in an American context, see Perl-Rosenthal, *Citizen Sailors*; Rouleau, *With Sails Whitening Every Sea*; Paul A. Gilje, *Free Trade and Sailors' Rights in the War of 1812* (New York: Cambridge University Press, 2013); Gilje, *Liberty on the Waterfront* (Philadelphia: Pennsylvania University Press, 2007); Jesse Lemisch, *Jack Tar vs. John Bull: The Role of New York's Seamen in Precipitating the Revolution* (New York: Garland, 1997).

58. Fusaro, "Northern Litigants," 31.

59. Denver Brunsman, *The Evil Necessity: British Naval Impressment in the Eighteenth Century Atlantic World* (Richmond: University of Virginia Press, 2013); Gilje, *Liberty on the Waterfront*, 157–58.

60. Marcus Rediker, "Toward a People's History of the Sea," in *Maritime Empires: British Maritime Trade in the Nineteenth Century*, ed. David Killingray et al. (London: Boydell Press, 2004), 195–206.

61. Isaacs, *Twenty Years Before the Mast*, 81.

62. Amélia Polónia, "Portuguese Seafarers: Informal Agents of Empire Building," in *Law, Labour, and Empire*, 215; See also Abdul Sheriff, *Slaves, Spices and Ivory in Zanzibar: Integration of an Eastern African Commercial Empire into the World Economy, 1770–1873* (Athens: Ohio University Press, 1987), 18.

63. Ann M. Carlos and Stephen Nicholas, "Agency Problems in Early Chartered Companies: The Case of the Hudson's Bay Company," *Journal of Economic History* 50, no. 4 (December 1990): 855.

64. A. C. Wood, *History of the Levant Company* (Oxford: Barnes and Noble, 1935); Paul Masson, *Histoire du commerce francais dans le Levant au XVIIIe siècle* (Paris: Hachette, 1911); Daniel Panzac, "International and Domestic Maritime Trade in the Ottoman Empire During the 18th Century," *International Journal of Middle East Studies* 24, no. 2 (May 1992): 191.

65. Kenneth Davies, *The Royal Africa Company* (New York: Longmans, Green, 1957), 165, 255.

66. Maurits van den Boogert, "Consular Jurisdiction in the Ottoman Legal System in the Eighteenth Century," *Oriente Moderno*, Nuova serie 83, no. 3 (2003): 613–34.

67. Frank Kitson, *Prince Rupert: Admiral and General-at-Sea* (London: Constable, 1999), 155, 261, 296–97, 348.

68. Matthew Taylor Raffety, "Our (Unhappy) Man in Havana: Nicholas P. Trist, American Networks of Capital and US Consular Authority in Cuba, 1831–1845," Society for Historians of American Foreign Relations Annual Conference, Arlington, VA, 2015.

69. Philip J. Stern, *The Company-State Corporate Sovereignty and the Early Modern Foundations of the British Empire in India* (New York: Oxford University Press, 2011).

70. Matthias van Rossum, "Claiming Their Rights? Indian Sailors Under the Dutch East India Company," in Fusaro et al., *Law, Labour, and Empire*, 274.

71. Preeti Nijhar, *Law and Imperialism: Criminality and Constitution in Colonial India and Victorian England* (New York: Routledge, 2008), 12, 81, 155, supra 25; Ravi Ahuja, "Networks of Subordination—Networks of the Subordinated: The Crowded Spaces of South Asian Maritime Labour in an Age of Imperialism (c. 1890–1947)," in *The Limits of British Control in South Asia: Spaces of Disorder in the Indian Ocean Region*, ed. Ashwini Tambe and Harold Fischer Tiné (New York: Routledge, 2008), 13–48.

72. Ewald, "Crossers of the Sea," 76.

73. "More Than a List of the Crew," Maritime History Archive, Memorial University, accessed August 31, 2018, https://www.mun.ca/mha/mlc/seafarers/lascars/remainder-of-crew.php.

74. David Warburton, "The Hadhramis, the Hadhramaut and European Colonial Powers in the Indian Ocean," in *The Indian Ocean Rim: Southern Africa and Regional Cooperation*, ed. Gwyn Campbell (New York: Routledge, 2003), 56.

75. *Parliamentary Papers, House of Commons and Command, Volume 62: Report of the Committee Appointed by the Board of Trade to Inquire into Certain Questions Affecting the Mercantile Marine* (London: Wyman & Sons, 1903), 193–94, 256–57.

76. Linda Boxberger, *On the Edge of Empire: Hadhramawt, Emigration, and the Indian Ocean, 1880s–1930s* (Albany: State University of New York Press, 2002), 51–52.

77. Sheriff, *Slaves, Spices and Ivory*, 22–23.

78. Gilje, *Free Trade and Sailors' Rights*, 163.

79. George W. Dalzell, *The Flight from the Flag: The Continuing Effect of the Civil War upon the American Carrying Trade* (Chapel Hill: University of North Carolina Press, 1940).

80. Maurits van den Boogert, "Ottoman Greeks in the Dutch Levant Trade: Collective Strategies and Individual Practice (c. 1750–1821)," *Oriente Moderno*, Nuova serie, Anno 25 (86), no. 1 (2006): 129–47.

81. Gerald Horne, *Race to Revolution: The United States and Cuba During Slavery and Jim Crow* (New York: Monthly Review Press, 2014), 48.

82. Dale T. Graden, *Disease, Resistance, and Lies: The Demise of the Atlantic Slave Trade to Brazil and Cuba* (Baton Rouge: Louisiana State University Press, 2014), 14, 38–39, 78; Horne, *Race to Revolution*, 14, 58.

83. R. R. Madden, *A letter to W. E. Channing, D.D., on the subject of the abuse of the flag of the United States in the Island of Cuba* (Boston: William D. Ticknor, 1839); H. R. Doc., 26th Cong., 1st Sess., Doc. 707, 1840, 63.

84. William Langewische, *The Outlaw Sea* (New York: North Point Press, 2004), 6.

85. Leslie Sklair, "Social Movements for Global Capitalism: The Transnational Capitalist Class in Action," *Review of International Political Economy* 4, no. 3 (January 1997): 518–38.

86. Nathan Lillie, *A Global Union for Global Workers: Collective Bargaining and Regulatory Politics in Maritime Shipping* (New York: Routledge, 2006), 9.

87. Lillie, *Global Union for Global Workers*, 25.

88. Fink, *Sweatshops at Sea*, 201.

89. Richard S. Horowitz, "International Law and State Transformation in China, Siam, and the Ottoman Empire During the Nineteenth Century," *Journal of World History* 15, no. 4 (December 2005): 445.

90. Fusaro, "Afterword," 305.

91. Horowitz, "International Law," 456.

92. Danilo Pedemonte, "Deserters, Mutineers and Criminals: British Sailors and Problems of Port Jurisdiction in Genoa and Livorno during the Eighteenth Century," in *Law, Labour and Empire*, 271.

93. Ibid.

94. Pedemonte, "Deserters, Mutineers and Criminals," 259–64.

95. See Palmira Brummett, "The Ottomans as a World Power: What We Don't Know About Ottoman Sea Power," *Oriente Moderno*, Nuova serie, Anno 20 (81), no. 20 (2001): 1–21; Brummett, *Ottoman Seapower and Levantine Diplomacy in the Age of Discovery* (Albany: State University of New York Press, 1994).

96. Patrick Wing, "Indian Ocean Trade and Sultanic Authority: The Nāẓir of Jedda and the Mamluk Political Economy," *Journal of the Economic and Social History of the Orient* 57, no. 1 (February 2014), 61; R. Stephen Humphreys, "Egypt in the World System of the Later Middle Ages," in *The Cambridge History of Egypt, vol. 1: Islamic Egypt, 640–1517*, ed.

Carl F. Petry (Cambridge: Cambridge University Press, 1998), 449; Albrecht Fuess, "Rotting Ships and Razed Harbors: The Naval Policy of the Mamluks," *Mamlūk Studies Review* 5 (2001), 45–71.

97. Brummett, "Ottomans as a World Power," 2, 7–10.

98. Joshua Michael White, "Catch and Release: Piracy, Slavery, and Law in the Early Modern Ottoman Mediterranean" (PhD diss., University of Michigan, 2012), 5.

99. Huri Islamoğulu and Çağlar Keyder, "Agenda for Ottoman History," *Review (Fernand Braudel Center)* 1, no. 1 (Summer 1977): 42, 43.

100. Horowitz, "International Law," 460.

101. Maurits van den Boogert, *The Capitulations and the Ottoman Legal System: Qadis, Consuls, and Beraths in the 18th Century* (Leiden: Brill, 2005); Feroz Ahmad, "Ottoman Perceptions of the Capitulations 1800–1914," *Journal of Islamic Studies* 11, no. 1 (February 2000): 1–20.

102. Horowitz, "International Law," 460.

103. Panzac, "Trade in the Ottoman Empire," 203; Suraiya Faroqhi, *Approaching Ottoman History: An Introduction to the Sources* (New York: Cambridge University Press, 1999), 178.

104. A. Smirnov, "Understanding Justice in an Islamic Context: Some Points of Contrast with Western Theories," *Philosophy East and West* 46, no. 3 (July 1996): 374.

105. White, "Catch and Release," 7, 20, 42.

106. Ayşe Devrim Atauz, "Trade, Piracy, and Naval Warfare in the Central Mediterranean: The Maritime History and Archaeology of Malta" (PhD diss., Texas A&M University, 2004); Daniel Panzac, *Barbary Corsairs: The End of a Legend, 1800–1820* (Leiden: Brill, 2005); on the Caribbean, see Peter Linebaugh and Marcus Rediker, *The Many Headed Hydra: Sailors, Slaves, Commoners, and the Hidden History of the Revolutionary Atlantic* (New York: Beacon, 2000), 161–73.

107. White, "Catch and Release," 42.

108. Sheriff, *Slaves, Spices and Ivory,* 18–23, 83.

109. Lidwien Kapteijns and Jay Spaulding, "Indian Ocean Diplomacy: Two Documents Relating to the Nineteenth-Century Mijertein Coast," *Sudanic Africa* 13: *Sudanic Africa: Texts and Sources: Fontes Historiae Africanae Bulletin of Information: Selected articles* 1979–1987 (2002): 21–28; Sugata Bose, "Space and Time on the Indian Ocean Rim: Theory and History," in *Modernity and Culture from the Mediterranean to the Indian Ocean*, ed. Leila Tazari Fawaz and C. A. Bayley (New York: Columbia University Press, 2002), 365–87; Warbutron, "The Hasdhramis," 54–55.

110. Richard B. Morris, *Government and Labor in Early America* (New York: Harper & Row, 1965), 225–62; Steven L. Snell, *Courts of Admiralty and the Common Law: Origins of American Experiment in Concurrent Jurisdiction* (Durham, NC: Carolina Academic Press, 2007), 211–31; Robertson, *Admiralty and Federalism,* 1–3, 6, 93.

111. McCormack, "Uniformity of Maritime Law," 1484.

112. *Constitution of the Republic of Texas,* 1836, Art. IV; *An act establishing regulations and instructions for the government of the naval service of Texas,* December 15, 1836; *An act to prescribe the mode of holding Courts of Admiralty,* June 7, 1837.

113. *Penal Code of the Hawaiian Kingdom, compiled from the Penal Code of 1850, And the Various Penal Enactments Since Made, Pursuant to Act of the Legislative Assembly, June 22d, 1868* (Honolulu, HI: Government Press, 1869), § LXXVI, LXXXI, LV.

114. *Penal Code for the Kingdom of Siam, R.S. 127* (Bangkok: A. P. Mission Press, 1908), § 10, 302. Notably, Siam limited its criminal maritime statutes primarily to piracy.

115. See David Armitage and Michael J. Braddick, eds., *The British Atlantic World, 1500–1800*, 2nd ed. (New York: Palgrave Macmillan, 2009); Bernard Bailyn, *Atlantic History: Concepts and Contours* (Cambridge, MA: Harvard University Press, 2005); John Thornton, *Africa and Africans in the Making of the Atlantic World*, 2nd ed. (New York: Cambridge University Press, 1998).

116. McCormack, "Uniformity of Maritime Law," 1483.

117. Daniel Vickers, "Beyond Jack Tar," *William and Mary Quarterly* 50, 3rd ser., no. 2 (April 1993): 418; Maria Fusaro, "Maritime History as Global History? The Methodological Challenges and a Future Research Agenda," in *Maritime History as Global History*, Research in Maritime History No. 42, ed. Maria Fusaro and Amélia Polónia (St. John's, NL: Liverpool University Press, 2010), 269.

Chapter 4

1. The case files are in *Vertumne*, HCA 32/471 and the seized correspondence is in *Vertumne*, HCA 30/301, both in the National Archives, Kew (hereafter TNA).

2. On the economic importance of privateering in the eighteenth century, see David J. Starkey, *British Privateering Enterprise in the Eighteenth Century* (Liverpool: Liverpool University Press, 1990).

3. C. M. Andrews called the determination of nationality one of the two "most perplexing problems that confronted the [prize] courts": see Charles McLean Andrews, *The Colonial Period of American History* (New Haven, CT: Yale University Press, 1934), 4:236. See also n. 35 below. The term "nationality" is an anachronism for the period in question in this essay. I use it as an analytic category signifying "allegiance" or "political belonging," for which see Nathan Perl-Rosenthal, *Citizen Sailors: Becoming American in the Age of Revolution* (Cambridge, MA: Belknap Press of Harvard University Press, 2015), 283n11.

4. See, e.g., David Hancock, *Citizens of the World: London Merchants and the Integration of the British Atlantic Community, 1735–1785* (Cambridge: Cambridge University Press, 1995); Cathy D. Matson, *Merchants & Empire: Trading in Colonial New York* (Baltimore, MD: Johns Hopkins University Press, 1998); Francesca Trivellato, *The Familiarity of Strangers: The Sephardic Diaspora, Livorno, and Cross-Cultural Trade in the Early Modern Period* (New Haven, CT: Yale University Press, 2009). For an excellent and unusual collection of these letters and a good introduction to some of their content, see L. M. Cullen, John Shovlin, and Thomas M. Truxes, eds., *The Bordeaux-Dublin Letters, 1757: Correspondence of an Irish Community Abroad* (Oxford: Oxford University Press for the Britsh Academy, 2013), esp. 59–71.

5. On the expansion of private correspondence, see Sarah M. S. Pearsall, *Atlantic Families: Lives and Letters in the Later Eighteenth Century* (Oxford: Oxford University Press, 2008); Roger Duchêne, *Comme une lettre à la poste: Le progrès de l'écriture personnelle sous Louis XIV* (Paris: Fayard, 2006); and Susan E. Whyman, *The Pen and the People: English Letter Writers, 1660–1800* (Oxford: Oxford University Press, 2009). See also Nathan Perl-Rosenthal, "Corresponding Republics: Letter Writing and Patriot Organizing in the Atlantic Revolutions, circa 1760–1792" (PhD diss., Columbia University, 2011).

6. There is a substantial literature on this subject: see Robert C. Ritchie, *Captain Kidd and the War Against the Pirates* (Cambridge, MA: Harvard University Press, 1986); Lauren

Benton, *A Search for Sovereignty: Law and Geography in European Empires, 1400–1900* (New York: Cambridge University Press, 2009), ch. 3; and Marcus Rediker, *Between the Devil and the Deep Blue Sea: Merchant Seamen, Pirates, and the Anglo-American Maritime World, 1700–1750* (Cambridge: Cambridge University Press, 1987).

7. On the slave trade, see especially Stephanie Smallwood, *Saltwater Slavery: A Middle Passage from Africa to American Diaspora* (Cambridge, MA: Harvard University Press, 2008); and Robert W. Harms, *The Diligent: A Voyage Through the Worlds of the Slave Trade* (New York: Basic Books, 2002), 82–85. See also Charles R. Foy, "Eighteenth-Century Prize Negroes: From Britain to America," *Slavery and Abolition* 31, no. 3 (September 2010): 379–93.

8. For an excellent discussion of this issue, see Andrews, *Colonial Period*, 4:224–37; and (for other empires) Perl-Rosenthal, *Citizen Sailors*, 297n32. The case of Lewis Morris is a valuable counterpoint to this general rule, for which see Michael Watson, "Judge Lewis Morris, the New York Vice-Admiralty Court, and Colonial Privateering, 1739–1762," *New York History* 78, no. 2 (1997): 117–46.

9. For an exhaustive discussion of this point in the U.S. context, see Henry J. Bourguignon, *The First Federal Court: The Federal Appellate Prize Court of the American Revolution, 1775–1787* (Philadelphia: American Philosophical Society, 1977), esp. 143–56.

10. Captains of privateers rarely had any formal training in prize law. Their practices were often based more on folk understandings than on the letter of the law. For instance, under interrogation a French privateering captain in the Indian Ocean asserted that even though captors could not despoil prizes, "il est cependant une exception a cette regle, puisqu'il y est Reputé que le coffre du Capitaine pris appartient de droit au Capitaine preneur." See "Interrogation de Crozet," September 16–17, 1780, Greffes, Ile Maurice: Procedures criminelles (6 dppc 3086–3088), Centre d'Archives d'Outre Mer, Aix-en-Provence. I discuss this case further in Nathan Perl-Rosenthal, "On Mobile Legal Spaces and Maritime Empires: The Pillage of the East Indiaman *Osterley* (1779)," *Itinerario* 42, no. 2 (August 2018): 183–201, esp. 189–92.

11. For a discussion of this issue, see Perl-Rosenthal, *Citizen Sailors*, 37–39.

12. November 16, 1757, in Burrell et al., *Reports of cases determined by the High court of admiralty: and upon appeal therefrom, temp. Sir Thomas Salusbury and Sir George Hay, judges, 1758–1774. By Sir William Burrell, bart. . . . Together with extracts from the books and records of the High court of admiralty and the Court of the judges delegates, 1584–1839. And a collection of cases and opinions upon admiralty matters, 1701–1781*, 392. Emphasis mine.

13. At the margins, the "character" of a vessel could also be affected by the maritime paperwork it carried (including sea letters and port clearances), the actual flag that it flew, and the place from where it habitually sailed. Cargo drew its "character" mainly from the "character" of its owner, but also from the "characters" of the person to whom it was to be sold and the supercargo entrusted with its care during shipment. Cargo also had two other qualities that could shape its fate. Where it had been originally produced or grown could determine its "national character" in some instances. And some types of cargo were deemed "contraband" that was subject to seizure by belligerents even if owned or shipped by neutrals. "Contraband" was a flexible and much debated category: though it clearly included such items as guns and ammunition, and excluded luxury goods, there was no consensus on its applicability to provisions, building materials and the like. See also the discussion in Perl-Rosenthal, *Citizen Sailors*, 314–316n5–8.

14. Across every empire, prize law required that "in the first instance" the admiralty courts were to rule on the question of ownership using only proofs that "come . . . from the ship taken, viz., the papers on board, and the examination on oath of the master" and seamen: see Sir William Scott and Sir John Nicoll to John Jay, September 10, 1794, in Joseph Story, *Notes on the Principles and Practice of Prize Courts* (London: W. Benning, 1854), 3. These papers might include charter parties, certificates and safe-conducts: see Dumas, *Etude sur le jugement des prises maritimes en France jusqu'à la supression de l'office d'amiral (1627)* (Paris: Larose, 1908), 183–86; and Richard Pares, *Colonial Blockade and Neutral Rights, 1739–1763* (Oxford: Clarendon Press, 1938), 108–111. On an exceptional basis, the courts might permit the parties to seek additional proofs of their subjecthood or the ownership of ship and cargo (an "interlocutory" order in the terms of the English admiralty courts): see Pares, *Colonial Blockade*, 112–13 and Dumas, *Etude*, 181–82.

15. See the case of the *Pruth*, described in Michel Rodigneaux, *La guerre de course en Guadeloupe, XVIIIe–XIXe siècles, ou, Alger sous les tropiques* (Paris: L'Harmattan, 2006), 254–55.

16. Story, *Practice of Prize Courts*, 36. In the event of a conflict between a ship's papers and the crew's depositions, French law required privateers and the courts to give greater weight to "the depositions of the officers and sailors of the captured vessel" because they were "singularly capable of illuminating the truth and uncovering fraud." Arret du Conseil d'Etat, October 26, 1692, in René-Josué Valin, *Nouveau commentaire sur l'Ordonnance de la marine, du mois d'août 1681*, New rev. ed., 4 vols. (La Rochelle: J. Legier, 1776), 2:246. Case law during the wars of the eighteenth century continued to support this preference for interrogations over paperwork, and that remained the case into the early revolutionary period: see Alphonse Pistoye and Charles Duverdy, *Traité des prises maritimes dans lequel on a refondu en partie le Traité de Valin en l'appropriant à la législation nouvelle* (Paris: A. Durand, 1855), 1:421–22.

17. See the case discussed in Perl-Rosenthal, *Citizen Sailors*, 92.

18. Charles Dudley to Germain, March 13, 1779 (London) in *Documents of the American Revolution, 1770–1783 (Colonial Office series)*, ed. K. G. Davies (Shannon: Irish University Press, 1972), 17:87. On this subject, see also Perl-Rosenthal, *Citizen Sailors*, chap. 1.

19. Burrell, ed., *Reports of cases determined by the High court of admiralty: and upon appeal therefrom, temp. Sir Thomas Salusbury and Sir George Hay . . .*, 182.

20. See *Minerva* (1778), *Decisions in the High Court of Admiralty: During the Time of Sir George Hay and Sir James Marriott . . .* (London, 1801), 1:238.

21. *Craig v. The Brig Richmond* (August 1776–January 1777), Pennsylvania, Records of the Court of Appeals in Cases of Capture, 1776–1787, M162, National Archives and Records Administration.

22. See correspondence of Herren Levy and Leman, Dossier 17, F7 4242B, Archives Nationales, France.

23. *Appendix to the Case of the Claimant, The Molly, Master James Young* (1793), HCA 45/18, TNA.

24. *The Molly, Master James Young* (1793).

25. *The Nancy, Master David Florence* (1793), HCA 45/19, TNA.

26. See Perl-Rosenthal, *Citizen Sailors*, 38 and works cited there.

27. *Appendix to the Case on Behalf of the Appellants, Brig Eagle, Master Hugh Manning*, HCA 45/18, TNA.

28. *Appendix to the Case of the Appellant, Brigantine Maryland, Master John Stran*, HCA 45/19, TNA.

29. See the regulations reprinted in J. Franklin Jameson, *Privateering and Piracy in the Colonial Period: Illustrative Documents* (New York: Macmillan, 1923), 347–50. This is the language in the 1739 privateering regulations, but similar language was present in British prize law throughout the century, as well as in the prize regulations of other powers.

30. On the appearance of letter writing manuals for merchants in the early eighteenth century, see esp. Eve Tavor Bannet, *Empire of Letters: Letter Manuals and Transatlantic Correspondence, 1688–1820* (Cambridge: Cambridge University Press, 2005), esp. chap. 3; see also Konstantin Dierks, *In My Power: Letter Writing and Communications in Early America* (Philadelphia: University of Pennsylvania Press, 2009), 68–76.

31. See *The Accomplished Letter-Writer; or, Universal Correspondent. Containing Familiar Letters on the Most Common Occasions in Life* . . . (London, 1779), iv. See also *The Complete Letter-Writer: or, New and Polite English Secretary. Containing Directions for Writing Letters on all Occasions* . . . (London, 1756), 2, 4.

32. See *Polly* (1800), in *Reports of Cases in the High Court of Admiralty . . . Judgements of . . . Sir William Scott*, 2:361. Vice-admiralty courts did not necessarily conform to this standard of proof. The New York vice-admiralty court in the mid-eighteenth century, for instance, seems at times to have taken the destruction of papers *ipso facto* as evidence of trading with the French: see *Anthony Rutgers et al. v. Ship* Isaac Galley (1758) in *Reports of Cases in the Vice Admiralty of the Province of New York and in the Court of Admiralty of the State of New York, 1715–1788, with an Historical Introduction and Appendix*, ed. Charles M. Hough (New Haven, CT: Yale University Press, 1925), 159.

33. For an example of translators and translation orders, see Jameson, *Privateering and Piracy*, 473–77. A letter of complaint from a translator asking for higher pay to offset unexpected costs of a large prize ship file can be found in Procès relatifs à la prise et à la confiscation du brick espagnol La Rose et du Bateau danois Le Jeremia, Carton 32, D XXV, Archives Nationales, Paris. For examples of the pay for translators by piecework, see 2L 183, Archives départementales de la Guadeloupe, Basse-Terre, Guadeloupe.

34. *Kinders Kinder* (1799), in *Reports of Cases in the High Court of Admiralty . . . Judgements of . . . Sir William Scott*, 2:90.

35. See, e.g., the principles in Emmerich de Vattel, *The Law of Nations* (G. G. and J. Robinson, 1797), Book 1, Ch. 19, §211–16. For excellent discussions of the issues involved in determining nationality, see Pares, *Colonial Blockade and Neutral Rights, 1739–1763*, 112–21; and Henry J. Bourguignon, *Sir William Scott, Lord Stowell, Judge of the High Court of Admiralty, 1798–1828* (New York: Cambridge University Press, 1987), chap. 4. There were complications that drew considerable attention from legal minds: What constituted "living" somewhere? Did a merchant living in a foreign country become "domiciled" there? When did naturalizations occur? What about partnerships between individuals of two nationalities? Yet these were questions about the application of the principle rather than the principle itself.

36. *Le Theodore*, in J. M. Howard et al., eds., *English Admiralty Reports: Reports of cases argued and determined in the High court of admiralty. Commencing with the judgments of the Right Hon. Sir William Scott. Michaelmas term, 1789[-1808] By Chr. Robinson* (Boston: Little, Brown, 1853), 258ff, emphasis added.

37. This was a doctrine promulgated by Scott, for which see the cases of the *Ospray* (1793) and *Vigilantia* (1798). Both cases are discussed in Bourguignon, *Sir William Scott*, 153–54.

38. See discussion of this case in Bourguignon, *Sir William Scott*, 155–57.

39. See *Harmony* (1800), in *Reports of Cases in the High Court of Admiralty . . . Judgements of . . . Sir William Scott*, 2:333–35.

40. *Harmony* (1800), 2:342.

41. *Conqueror* (1800), 2:303–6.

42. Ibid., 2:307.

43. Ibid., 2:321.

44. See Schooner *Hannah*, Master Benjamin Rice, HCA 45/18, TNA.

45. These problems with the documentation of ships paralleled similar difficulties that governments had during the eighteenth century in identifying mariners who were eligible for enlistment in naval service. See Perl-Rosenthal, *Citizen Sailors*, passim.

Chapter 5

1. "A Certaine Relation Concerning the Late Shipwracke of One of the King's Ships Called the Speedwell Which Perished upon the Sands Neere Flushing. Wherein Count Mansfield Was to Have Been Transported over into England," *The Continuation of Our Weekly Newes*, December 4, 1624, Issue 43, Burney Collection.

2. See E. G. R. Taylor, *Mathematical Practitioners of Tudor and Stuart England* (Cambridge: Institute of Navigation at the University Press, 1954) for the classic account of the shift from coastal to transoceanic sailing. On the introduction of new nautical technologies, see C. A. Davids, *Zeewezen en Wetenschap: De Wetenschap en de Ontwikkeling van de Navigatietechniek in Nederland Tussen 1585 en 1815* (Amsterdam: De Bataafsche Leeuw, 1986); David W. Waters, *The Art of Navigation in England in Elizabethan and Early Stuart Times* (New Haven, CT: Yale University Press, 1958).

3. Mariners are omitted from most standard accounts of the Scientific Revolution published prior to 1990. Two important early exceptions are: R. K. Merton, *Science, Technology and Society in Seventeenth Century England* (Bruges, Belgium: Saint Catherine Press, 1938); E. Zilsel, "The Origins of William Gilbert's Scientific Method," *Journal of the History of Ideas* 2, no. 1 (January 1941): 1–32.

4. For instance, the magisterial and prolific maritime historian Samuel Eliot Morison made grand pronouncements about the timelessness of sailing: "Navigational methods in effect around 1500 lasted, with many refinements but no essential changes, until 1920–30" (*The Great Explorers: The European Discovery of America* [New York: Oxford University Press, 1978], 32). Similarly, Olaf Janzen, "The Oceans as Highways," in *Maritime History as World History*, ed. D. Finamore (Salem, MA: Peabody Essex Museum, 2004), 103.

5. There were other contemporary projects that were similarly large-scale and systematic, but which focused on political economy rather than technical or scientific matters. These include William Petty's survey of Ireland, *Political Arithmetick, Or, A Discourse Concerning the Extent and Value of Lands, People . . . Shipping, Power at Sea, &c.* (London: for R. Clavel and H. Mortlock, 1691); and Colbert's drive to acquire and control political information, described by Jacob Soll, *The Information Master: Jean-Baptiste Colbert's Secret State Intelligence System* (Ann Arbor: University of Michigan Press, 2009).

6. While not discussed here, Spain also fits this category.

7. *Ordonnance de Louis XIV, donnée à fontainebleau au mois d'Aoust 1681, touchant la Marine* (Paris: Charles Osmont, 1714), "Preface."

8. Dirk Makreel, *Lichtende leydt-starre der groote zeevaert* (Amsterdam: Hendrick Doncker, 1671), "Voor-reden."

9. Pamela Long, *Openness, Secrecy, Authorship* (Baltimore: Johns Hopkins University Press, 2001), on the term "artifice."

10. E.g., Pedro Nunes, *De arte atque ratione navigandi* (Coimbra, 1573); Martín Cortés, *Arte of Navigation*, trans. Richard Eden (London: Richard Jugge, 1561). Numerous seventeenth-century texts follow these early examples, particularly in French: e.g., Guillaume Denys, *L'art de naviguer* . . . (Dieppe: N. du Buc, 1666); Claude-François Milliet de Chales, *L'art de naviger, demontré par principes* . . . (Paris: E. Michallet, 1677).

11. Michiel Coignet, *Nieuwe Onderwijsinghe op de principaelste puncten der Zee-vaert* (Antwerp: H. Hendricksen, 1580), fol. 3.

12. F. Dassié, *L'Architecture Navale* (Paris: Jean de la Caille, 1677), 7: "l'art de naviger & de conduire un Navire, qui aura pour son Titre, La Science du Pilote." The French used "pilotage" to refer to steering any vessel, whether in harbor or on the open water.

13. Daniell Sephtonal, "Navigation Workbook" (ca. 1713) NVT/6, NMM Greenwich, f. [4]v.

14. The *Encyclopédie* (Paris, 1751–72), 11:54 defined "Navigation proprement dit": construction, loading, and steering (*conduire*) at sea. Georges Fournier, S.J., a French royal hydrographer, took a much broader view of the "theory and practice of all the parts of navigation." His *Hydrographie* (Paris, 1643), the earliest substantial French work on the subject, included magnetic compasses, the history and natural properties of the lodestone, religious homilies, and accounts of France's nautical superiority. See Flamsteed's far narrower definition below.

15. Capt. Charles Saltonstall explicitly set out to write a *theoretical* introduction to "the proper way of working a Ship in all Weathers," claiming that the lack of such an explanation has "perchance hither unto . . . hindred it [the science of "seamanship"] from the publicke view." Saltonstall, *The Nauigator Shewing and Explaining All the Chiefe Principles and Parts Both Theoricke and Practicke* (London: for Geo[rge] H[u]rlock, 1636), 2, 3.

16. E.g., Jacob Aertsz Colom, *The Nevv Fierie Sea-Colomne* (Amsterdam: Jacob Colom, 1649), f. [a]*v*. Readers could "looke upon this following little Table" if they wanted to "know the same without account" [i.e., computation]. Henry Phillippes, *The Geometrical Sea-Man: Or, the Art of Navigation Performed by Geometry* (London: R. and W. Leybourn, for George Hurlock, 1652), promising in the subtitle that "all three kinds of sailing . . . may be easily and exactly performed by a plain ruler and a pair of compasses, without arithmeticall calculation."

17. On the navigational textbook as a genre, see Annie Charon, Thierry Claerr, and François Moureau, eds., *Le livre maritime au siècle des Lumières* (Paris: Presses de l'Université de Paris-Sorbonne, 2005); Djoeke van Netten, "Een boek als carrière-vehikel. De zeemansgidsen van Blaeu," *De Zeventiende Eeuw. Cultuur in de Nederlanden in interdisciplinair perspectief* 27, no. 2 (March 14, 2012): 214–31.

18. Navigators were roundly criticized for underestimating the length of a nautical mile, but captains nearing shore preferred their estimates of speed and distance to be somewhat aggressive, since it was far better to overestimate and begin dropping a sounding line a few

days early than to run aground. "Memoire" (Havre-de-Grace, 1682), Mar G86, AN-Paris, fol. 22, "L'on fait remarquer l'Importance quil y a lorsque lon va chercher une terre de se faire de l'Avant en sa routte affin de se deffier du mal qui pourroit arriver d'une estime trop foible." See also William Bourne, *A Regiment for the Sea* (London, 1574), fol. 49v.

19. Few texts discussed the extremely uncertain art of weather prediction, but those that did simply recycled time-honored indicators from Pliny; see Pierre Cauvette, *Nouveaux elemens d'hydrographie* (Paris; Dieppe, 1685), "Signes du changement de tems." Early seventeenth-century texts, such as John Smith's *A Sea Grammar* (London, 1627) and Henry Mainwaring's *Sea-Mans Dictionary* (London, 1644), mentioned but did not illustrate or explain knots and rope work; diagrams of the most common knots did not appear in manuals until the mid-eighteenth century, e.g., T. R. Blanckley, *A Naval Expositor* (London, 1750); William Falconer, *An Universal Dictionary of the Marine* (London, 1769).

20. E.g., William Bourne, *A Regiment for the Sea Conteyning Most Profitable Rules, Mathematical Experiences, and Perfect Knowledge of Nauigation* (London: [Henry Bynneman for] Thomas Hacket, 1574).

21. Georges Fournier devoted ten pages of his magnum opus, *Hydrographie* (Paris, 1667), 376–83 to the proper means of graduating the scale on a cross-staff, and warned against the inexplicable, "dangerous" convention of shortening the staff by 2.5 degrees. Radouay, "Nouvelle pratique de navigation" (ca. 1727), SH 284, SHD-Vincennes, p. 12: "A pilot needed to use the same instrument for a long time to be assured of such precision."

22. J. A. Bennett, *The Divided Circle: A History of Instruments for Astronomy, Navigation and Surveying* (Oxford: Phaidon Christie's, 1987); and see Norton Wise, *The Values of Precision* (Princeton, NJ: Princeton University Press, 1995), 9 for the socially constructed standards of precision that guide the use of every "carefully constructed instrument."

23. See Margaret Schotte, "Expert Records: Nautical Logbooks from Columbus to Cook," *Information & Culture: A Journal of History* 48, no. 3 (2013): 281–322.

24. Schotte, *Sailing School: Navigating Science and Skill, 1550–1800* (Baltimore: Johns Hopkins University Press, 2019). See, e.g., Daniel Newhouse, *VVhole Art of Navigation* (London: for the author, 1685), 3. "S[cholar]: Is it necessary for a Pilot to carry to Sea a Cross-Staff, a Quadrant and an Astronomical Ring or Astrolabe? T[utor]: Yes, in long Voyages; since many good Observers have found by experience, that the Quadrant is best when the Sun is near the Zenith, but that otherwise the Cross-Staff is better. The Astronomical Ring & Astrolabe is also necessary to take observation, when there is no clear Horizon."

25. Peter Galison and Bruce Hevly, eds., *Big Science: The Growth of Large-Scale Research* (Stanford, CA: Stanford University Press, 1992), 355. See also Mariana Mazzucato, *The Entrepreneurial State: Debunking Public vs. Private Sector Myths* (London; New York: Anthem Press, 2013).

26. This phenomenon was widespread enough in Britain's Royal Navy that a debate raged over the relative merits of "tarpaulins," officers who rose through the ranks, compared to the far more common "gentlemen," who received their commissions without having been to sea. J. D. Davies, *Gentlemen and Tarpaulins: The Officers and Men of the Restoration Navy* (Oxford: Clarendon Press, 1991).

27. The cleric William Barlow candidly admitted: "Touching experience in these matters, of my selfe I have none." *The Navigators Supply* (London, 1597), fol. [a4v]. On "liefhebbers" (lovers or enthusiasts) as an audience for and promoters of science, see Vera Keller, "Art Lovers and Scientific Virtuosi?," *Nuncius* 31, no. 3 (January 1, 2016): 523–48.

28. On the intellectual divide between nautical educators and their pupils in sixteenth-century Spain, see Ursula Lamb, *Cosmographers and Pilots of the Spanish Maritime Empire* (Aldershot, Hampshire; Brookfield, VT: Ashgate Variorum, 1995); Alison D. Sandman, "Cosmographers vs. Pilots: Navigation, Cosmography, and the State in Early Modern Spain" (PhD diss., University of Wisconsin, Madison, 2001).

29. Fournier, *Hydrographie* (1667), 124: "une franche beste"; chap. XXIII, "Yvrognerie." English authors were equally critical: Nathaniel Boteler, *Six Dialogues About Sea-services Between an High-admiral and a Captain at Sea* . . . (London: for Moses Pitt, 1685), 45: "the loose Liberty and uncontrouled Life that they lead." Charles Saltonstall, *The Nauigator* (London: G. H[u]rlock, 1636), 13, "many hundreds of Ignorant Asses."

30. For early literary examples of the mariner as a useful eyewitness, see Thomas More, *Utopia* (Louvain, 1516); André Thevet, *Cosmographie universelle* (Paris, 1575); and Francis Bacon, *New Atlantis* (London, 1620). John Flamsteed, "Doctrine and Practice of Navigation" (1697), Pepys MS 2184, p. 1, "discreet saylor"; Samuel Pepys, *Tangier Papers*, ed. E. Chappell (London: Printed for the Navy Records Society, 1935), 110, 120.

31. In contrast to the negative descriptions in French and English texts (note 29 above), popular Dutch literature idealized the figure of the wise navigator, and even pirates were regarded with veiled patriotism: Karel Porteman and Mieke Smits-Veldt, *Nieuw Vaderland voor de Muzen* (Amsterdam: Bert Bakker, 2008); Virginia West Lunsford. *Piracy and Privateering in the Golden Age Netherlands* (Houndmills, Basingstoke, Hampshire: Palgrave Macmillan, 2005).

32. Pepys worked his way up within the Royal Navy's bureaucracy over the course of the 1670s and 1680s, from Clerk of the Acts to Secretary of the Admiralty Board. See Norman Thrower, "Samuel Pepys FRS (1633–1703) and the Royal Society," *Notes and Records of the Royal Society of London* 57, no. 1 (2003): 3–13.

33. Pepys's mathematics lessons with Cooper extended through the summer of 1662; see Robert Latham and William Matthews, *Diary of Samuel Pepys: A New and Complete Transcription* (London: Bell, 1970), 3/128–4/85, passim; Deane, 3/151, 163, 169; other lessons 4/189–90, 4/7, 5/115. Notes for his unfinished history of the Royal Navy (Pepys MS 2866) have been published as *Samuel Pepys's Naval Minutes*, ed. J. R. Tanner (London: Printed for the Navy Records Society, 1926).

34. Edward J. Phillips, *The Founding of Russia's Navy: Peter the Great and the Azov Fleet, 1688–1714* (Westport, CT: Greenwood Press, 1995), 54; Jozien J. Driessen-van het Reve, "Wat tsaar Peter de Grote (1672–1725) leerde van Holland en de Hollanders," *Leidschrift Rusland en Europa. Westerse invloeden op Rusland*, 24, no. 2 (2009); 15–33.

35. Bernard de Fontenelle, "Eloge of N. Hartsoeker [1699]" in *Oeuvres de Fontenelle. Éloges* (Paris: Salmon, 1825), 150.

36. Arthur MacGregor, "The Tsar in England: Peter the Great's Visit to London in 1698," *Seventeenth Century* 19, no. 1 (Spring 2004): 116–47; and see note 75 below. Phillips, *The Founding of Russia's Navy*, 174, contends that Peter chose the English model for shipbuilding rather than the Dutch one, claiming that the mathematical approach of the former was easier to learn than the time-consuming craftsmanship of the latter.

37. Jan de Boer, *Zeemans Oeffening* (Amsterdam: Joh. van Keulen en Zoonen, 1769), vi, "Voorreden."

38. E.g., Jan de Boer, "Extract uit de 'Zeemansoefening over de groote zeevaart,' memorie" (1773), VOC 5022, NL-HaNA. "Idées d'un marin sur les connaissances théoriques et

pratiques à exiger des officiers de la Marine royale et sur les avantages que présenteraient un collège de Marine établi à Port-Louis pour l'instruction des élèves" (ca. 1802), MS 516, SHD-Vincennes.

39. [Guillaume Clément de] Viviers, "Memoire sur les Ecoles de Pilotes" (April 1681) in "Mémoires et projets [des] Ecoles de Marine diverses" (1681–1795), Mar G86, AN-Paris, fols. 47–54v.

40. Waters, *Art of Navigation* (1958), 103–5; J. B. P. Willaumez, *Project pour former des Élèves Marines, a Paris même* (n.p., [1800]).

41. Radouay, "Nouvelle pratique de navigation" (ca. 1727), SH 284, SHD-Vincennes; Martinus Martens and Jan de Marre, "Kopie-memoires . . . over . . . verbeteringen in kaarten en scheepsinstructie" (1746), VOC 5020, NL-HaNA. Jaap R. Bruijn, *Schippers van de VOC in de achttiende eeuw aan de wal en op zee* (Amsterdam: Bataafsche Leeuw, 2008), 122, notes that the company took their advice and adopted the octant and azimuth compass.

42. E.g., Léonard Duliris, *La Theorie des longitudes, reduite en pratique sur le globe céleste . . .* (Paris: Jean Guillemot, 1647); Jane Squire, *A Proposal for Discovering Our Longitude* (London: for the author, 1742). The Dutch committee issued payments for several promising designs, although none proved definitively effective; see Davids, *Zeewezen en Wetenschap* (1986), 82.

43. Dava Sobel, *Longitude: The True Story of a Lone Genius Who Solved the Greatest Scientific Problem of His Time* (New York: Walker, 1995).

44. Richard Dunn and Rebekah Higgitt, *Ships, Clocks, and Stars: The Quest for Longitude* (New York, NY: Harper Design, 2014).

45. See Galison and Hevly, *Big Science*; John Brewer, *The Sinews of Power: War, Money, and the English State, 1688–1783* (London: Unwin Hyman, 1989); N. A. M. Rodger, *The Command of the Ocean: A Naval History of Britain 1649–1815* (London: Allen Lane/National Maritime Museum, 2004); N. A. M. Rodger, "From the 'Military Revolution' to the 'Fiscal-Naval State,'" *Journal for Maritime Research* 13, no. 2 (2011): 119–28.

46. See, among myriad examples, William Gilbert, *De Magnete* (London: P. Short, 1600); he consulted with mariners as part of his experimental research into magnetism. On an early effort to assess the accuracy of timekeepers, see John W. Olmsted, "The Voyage of Jean Richer to Acadia in 1670: A Study in the Relations of Science and Navigation under Colbert," *Proceedings of the American Philosophical Society* 104, no. 6 (December 15, 1960): 612–34.

47. "Directions for Sea-Men, Bound for Far Voyages," *Philosophical Transactions* (1665–66): 1.140–43; "Directions for Observations and Experiments to Be Made by Masters of Ships, Pilots, and Other Fit Persons in Their Sea-Voyages," *Philosophical Transactions* (1666–67): 2.24: 433–48.

48. Journals from eighteen voyages to Cape of Good Hope: Records of Waterworks (1693–94), VOC 5058, NL-HaNA; see Margaret Schotte, "Distilling Water, Distilling Data: Questionnaires in Dutch East India Company Record-keeping," *European History Quarterly* (forthcoming 2021).

49. Lucas J. Waghenaer, *Spiegel der Seefahrt* (Amsterdam: Cornelis Claesz., 1589), "Der Autor zum Leser." On positive representations, see note 31 above.

50. Abbé Bernou, "Pieces sur le Flux et Reflux, mouvement et courans de la Mer, avec des Extraits de Voyages en Asie, Affrique, et Amerique, et autres traitez sur cette matiere" (n.d.), Mss. Clair. 848, BnF-Richelieu.

51. Pepys, *Naval Minutes,* 421–22 (ca. 1695). Pepys also singled out Edward Halley ("Mr. Hawley") as the "first Englishman (and possibly any other) that had . . . any competent degree . . . of the science and practice (both) of navigation?" Ibid., 420.

52. Alexander Justice, *A General Treatise of the Dominion of the Sea: and a Compleat Body of the Sea-Laws . . .* (London: D. Leach, for J. Nicholson, and J. and B. Sprint; and R. Smith, 1709), 632.

53. Nathaniel Boteler, *Six Dialogues About Sea-services Between an High-admiral and a Captain at Sea . . .* (London: Printed for Moses Pitt, 1685), 62; *Considerations on the nurseries for British seamen* ([London]: n.p., 1766).

54. In traditional maritime industries, men tended to follow in their fathers' footsteps, and often apprenticed with family members. P. C. van Royen, "Mariners and Markets," in *Market for Seamen in the Age of Sail,* ed. Lewis R. Fischer (Liverpool: Liverpool University Press, 1994), 50: in 1680, 50,000 sailors (of a population of 2 million) manned all the merchantmen, VOC, and naval vessels.

55. Des Nos, "L'Escole du canon au port de Brest que Monseigneur Le Marquis de Seignelay aura s'il luy plaist agreable d'examiner" (Brest, February 2, 1682), Mar G86, AN-Paris, No. 2; T. J. A. Le Goff, "Labour Market for Sailors in France," in *"Those Emblems of Hell"?: European Sailors and the Maritime Labour Market, 1570–1870* (St. John's, NL: International Maritime Economic History Association, 1997), 300: 15,000 men in the navy at the 1690 peak (the bulk of whom were oarsmen); 43,000 skilled seafarers in France in the late seventeenth century, of a population of approximately 25 million.

56. Colbert Papers, NAFr. 9479, BnF-Richelieu, fol. 21, cited in Thomas Chapais, *Jean Talon* (Québec: Impr. de S.-A. Demers, 1904), 422–23. Intendant Talon reported that given their "natural disposition to these occupations," the inclination of "the young people of Canada [to] devote themselves, indeed throw themselves, into the study of the arts and sciences and the learning of trades, especially the seafaring ones," needed only to be "fostered a little" to have a substantial benefit to the French state.

57. Des Nos, "L'Escole du canon au port de Brest" (1682), fol. 7. "Si toutefois parmi ces gens la Il s'en presentes quelques uns portés de bonne volonté en qui on trouvast de la disposition Il les faudroit preferer parceque l'Inclination y faict beaucoup et Je croy mesme qu'en ce cas la Il ne faudroit pas avoir egard aux classes."

58. "Lettre de Maurepas du 14 nov. 1734," cited in René-Josué Valin, *Nouveau Commentaire sur l'Ordonnance de La Marine, du mois d'août 1681,* 2 vols. (La Rochelle: J. Legier, 1760), I.212–13; Bernard Lutun, "Des Ecoles de marine et principalement des écoles d'hydrographie (1629–1789)," *Sciences et Techniques en Perspective* 34 (1995): 9, no. 47. See below on the main British naval school, the Royal Mathematical School, which was also associated with a charitable institution for poor children.

59. On the history of the pathbreaking Spanish and Portuguese navigators, see, among others: Maria Portuondo, *Secret Science* (Chicago: University of Chicago Press, 2009); Lamb, *Cosmographers and Pilots*; Sandman, "Cosmographers vs. Pilots."

60. Pepys, *Naval Minutes,* 240, 355; Viviers, "Memoire sur les Ecoles de Pilotes" (April 1681), Mar G86, AN-Paris, f. 47.

61. Although the northern core of the country was not oriented to the sea, the southern periphery did have a longstanding maritime industry, e.g., Basque fishermen, and the Roman port of Marseille.

62. René Mémain, *La marine de guerre sous Louis XIV. Le materiel. Rochefort, arsenal modele de Colbert* (Paris: Librairie Hachette, 1937); James S. Pritchard, *Louis XV's Navy, 1748–1762* (Kingston and Montreal: McGill-Queen's University Press, 1987). The Académie royale des sciences sponsored overseas expeditions that had explicitly scientific purposes (e.g., J. Richer to Acadia, J. Deshayes et al. to Africa, as well as numerous eighteenth-century ventures); these were separate from naval and trade activities.

63. Michel Vergé-Franceschi, *Marine et éducation sous l'ancien régime* (Paris: Editions du Centre national de la recherche scientifique, 1991), 94; Albert Anthiaume, *Evolution et enseignement* (Paris: E. Dumont, 1920). The guards were being groomed for naval careers, but were still subordinate to any officers who may also have taken classes at the same schools.

64. Only a small number of these teachers had maritime experience, and it was not uncommon for sons to take over from their fathers. Although Colbert had initially engaged instructors from Holland rather than clerics "who had never been to sea," in 1686 Louis XIV gave Jesuits the exclusive right to teach hydrography to the *gardes*; see François de Dainville, *La géographie des humanistes* (Paris: Beauchesne et ses fils, 1940), 435, 439; L.-P. Audet, "Hydrographes du Roi . . ." *Cahiers de Dix* 35 (1970): 13–37, 15.

65. "Projet d'examen et d'amelioration de l'enseignement maritime theorique et pratique; projet de redaction d'un nouveau manuel de navigation et de pilotage" (1771), Mar G89, AN-Paris; "Mémoires et projets [des] Ecoles de Marine diverses" (1682–1700), Mar G86, AN-Paris.

66. See Eugene L. Asher, *The Resistance to the Maritime Classes: The Survival of Feudalism in the France of Colbert* (Berkeley: University of California Press, 1960).

67. François de Dainville, "L'instruction des Gardes de la Marine à Brest en 1692," *Revue d'histoire des sciences et de leurs applications* 9, no. 4 (1956): 323–38, 338. In the 1690s, French schools ended up having to dock cadets' wages to punish them for skipping class or selling their textbooks.

68. The first French "floating school" was launched at Le Havre during the summer of 1774, but illness plagued the students. Michel Vergé-Franceschi, "Un enseignement éclairé au xviiie siècle: l'enseignement maritime dispensé aux gardes," *Revue Historique* (France) 276, no. 1 (1986): 29–56, 53.

69. The Portsmouth Naval Academy, dedicated to educating officers, would be founded sixty years later in 1733; Harry W. Dickinson, *Educating the Royal Navy: Eighteenth- and Nineteenth-Century Education for Officers* (Hove, Sussex: Psychology Press, 2007).

70. Stephen Johnston, "Making Mathematical Practice: Gentlemen, Practitioners and Artisans in Elizabethan England" (PhD diss., Cambridge University, 1994); Deborah E. Harkness, *The Jewel House: Elizabethan London and the Scientific Revolution* (New Haven: Yale University Press, 2007).

71. Rob Iliffe, "Mathematical Characters: Flamsteed and Christ's Hospital Royal Mathematical School," in *Flamsteed's Stars: New Perspectives on the Life and Work of the First Astronomer Royal, 1646–1719*, ed. Frances Willmoth (Woodbridge, Suffolk: Boydell Press/National Maritime Museum, 1997), 115–44.

72. Pepys is often credited with substantially improving the Royal Navy through his administrative reforms, e.g., pensions for sailors. However, his financial and political clout were far lower than Colbert's, so he did not effect the same degree of change. In addition to his meticulous notes about nautical developments abroad he sought accounts of the Casa de la

Contratación in Seville, see *Naval Minutes,* Pepys MS 2866; "Schemes of Learning" preserved in "Matters Pertaining to Christ's Hospital" (ca. 1684), Pepys MS 2612.

73. J. Flamsteed to S. Pepys, correspondence (April 21, 1697), Pepys MS 2184, p. 1.

74. Isaac Newton/Roger Cotes, *Correspondence of Sir Isaac Newton and Professor Cotes: Including Letters of Other Eminent Men*, ed. J. Edleston (London: J. W. Parker, 1850), 292.

75. Graduates seem to have been hired for their mathematical training rather than their nautical skills. Two young men went to teach navigation in St. Petersburg and one in Bremen, while another was recruited to a bookkeeping post in Virginia. Ms. 12873-A, Guildhall/London Metropolitan Archives, Christ's Hospital School Cttee. Minutes (1681–88), September 7, 1687.

76. In the eighteenth century, a fairly robust program of shipboard classes was established, although very little is known about the lessons; see Dickinson, *Educating the Royal Navy* (2007).

77. The VOC briefly ran a school in Amsterdam (1743–53) and also operated the Académie de Marine in Batavia (1743–1755), the latter focusing on equipping local men to be common seamen rather than navigators or officers. F. C. van Oosten, "'Hear Instruction and Be Wise': The History of a Naval College on Java in the Eighteenth and Nineteenth Century," *Mariner's Mirror* 55, no. 3 (August 1969): 247–62.

78. Ernst Crone, "Pieter Holm en zijn Zeevaartschool," *De Zee: Zeevaartkundig Tijdschrift* 52 (1930); Willem F. J. Mörzer Bruyns, *Schip Recht door Zee: De octant in de Republiek in de achttiende eeuw* (Amsterdam: Koninklijke Nederlandse Akademie van Wetenschappen, 2003).

79. Jan Willem Sleutel, "Konstige oefeningen begrepen in drie boecken," Manuscript workbook, Hoorn (1675–77), H631, Maritiem Museum Rotterdam, 125.

80. J. A. Bennett, "Shopping for Instruments in Paris and London," in *Merchants and Marvels: Commerce and the Representation of Nature in Early Modern Europe*, ed. Paula Findlen and Pamela H. Smith (New York: Routledge, 2002), 370–95.

81. The Amsterdam Admiralty adopted the textbook of Pybo Steenstra, *Grond-beginzels der stuurmans-kunst* (Amsterdam: G. Hulst Van Keulen, 1779).

82. Johan S. Stavorinus and Samuel H. Wilcocke, *Voyages to the East-Indies* (London: G. G. and J. Robinson, 1798), III.465–67.

83. Pamela Long, *Artisan/Practitioners and the Rise of the New Sciences, 1400–1600* (Portland, OR: Oregon State University Press, 2011), 3.

84. For instance, even after the popularization of cheap almanacs, mariners continued to rely on mnemonic rhymes and spinning volvelles, tools that seemed outdated but which remained important for daily calendrical and tidal calculations.

85. Lissa L. Roberts, Simon Schaffer, and Peter Robert Dear, eds., *The Mindful Hand: Inquiry and Invention from the Late Renaissance to Early Industrialisation* (Amsterdam: Koninklijke Nederlandse Akademie van Wetenschappen, 2007) offers a model for bridging this divide.

Chapter 6

1. Kadu receives only brief attention in the literature. See Paul D'Arcy, "Connected by the Sea: Towards a Regional History of the Western Caroline Islands," *Journal of Pacific History* 36, no. 2 (September 2001): 173–78; Ilya Vinkovetsky, *Russian America: An Overseas Colony of a Continental Empire, 1804–1867* (New York: Oxford University Press, 2011), 119–20;

Harry Liebersohn, *The Travelers' World: Europe to the Pacific* (Cambridge, MA: Harvard University Press, 2006), 157–61; and David Igler, *The Great Ocean: Pacific Worlds from Captain Cook to the Gold Rush* (New York: Oxford University Press, 2013), 139–40.

2. On Choris, see James W. Vanstone, "An Early Nineteenth-Century Artist in Alaska," *Pacific Northwest Quarterly* 51, no. 4 (October 1960): 145–58; Harry Liebersohn, "Images of Monarchy: Kamehameha I and the Art of Louis Choris," in *Double Vision: Art Histories and Colonial Histories in the Pacific*, ed. Nicholas Thomas and Diane Losche (Cambridge: Cambridge University Press, 1999), 44–63; Porter Garnett, *San Francisco One Hundred Years Ago* (San Francisco: A. M. Robertson, 1913); Liebersohn, *The Travelers' World*, 93–97.

3. Louis Choris, *Voyage pittoresque autour du monde: Avec des portraits de sauvages d'Amérique, d'Asie, d'Afrique, et des Îles du Grand océan; des paysages, des vues maritimes, et plusieurs objets d'histoire naturelle* (Paris: Firmin Didot, 1822). On *Voyage pittoresque*, William Reese states the first-edition volume was produced in three different varieties, from monochrome to full hand-colored. The Reese catalogue includes a full-color first edition listed at $155,000, one of fifty copies produced. See *Catalogue 322 Forty Years a Bookseller* (New Haven, CT: William Reese, 2015), item #25, n.p. Copies of this volume at different archives demonstrate not only these three different varieties but also a range in hand-colored image quality.

4. For one example of this ethnography, see Sally Engle Merry, "Kapi'olani at the Brink: Dilemmas of Historical Ethnography in 19th-Century Hawai'i," *American Ethnography* 30, no. 1 (February 2003): 44–60. In his highly regarded survey of Pacific representation, Bernard Smith suggests that Choris did not provide honest portrayals of Pacific peoples; see Smith, *European Vision and the South Pacific* (New Haven: Yale University Press, 1985), 206–11.

5. Epeli Haúofa, "Our Sea of Islands," *Contemporary Pacific* 6, no. 1 (Spring 1994): 153.

6. Thomas Bender, *A Nation Among Nations: America's Place in World History* (New York: Hill and Wang, 2006), 16.

7. David Chappell, *Double Ghosts: Oceanian Voyagers on Euroamerican Ships* (Armonk, NY: M. E. Sharpe, 1997).

8. Felipe Fernández-Armesto, *Pathfinders: A Global History of Exploration* (New York: W. W. Norton, 2006), 241.

9. On Christian-Muslim trade routes across the Indian Ocean, see Anthony Disney and Emily Booth, eds., *Vasco da Gama and the Linking of Europe and Asia* (New York: Oxford University Press, 1997), especially the chapters by Felipe Fernández-Armesto, John Villiers, and Om Prakesh. See also Sanjay Subrahmanyam, *The Career and Legend of Vasco da Gama* (Cambridge: Cambridge University Press, 1997), 76–164.

10. Philip Carteret, *Carteret's Voyage Round the World, 1766–1769*, ed. Helen Wallis (Cambridge, England: Published for the Hakluyt Society, 1965), 200-201.

11. On death rates for indigenous crewmembers, see Chappell, *Double Ghosts*, 31–34, 159–65.

12. Joseph Banks, in *The Journals of Captain James Cook on His Voyages of Discovery*, ed. J. C. Beaglehole (Cambridge: Hakluyt Society, 1955–1974): v. 1: 312.

13. Cook admitted this lack of understanding to James Boswell following his return to London. See Charles Ryskamp, *Boswell: The Ominous Years* (New York: McGraw-Hill, 1963), 341.

14. Anne Salmond, *Two Worlds: First Meetings Between Maori and Europeans, 1642–1772* (Honolulu: University of Hawai'i Press, 1991), 253.

15. James Belich, *Making Peoples: A History of the New Zealanders from Polynesian Settlement to the End of the Nineteenth Century* (Honolulu: University of Hawaiʻi Press, 1996), 20.

16. Alden T. Vaughan, *Transatlantic Encounters: American Indians in Britain, 1500–1776* (New York: Columbia University Press, 2008), especially chaps. 3 and 4.

17. Bartolomé de las Casas, quoted in Fernández-Armesto, *Pathfinders*, 240.

18. "The Voyage of Juan Rodriquez Cabrillo up the Pacific Coast," in *New American World: A Documentary History of North America to 1612*, ed. David B. Quinn (New York: Arno Press, 1979), vol. 1, 453, 455, 460. On other Spanish expeditions to California and hostage taking, see Kent Lightfoot and William Simmons, "Culture Contact in Protohistoric California: Social Contexts of Native and European Encounters," *Journal of California and Great Basin Anthropology* 20, no. 2 (1998): 138–69.

19. Adelbert von Chamisso, *A Voyage Around the World with the Romanzov Expedition in the Years 1815–1818 in the Brig* Rurik, *Captain Otto von Kotzebue*, ed. and trans. Henry Kratz (Honolulu: University of Hawaiʻi Press, 1986 [1836]), 129. Chamisso also authored large portions of the official three-volume account of the *Rurik*'s voyage published in 1821.

20. Chamisso, *Voyage*, 159.

21. Chamisso, *Voyage*, 161. Chamisso would donate the skulls to a Berlin museum. One of these skulls resides today in Berlin's Anatomical Institute. The skull goes by the scientific marker "A 685," an Aleut male whose tomb was "ransacked," according to Chamisso, who did the ransacking. Matthias Glaubrecht, Nils Seethaler, Barbara Tebman, and Katrin Koel-Abt, "The Potential of Biohistory: Re-discovering Adelbert von Chamisso's Skull of an Aleut Collected During the '*Rurik*' Expedition 1815–1818 in Alaska," *Zoosystematics and Evolution* 89, no. 2 (September 2013): 317–36. On skull collecting, see Ann Fabian, *The Skull Collectors: Race, Science, and America's Unburied Dead* (Chicago: University of Chicago Press, 2010).

22. Chamisso, *Voyage*, 140.

23. Choris, *Voyage pittoresque*, 18–22.

24. Vanstone, "An Early Nineteenth-Century Artist in Alaska," 151.

25. Ryan Tucker Jones, *Empire of Extinction: Russians and the North Pacific's Strange Beasts of the Sea, 1741–1867* (New York: Oxford University Press, 2014), 155–66.

26. Chamisso, *Voyage*, 266–67.

27. Chamisso, *Voyage*, 267; Louis Choris, *Journal des Malers Ludwig Choris*, ed. Niklaus R. Schweizer (New York: Lang, 1999), 268.

28. Adelbert von Chamisso, *The Alaskan Diary of Adelbert von Chamisso, Naturalist on the Kotzebue Voyage, 1815–1818*, ed. and trans. Robert Fortuine (Anchorage, AK: Cook Inlet Historical Society, 1986), 14.

29. Chamisso, *Alaskan Diary*, 25.

30. Choris's diary entries at this point in the voyage are filled with commentary about Kadu. Choris is actively gathering information about Kadu's background and beliefs, and the artist is especially interested in Kadu's thoughts about the different people they encounter in the North as well as the different cultural practices in the Marshall and Caroline Islands. Choris, *Journal*, 264–69.

31. Vanstone, "An Early Nineteenth-Century Artist in Alaska," 156.

32. Matt K. Matsuda, "AHR Forum: The Pacific," *American Historical Review* 111, no. 3 (June 2006): 758; Matsuda, *Pacific Worlds: A History of Seas, Peoples, and Cultures* (Cambridge: Cambridge University Press, 2012).

33. The *Rurik* visited Alta California during the late fall of 1816, the season prior to Kadu joining the ship's company.

34. Steven W. Hackel, *Children of Coyote, Missionaries of Saint Francis: Indian-Spanish Relations in Colonial California, 1769–1850* (Chapel Hill: University of North Carolina Press, 2005), 96–123.

35. Daniela Bleichmar, "A Visible and Useful Empire: Visual Culture and Colonial Natural History in the Eighteenth-Century Spanish World," in *Science in the Spanish and Portuguese Empires, 1500–1800*, ed. Daniela Bleichmar, Paula DeVos, Kristin Huffine, and Kevin Sheehan (Stanford, CA: Stanford University Press, 2008), 304.

36. Chamisso, *Voyage*, 198.

37. Liebersohn, "Images of Monarchy," 57.

38. Choris, *Journal*, 269; Chamisso, *Voyage*, 263–64; also see S. H. Reisenberg, "Table of Voyages Affecting Micronesian Islands," *Oceania* 36, no. 2 (December 1965): 155–70.

39. Chamisso, *Voyage*, 119–20.

40. Choris's diary includes lengthy descriptions of the Hawaiian people as well as Hawaiian royalty, most of whom he communicated with in English. Choris, *Journal*, 366–71.

41. Otto von Kotzebue, *A Voyage of Discovery: Into the South Sea and Bering's Straits for the Purpose of Exploring a North-East Passage, Undertaken in the Years 1815–1818* (London, 1821), vol. 1, 315. Kotzebue wrote: King Kamehameha "had attracted the attention of all Europe, and . . . inspired me with the greatest confidence by his unreserved and friendly behavior," 300–301.

42. Choris, *Journal*, 366.

43. Chamisso, *Voyage*, 124.

44. Ibid., 119.

45. Ibid., 181.

46. For extensive commentary by these two men on their subsequent careers, see the unpublished letters contained in Tatiana Arkadevna Lukina, *Johann Friedrich Eschscholtz, 1793–1831*, trans. Wilma C. Follette, unpublished manuscript, 2009.

47. Harold J. Cook, *Matters of Exchange: Commerce, Medicine, and Science in the Dutch Golden Age* (New Haven: Yale University Press, 2007), 41.

48. Otto Von Kotzebue, *A New Voyage Round the World in the Years 1823, 1824, 1825, 1826* (London: Henry Colburn and Richard Bentley, 1830), vol. 1, 317; 307.

49. Chamisso, *Voyage*, 199.

50. Chamisso made this remark in reference to the "natural investigations" they conducted together. Chamisso, *Voyage*, 161.

Chapter 7

1. *Antigua Gazette*, August 2, 1798, front page. Available in the Caribbean Newspapers collection of the American Antiquarian Society (henceforth AAS).

2. The term "maritime marronage" was coined by Neville Hall in his pioneering work on the Danish West Indies. See Hall, "Maritime Maroons: 'Grand Marronage' from the Danish West Indies," *William and Mary Quarterly* 42, no. 4 (October 1985): 476–98; Hall, *Slave Society in the Danish West Indies* (Mona, Jamaica: University of the West Indies Press, 1992), chap. 7. For the larger body of scholarship on marronage, see, e.g., Richard Price, *The Guiana Maroons: A Historical and Bibliographical Introduction* (Baltimore: Johns Hopkins University

Press, 1976); John Hope Franklin and Loren Schweninger, *Runaway Slaves: Rebels on the Plantation* (New York: Oxford University Press, 1999); Sylviane A. Diouf, *Slavery's Exiles: The Story of the American Maroons* (New York: New York University Press, 2014). The best overview of the literature on marronage and one of the few works to cover the entirety of the Americas and the Caribbean is Alvin O. Thompson, *Flight to Freedom: African Runaways and Maroons in the Americas* (Mona, Jamaica: University of the West Indies Press, 2006). For a newer comparative analysis, see Simon P. Newman, "Rethinking Runaways in the British Atlantic World: Britain, the Caribbean, West Africa, and North America," *Slavery and Abolition* 38, no. 1 (2017): 49–75.

3. Free people of color here refers to nonenslaved individuals of either African or multiracial descent, rather than narrowly to those of mixed European and African descent.

4. David William Cohen and Jack P. Greene, eds., *Neither Slave nor Free: The Freedmen of African Descent in the Slave Societies of the New World* (Baltimore: Johns Hopkins University Press, 1972); Jane Landers, ed., *Against the Odds: Free Blacks in the Slave Societies of the Americas* (London: Routledge, 1996); Rosemary Brana-Shute and Randy J. Sparks, eds., *Paths to Freedom: Manumission in the Atlantic World* (Columbia, SC: University of South Carolina Press, 2009).

5. Richard Price, "Introduction: Maroons and Their Communities," in *Maroon Societies: Rebel Slave Communities in the Americas*, ed. Richard Price (Baltimore: Johns Hopkins University Press, 1996), 13–15.

6. See R. K. Kent, "Palmares: An African State in Brazil," *Journal of African History* 6, no. 2 (1965): 161–75; Stuart B. Schwartz, "'The 'Mocambo': Slave Resistance in Colonial Bahia," *Journal of Social History* 3, no. 4 (July 1970): 313–33.

7. Francisco Pérez de la Riva, "Cuban *Palenques*," in *Maroon Societies*, 49–59; Gabriel Debien, "Marronage in the French Caribbean," ibid., 107–134.

8. Neil Roberts, *Freedom as Marronage* (Chicago: University of Chicago Press, 2015). For an example of the debate sparked by the book, see the roundtable hosted by the *African American Intellectual History Society Blog*, June 13–18, 2016, http://www.aaihs.org/the-political-worlds-of-the-enslaved-and-marginalized/.

9. In Jamaica, the colonial state required eighteenth-century maroon communities to assist in hunting down other escaped slaves. The practice was also employed in Dominica, and there is some evidence of its use in the British Leeward Islands. In some cases maroons used military enlistment as a method of securing their future freedom, especially in South American colonies. See Greg Childs, "Revolving Doors of Fugitivity: Marronage and the Military," *African American Intellectual History Society Blog*, October 15, 2016, http://www.aaihs.org/revolving-doors-of-fugitivity-marronage-and-the-military/; Nathaniel Millett, *The Maroons of Prospect Bluff and Their Quest for Freedom in the Atlantic World* (Gainesville: University of Florida Press, 2013), 97–126; Jane Landers, "Transforming Bondsmen into Vassals: Arming Slaves in Colonial Spanish America," in *Arming Slaves: From Classical Times to the Modern Age*, ed. Christopher Brown and Philip Morgan (New Haven, CT: Yale University Press, 2006), 120–45.

10. Franklin and Schweninger, *Runaway Slaves*, 149–64. These hounds were specially trained to hunt down runaway slaves, and while not as common in the Caribbean as they were on the continent, they were in fact used against maroons on larger islands including Cuba, Jamaica, and Saint Domingue.

11. Marcus Rediker, "History from Below the Water Line: Sharks and the Atlantic Slave Trade," *Atlantic Studies* 5, no. 2 (August 2008): 285–97; Stuart B. Schwartz, *Sea of Storms: A History of Hurricanes in the Greater Caribbean from Columbus to Katrina* (Princeton, NJ: Princeton University Press, 2015).

12. Hall, *Slave Society in the Danish West Indies*, 134.

13. Jorge L. Chinea, "A Quest for Freedom: The Immigration of Maritime Maroons into Puerto Rico, 1656–1800," *Journal of Caribbean History* 31, no. 1 (January 1997): 73–74. It seems that the Spanish governor refused most of the requests to hand over fugitive slaves, citing earlier sanctuary decrees. See below for more on the tensions between the Spanish and other colonies on this issue.

14. Notably this was the case for men as well as women. Quoted in Hall, *Slave Society in the Danish West Indies,* 103.

15. Reports on the difficulties caused by slaves fleeing to the Dutch and Danish islands from the British Leewards were frequent. See, e.g., "Report from St. Christopher on Fugitive Slaves," August 29, 1827, in the British National Archives (henceforth TNA), Colonial Office (CO) 239/17, fol. 118.

16. For a somewhat optimistic take on this dynamic in the French Caribbean, see Gabriel Debien, "Marronage in the French Caribbean," in *Maroon Societies*, 124-26. For a more critical discussion of the relative anonymity of urban ports vis-à-vis the rural hinterland, and the importance of smaller farms offering shelter and possible employment to runaways, see Thompson, *Flight to Freedom*, 103–8.

17. For more on these networks, see Jeppe Mulich, "Microregionalism and Intercolonial Relations: The Case of the Danish West Indies, 1730–1830," *Journal of Global History* 8, no. 1 (March 2013): 72–94.

18. See W. Jeffrey Bolster, *Black Jacks: African American Seamen in the Age of Sail* (Cambridge, MA: Harvard University Press, 1997); Michael J. Jarvis, *In the Eye of All Trade: Bermuda, Bermudians, and the Maritime Atlantic World, 1680–1783* (Chapel Hill: University of North Carolina Press, 2010).

19. Police Journal, Sheriff of Christiansted, September 19, 1805, Rigsarkivet (henceforth RA), West Indian Local Archives (WILA) 38.31.2.

20. Police Journal, Sheriff of Christiansted, September 21, 1805, RA, WILA 38.31.2.

21. Mulich, "Microregionalism and Intercolonial Relations."

22. *St. Thomas Gazette*, August 23, 1810, 3, in AAS. It is worth noting that forty dollars per man was significantly higher than the normal rate promised for the return of maroons, which was closer to ten dollars in notices posted on August 23, 1810 in the *St. Thomas Gazette* and September 25, 1810 in the *St. Thomas Monday's Advertiser* (AAS).

23. Lauren Benton and Jeppe Mulich, "The Space Between Empires: Coastal and Insular Microregions in the Early Nineteenth-Century World," in *The Uses of Space in Early Modern History*, ed. Paul Stock (New York: Palgrave Macmillan, 2015), 151–71. For more on borderlands, see Jeremy Adelman and Stephen Aron, "From Borderlands to Borders: Empires, Nation-States, and the Peoples in Between in North American History," *American Historical Review* 104, no. 3 (June 1999): 814–41; Paul Readman, Cynthia Radding, and Chad Bryant, eds., *Borderlands in World History, 1700–1914* (New York: Palgrave Macmillan, 2014); for more on interpolity zones, see Lauren Benton and Adam Clulow, "Empires and Protection: Making Interpolity Law in the Early Modern World," *Journal of Global History* 12, no. 1 (March 2017): 74–92.

24. See Kären Wigen, "Cartographies of Connection: Ocean Maps as Metaphors for Inter-area History," in *Interactions: Transregional Perspectives on World History*, ed. Jerry Bentley, Renate Bridenthal, and Anand Yang (Honolulu: University of Hawai'i Press, 2005), 150–66.

25. For a range of historical examples, see Price, *Maroon Societies*. See also Thomas Flory, "Fugitive Slaves and Free Society: The Case of Brazil," *Journal of Negro History* 64, no. 2 (April 1979): 116–30; Yuko Miki, "Fleeing into Slavery: The Insurgent Geographies of Brazilian Quilombolas (Maroons), 1880–1881," *Americas* 68, no. 4 (April 2012): 495–528.

26. John Julius to the Earl of Bathurst, January 20, 1814, TNA, CO 152/104, fol. 4.

27. Richard Hetherington to John Julius, January 17, 1814, TNA, CO 152/104, fol. 5.

28. Despite the date on the document it is unclear whether this memorial was indeed authored in 1811 or rather made for the occasion in 1814 in order to avoid any competing territorial claims. "Memorial of the Council and Commons House of Assembly of the Virgin Islands," September 17, 1811, TNA, CO 152/104, fol. 5.

29. On the larger islands of the Caribbean maroon communities sometimes grew to such a size that they became a force to be reckoned with by colonial states, leading to large-scale military confrontations like the Jamaica Maroon Wars. See Michael Craton, *Testing the Chains: Resistance to Slavery in the British West Indies* (Ithaca, NY: Cornell University Press, 1983), 70–92; Orlando Patterson, "Slavery and Slave Revolts: A Socio-historical Analysis of the First Maroon War of Jamaica, 1655–1740," *Social and Economic Studies* 19, no. 3 (September 1970): 311–13. Other major maroon insurgencies of the eighteenth century included a series of conflicts in Dutch Surinam and French Guiana. See Thompson, *Flight to Freedom*, 115–16; Silvia W. de Groot, "The Boni Maroon War 1765–1793, Surinam and French Guiana," *Boletín de Estudios Latinoamericanos y del Caribe* 18 (1975): 30–48.

30. An example of such local measures is an ordinance adopted by the British colonial government of St. Lucia on the very eve of emancipation. It stated that any person or persons harboring runaway slaves "shall, on conviction, in a summary manner, before any Magistrate of this Island, be adjudged to pay a fine which shall not be less than Fifty Livres nor exceed Two Hundred and Fifty Livres current money, for each and every offence." See "An Ordinance Enacted by the Governor and Legislative Council of St. Lucia—for repressing the practice of Harboring Runaway Slaves," printed in the *Saint Lucia Gazette*, March 12, 1834, front page, in AAS.

31. Julius Scott, "Crisscrossing Empires: Ships, Sailors, and Resistance in the Lesser Antilles in the Eighteenth Century," in *The Lesser Antilles in the Age of European Expansion*, ed. Robert L. Paquette and Stanley L. Engerman (Gainesville: University Press of Florida, 1996), 128–43.

32. TNA CO 239/12, f. 180.

33. Thompson, *Flight to Freedom*, 278.

34. This tension between colonial and imperial levels was also reflected in the responses to slave uprisings and conspiracies during the same period. See Mulich, "Microregionalism and Intercolonial Relations," 84–88.

35. See Linda Rupert, "'Seeking the Waters of Baptism': Fugitive Slaves and Imperial Jurisdiction in the Early Modern Caribbean," in *Legal Pluralism and Empire, 1500–1850*, ed. Richard J. Ross and Lauren Benton (New York: New York University Press, 2013), 201–6; Chinea, "A Quest for Freedom." For similar sanctuary policies in a different part of the Spanish Atlantic, see Matthew Restall, "Crossing to Safety? Frontier Flight in Eighteenth Century Belize and Yucatan," *Hispanic American Historical Review* 94, no. 3 (August 2014): 381–419.

36. Quoted in Elsa Goveia, *Slave Society in the British Leeward Islands at the End of the Eighteenth Century* (New Haven, CT: Yale University Press, 1965), 255.

37. See Francisco A. Scarano, *Sugar and Slavery in Puerto Rico: The Plantation Economy of Ponce, 1800–1850* (Madison: University of Wisconsin Press, 1984).

38. See Lauren Benton and Lisa Ford, *Rage for Order: The British Empire and the Origins of International Law 1800–1850* (Cambridge, MA: Harvard University Press, 2016), chap. 2; Benton and Mulich, "The Space Between Empires."

39. *An Act more effectually to provide for the Support and to Extend certain Regulations for the Protection of Slaves; to Promote and Encourage their Increase, and generally to Meliorate their Condition* (Basseterre, St. Kitts and Nevis: Richard Cable, 1799), 8–9.

40. A different and earlier destination was, of course, Haiti, which made a concerted effort to attract Caribbean maroons to its shores in the wake of independence. See Ada Ferrer, "Haiti, Free Soil, and Antislavery in the Revolutionary Atlantic," *American Historical Review* 117, no. 1 (February 2012): 40–66.

41. "Expelled and wanted persons," in the Caribbean Collection: Virgin Island Documents, The Florence Williams Library, Christiansted, St. Croix. Some of these cases are described in more detail in Hall, *Slave Society in the Danish West Indies*, 136–38.

42. Peter von Scholten to the King of Denmark, January 15, 1841, RA, WILA 2.7.3.

43. Peter von Scholten to the King of Denmark, November 11, 1843, RA, WILA 2.7.3.

44. Report from the brig *Mercurius*, August 11, 1840, RA, WILA, 2.7.3.

45. "Slavery Abolition Act of 1833," Section IV. For a broader discussion of the issue of postemancipation labor in the Caribbean, see in particular Thomas C. Holt, *The Problem of Freedom: Race, Labor, and Politics in Jamaica and Britain, 1832–1938* (Baltimore: Johns Hopkins University Press, 1992); Michael Craton, *Empire, Enslavement and Freedom in the Caribbean* (Kingston, Jamaica: Ian Randle, 1997), 356–438.

46. *Saint Lucia Gazette*, March 18, 1835, p. 2, in AAS.

47. Lauren Benton, *Law and Colonial Cultures: Legal Regimes in World History, 1400–1900* (Cambridge: Cambridge University Press, 2002), 59–66.

48. Craton, *Testing the Chains*, 90. Benton takes some issue with this argument, pointing instead to the fragmented and partial nature of colonial dominance, especially during the earlier period. See Benton, *Law and Colonial Cultures*, 64–65.

49. Rupert, "'Seeking the Waters of Baptism,'" 215–16; Chinea, "A Quest for Freedom," 72.

50. Thompson, *Flight to Freedom*, 272–78.

51. Linda Rupert, *Creolization and Contraband: Curaçao in the Early Modern Atlantic World* (Athens: University of Georgia Press, 2012), 4–6.

52. Ibid., 156–60; Rupert, "Marronage, Manumission, and Maritime Trade in the Early Modern Caribbean," *Abolition and Slavery* 30, no. 3 (2009): 361–82.

53. Marie-Louise Marchand-Thébault, "L'Esclavage en Guyane sous l'Ancien Régime," *Revue Française d'Histoire d'Outre-mer* 47, no. 166 (1960): 5–75; Wim Hoogbergen, "The History of the Suriname Maroons," in *Resistance and Rebellion in Suriname*, ed. Gary Brana-Shute (Williamsburg, VA: College of William and Mary, 1990), 65–102; Miranda Frances Spieler, *Empire and Underworld: Captivity in French Guiana* (Cambridge, MA: Harvard University Press, 2012); Bram Hoonhout and Thomas Mareite, "Freedom at the Fringes? Slave Flight and Empire-Building in the Early Modern Spanish Borderlands of Essequibo-Venezuela and Louisiana-Texas," *Slavery and Abolition*, advance online publication (2018): 1–26.

54. See De Groot, "The Boni Maroon War," 30–48; Hoogbergen, "Marronage and Slave Rebellion in Surinam," in *Slavery in the Americas*, ed. Wolfgang Binder (Würzburg: Königshausen und Neumann, 1993), 165–95.

55. See Richard B. Allen, "Marronage and the Maintenance of Public Order in Mauritius, 1721–1825," *Slavery and Abolition* 4, no. 3 (1983): 214–31; Allen, "A Serious and Alarming Daily Evil: Marronage and Its Legacy in Mauritius and the Colonial Plantation World," *Slavery and Abolition* 25, no. 2 (2004): 1–17.

56. Allen, "Licentious and Unbridled Proceedings: The Illegal Slave Trade to Mauritius and the Seychelles during the Early Nineteenth Century," *Journal of African History* 42, no. 1 (March 2001): 91–116.

Chapter 8

Acknowledgments: I would like to thank Kären Wigen and Noell Wilson as well as Lauren Benton and Nathan Perl-Rosenthal for their valuable feedback on earlier versions of this chapter.

1. Takahiro Yamamoto also considers the question of how this was possible in his dissertation, "Balance of Favour: The Emergence of Territorial Boundaries around Japan, 1861–1875" (PhD diss., London School of Economics and Political Science, 2015).

2. W. G. Beasley, *Japanese Imperialism: 1894–95* (New York: Oxford University Press, 1987), 17, uses the idea of "cooperative imperialism" in specific relation to the Most Favored Nation Clause of the unequal treaties, but I would argue it has broader application to the situation in Northeast Asia during this era.

3. Bob T. Wakabayashi, *Anti-Foreignism and Western Learning in Early-Modern Japan: The New Theses of 1825* (Cambridge, MA: Council on East Asian Studies, Harvard University, 1999), 66. England and Portugal tried in 1674 and 1685, respectively. Donald Keene, *The Japanese Discovery of Europe, 1720–1830*, rev. ed. (Stanford, CA: Stanford University Press, 1952, 1969), 53.

4. George Alexander Lensen, *The Russian Push Toward Japan: Russo-Japanese Relations, 1697–1875* (Princeton, NJ: Princeton University Press, 1959), 98.

5. Matsumae was Tokugawa Japan's northernmost castle town, located on the southern tip of Ezo. David L. Howell, "Ainu Ethnicity and the Boundaries of the Early Modern Japanese State," *Past & Present*, 142 (February 1994): 69–93. See also Brett L. Walker, *The Conquest of Ainu Lands: Ecology and Culture in Japanese Expansion, 1590–1800* (Berkeley: University of California Press, 2006), 132, on the position of Ezo at the "boundary of the Chinese tribute system."

6. Lensen, *Russian Push Toward Japan*, 102–20. The Russians would again attempt to open trade with Japan in 1804 when Nikolai Rezanov took the Nagasaki permit given to Laxman with him, but the shogunate refused his overtures.

7. On the Satsuma domain's role in coastal defense and its cooptation of smuggling in that effort, see Robert I. Hellyer, "The Missing Pirate and the Pervasive Smuggler: Regional Agency in Coastal Defense, Trade, and Foreign Relations in 19th-Century Japan," *International History Review* 27.1 (March 2005): 1–24.

8. Matsumae's Japanese inhabitants mostly traded with the Ainu people through coastal trading territories, which extended all the way into Sakhalin and the Kuril island chain, where their trade further linked them to a variety of Northeast Asian populations. Richard M.

Siddle, "The Ainu: Indigenous People of Japan," in *Japan's Minorities: The Illusion of Homogeneity*, ed. Michael Weiner (London: Routledge, 1997), 25–26.

9. Wakabayashi, *Anti-Foreignism and Western Learning in Early-Modern Japan*, 59–64.

10. Even before 1792, scholars and officials alike had been concerned about conditions to the north and had active discussions about expansion. For information on scholars, such as Hayashi Shihei and Honda Toshiaki, who had early concerns about Japan's outer boundaries and defenses, see, e.g., Jonas Rüegg, "Mapping the Forgotten Colony: The Ogasawara Islands and the Tokugawa Pivot to the Pacific," *Cross-Currents: East Asian History and Culture Review*, E-Journal no. 23 (June 2017): 108–157.

11. Tessa Morris-Suzuki, "Lines in the Snow: Imagining the Russo-Japanese Frontier," *Pacific Affairs* 72, no. 1 (Spring 1999): 60.

12. Walker argues that cartographer Ino Tadataka's (1745–1818) early modern surveys and mapping of Japan's full coastline was a "cartographic fortification of the nation against the real threat of Western imperialism." Brett L. Walker, "Mamiya Rinzō and the Japanese Exploration of Sakhalin Island: Cartography and Empire," *Journal of Historical Geography*, 33 (2007): 285.

13. David L. Howell, "Early 'Shizoku' Colonization of Hokkaidō," *Journal of Asian History* 17 (1983): 40–67. In the 1875 Treaty of St. Petersburg, Japan and Russia agreed that the Kuril archipelago would go to the former and Sakhalin to the latter. These territories have subsequently changed hands a number of times, and the status of the Kuril Islands remains the source of an ongoing territorial dispute between Russia and Japan.

14. These include: Rezanov (1804), Raffles (1813, 1814), Morrison (1937), Biddle (1846). The French did not seek entry to Japan in the first half of the century, although they and the British had tried to gain trade privileges in the Ryukyus in the decade before Perry landed at Naha during the Japan expedition.

15. See, e.g., W. G. Beasley, *Great Britain and the Opening of Japan, 1834–1858* (London: Luzac, 1951); Hellyer, "The Missing Pirate and the Pervasive Smuggler"; David L. Howell, "Foreign Encounters and Informal Diplomacy in Early Modern Japan," *Journal of Japanese Studies* 40, no. 2 (Summer 2014): 295–327; Luke S. Roberts, "Shipwrecks and Flotsam: The Foreign World in Edo-Period Tosa," *Monumenta Nipponica* 70, no. 1 (2015): 83–122; and Noell Wilson, "Tokugawa Defense Redux: Organizational Failure in the *Phaeton* Incident of 1808," *Journal of Japanese Studies* 36, no. 1 (Winter 2010): 1–32.

16. See Noell Wilson, *Defensive Positions: The Politics of Maritime Security in Tokugawa Japan* (Cambridge, MA: Harvard University Asia Center, 2015), on efforts that were made to increase coastal defenses.

17. W. G. Beasley, trans. and ed., "Ii Naosuke to Bakufu, 1 October 1853," *Select Documents on Japanese Foreign Policy, 1853–1868* (London: Oxford University Press, 1955), 119.

18. Russian vice-admiral Evfimii Vasil'evich Putiatin tried to reach Japan ahead of Perry but delays in his mission meant he arrived a month after the Americans. Putiatin negotiated the 1855 Treaty of Shimoda. This treaty was similar to the U.S.-Japan Treaty of Kanagawa but also attempted to address the demarcation of national borders with regard to Sakhalin and the Kuril Islands.

19. On April 24, 1852, the *New York Times* published "The Japanese Expedition—Instructions to Com. Aulick," which was originally from the Department of State, Washington, D.C., Tuesday, June 10, 1851, https://timesmachine.nytimes.com/timesmachine

/1852/04/24/75116237.html. The statement was made to John H. Aulick who was originally expected to lead the Japan expedition. Fillmore's letter to the Japanese emperor echoed these sentiments.

20. "Japan: Character of the Country—Relations with the World, the United States Expedition," *New York Times*, October 1, 1852, p. 3, https://timesmachine.nytimes.com/timesmachine/1852/10/01/75116982.html?pageNumber=3.

21. The U.S. Japan expedition used information about Uraga Bay and its defenses that had been gathered on earlier excursions, notably from when James Biddle, also an American commodore, attempted to open trade in 1846 and James Glynn rescued stranded American whalers in 1850. Clifford M. Drury, "Early American Contacts with the Japanese," *Pacific Northwest Quarterly* 36, no. 4 (October 1945): 319–30. Perry had also acquired information and a copy of Inō Chukei's 1832 map of Japan from the Dutch. Allan B. Cole, "The Ringgold-Rodgers-Brooke Expedition to Japan and the North Pacific, 1853-1859," *Pacific Historical Review* 16, no. 2 (May 1947): 155.

22. Letters from the U.S. President Millard Fillmore and U.S. Navy Commodore Matthew C. Perry to the Emperor of Japan, 1852–1853, accessed July 15, 2018, http://afe.easia.columbia.edu/ps/japan/fillmore_perry_letters.pdf.

23. The core of the twelve-article document restricted the Americans to the use of two ports (Shimoda and Hakodate), addressed the handling of shipwrecked vessels and crews, established most favored nation status, and granted the United States the right to appoint a consul. Additionally, shipwrecked Americans would be allowed to temporarily reside (within seven-mile limits) at these ports, and consuls or agents appointed by the United States would be allowed to reside in Shimoda. Beasley, *Select Documents on Japanese Foreign Policy*, 119–22.

24. Hiroshi Mitani, *Escape from Impasse: The Decision to Open Japan*, trans. David Noble (Tokyo: International House of Japan, 2006), 188–89.

25. Martha Chaiklin, "Monopolists to Middlemen: Dutch Liberalism and American Imperialism in the Opening of Japan," *Journal of World History* 21, no. 2 (June 2010): 249–69.

26. After coming down on the number of ports, Perry wanted one port in Ezo, one in the Ryukyus, plus either Kagoshima (southern Kyushu) or Uraga (much closer to Edo than Shimoda). He also refused to use Nagasaki, believing it to be a sign of Dutch submission, but would later recant after the Russians accepted it as a third port in their 1855 treaty with Japan. Mitani, *Escape from Impasse*, 189–91.

27. On the 1858 negotiations, see Michael R. Auslin, *Negotiating with Imperialism: The Unequal Treaties and The Culture of Japanese Diplomacy* (Cambridge, MA: Harvard University Press, 2006). Makimura argues that the decision to open Japan to trade had been made a full year before the 1858 treaties were signed, giving great agency to Hotta Masayoshi and his political efforts at home in making this a relatively easy process. Yasuhiro Makimura, *Yokohama and the Silk Trade:How Eastern Japan Became the Primary Economic Region of Japan, 1843–1893* (Lanham, MD: Lexington Books, 2017), 55.

28. Lauren Benton argues that most empires were not primarily seeking territorial control, and that was the case with Japan. "Legal Spaces of Empire: Piracy and the Origins of Ocean Regionalism," *Comparative Studies in Society and History* 47, no. 4 (October 2005): 700.

29. See, for example, Catherine L. Phipps, *Empires on the Waterfront: Japan's Ports and Power, 1858–1899* (Cambridge, MA: Harvard University Asia Center, 2015). 179–84; and

Harald Fuess, "Informal Imperialism and the 1879 *Hesperia* Incident: Containing Cholera and Challenging Extraterritoriality in Japan," *Japan Review* 27 (2014): 103–140.

30. Benton, "Legal Spaces of Empire," 706.

31. Douglas Howland, *International Law and Japanese Sovereignty: The Emerging Global Order in the 19th Century* (Houndmills, Basingstoke, Hampshire: Palgrave Macmillan, 2016), 1–26. Ultimately (following the Battle of Tsushima in the 1904–1905 Russo-Japanese War), Japan would gain maritime dominance in East Asian waters.

32. The illegality of imposing an indemnity on Japan for protecting its territorial waters was later recognized when, in 1876, after years of congressional discussion in the United States, an agreement was reached to return the amount paid to the United States. Payson J. Treat, "The Return of the Shimonoseki Indemnity," *Journal of Race Development* 8, no. 1 (July 1917): 1–12. See also Albert Craig, *Chōshū in the Meiji Restoration* (Cambridge, MA: Harvard University Press, 1967), 178–204.

33. On the unsettled nature of the international system see, e.g., Oona A. Hathaway and Scott J. Shapiro, *The Internationalists: How a Radical Plan to Outlaw War Remade the World* (New York: Simon & Schuster, 2017). The status of the Inland Sea, and whether it was an international passageway to the treaty ports or Japan's territorial waters, would again be called into question in 1894 in the court case over the *Chishima* incident. See Phipps, *Empires on the Waterfront*, 179–85.

34. Treat, "The Return of the Shimonoseki Indemnity," 4–9.

35. Legend has it that the Japanese discovered Ogasawara in 1593, but the islands are believed to have first been sighted by the Spanish in 1543. See Bernhard Welsch, "Was Marcus Island Discovered by Bernardo de la Torre in 1543?" *Journal of Pacific History* 39, no. 1 (June 2004): 109–122.

36. David Chapman, "Inventing Subjects and Sovereignty: Early History of the First Settlers of the Bonin (Ogasawara) Islands," *Asia-Pacific Journal—Japan Focus* 7 (24), no. 1 (June 15, 2009): 1–22; Chapman, "Britain and the Bonins: Discovery, Recovery and Reclamation," *Japan Forum* 29, no. 2 (June 2017): 154–79.

37. Hayashi discussed this in the same 1785 work, *An Ilustrated Description of Three Countries*, in which he made an early argument for the colonization of Hokkaido. Rüegg, "Mapping the Forgotten Colony," 121.

38. Mizuno had originally opposed opening the country and when he was governor of Nagasaki helped buy ships for the shogunate to establish a navy. Makimura, *Yokohama and the Silk Trade*, 53.

39. Hyman Kublin, "The Ogasawara Venture (1861–1863)," *Harvard Journal of Asiatic Studies* 14, no. 1/2 (June 1951): 275–78.

40. Rüegg, "Mapping the Forgotten Colony," 109. Rüegg also argues that these Tokugawa efforts in the Bonins joined Japan's earlier colonization effort in Ezo with Western imperial strategies, 111.

41. David Chapman, "Britain and the Bonins: Discovery, Recovery and Reclamation," *Japan Forum* 29, no. 2 (2017): 154-79; Yamamoto, "Balance of Favour," ch. 6.

42. Due to domestic turmoil leading to the Meiji Restoration, Japan did not formally annex the islands until 1875. Beasley, *Great Britain and the Opening of Japan*, 95–96. See also Yamamoto, "Balance of Favour," 188–210.

43. Alison Bashford, "Terraqueous Histories," *Historical Journal* 60, no. 2 (June 2017): 253.

44. Ōkurashō, ed., *Kōbushō enkaku hōkoku* (Tokyo: Ōkurashō, 1888), 1.

45. Such efforts also involved dealing with local specificity as well as complex issues of identity formation. See, e.g., Yamamoto, "Balance of Favour"; and Chapman, "Inventing Subjects and Sovereignty."

46. Matthew Edney, *Mapping an Empire: The Geographical Construction of British India, 1765–1843* (Bloomington: Indiana University Press, 1999).

47. Gotō Atsushi, "19 seiki America gasshūkoku ni yoru sokuryō jigyō to bakumatsu Nihon—Perry, Rogers, Brooke," *Nihonshi Kenkyū*, no. 634 (June 2015): 32–51.

48. Japanese pilots were apparently aboard the French and American vessels when they were fired upon after entering the Shimonoseki Straits in 1863. W. G. Beasley, "From Conflict to Co-operation: British Naval Surveying in Japanese Waters, 1845–82," in *The History of Anglo-Japanese Relations, 1600–2000*, vol. 1, ed. Ian Nish and Yoichi Kibata (Basingstoke: Palgrave Macmillan, 2000), 100–103.

49. Beasley, "From Conflict to Co-operation," 104.

50. Kobayashi Teruo, *Nihon no minato no rekishi: sono genjitsu to kadai* (Tokyo: Kōtsū Kenkyū Kyōkai, 1999), 47.

51. Japan, *Treaties and Conventions, Concluded between Japan and Foreign Nations, Together with Notifications & Regulations Made from Time to Time, 1854–1870* (Yokohama: "Daily Japan Herald" Office, 1871), 109.

52. R. Henry Brunton, edited and annotated by Edward R. Beauchamp, *Schoolmaster to an Empire: Richard Henry Brunton in Meiji Japan, 1868–1876* (New York: Greenwood Press, 1991), 1–5.

53. PRO FO 46/544, "Notes on the Foreign Trade and Shipping of Japan, 1872–1900," sent by Joseph N. Longford to Evelyn Cecil on July 17, 1901. United Kingdom, Public Record Office, Foreign Office, General Correspondence and Consular Court Records for Japan, 1888–1920. The same statistic is given in Tomohei Chida and Peter N. Davies, *The Japanese Shipping and Shipbuilding Industries* (London: Athlone Press, 1990), 17.

54. For the Special Trading Ports, see Phipps, *Empires on the Waterfront*, esp. chap. 2.

55. Ronald P. Toby, *State and Diplomacy in Early Modern Japan: Asia in the Development of the Tokugawa Bakufu* (Princeton, NJ: Princeton University Press, 1984).

56. David C. Evans and Mark R. Peattie, *Kaigun: Strategy, Tactics, and Technology in the Imperial Japanese Navy, 1887–1941* (Annapolis: Naval Institute Press, 1997), 7–8.

57. For a revised view of the Matsukata deflation's importance, see Steven J. Ericson, "The 'Matsukata Deflation' Reconsidered: Financial Stabilization and Japanese Exports in a Global Depression, 1881–85," *Journal of Japanese Studies* 40, no. 1 (Winter 2014): 1–28.

58. Nine years later, two more were added to cover the coasts of Suō and Nagato. *Nagasaki zeikan enkaku*, vol. 3 (Yokohama: Tokyo Insatsu Kabushiki Gaisha, 1902), 219–20.

59. The biggest challenge to Japan's expansion during the nineteenth century was the Triple Intervention of 1895 when Russia, together with Germany and France, took back Japan's war prize, the Liaodong Peninsula, in order to ensure Russian access to East Asian waters and gain a warm water port.

60. *Japan Weekly Mail*, September 2, 1893, 281.

61. *Nagasaki zeikan enkakushi*, 220. Here the customs history uses the term figuratively, but providing sufficient lighthouses along the coast was another long-term endeavor.

62. *Nagasaki zeikan enkakushi*, 220.

63. At this time, Hakodate was a treaty port and Nemuro was a domestic port without any special commercial or military functions.

64. *Moji shinpō*, October 13 and 14, 1893.

65. The number of Japanese fishers had also been increasing in this region. In Sakhalin alone they jumped more than twentyfold from roughly three hundred in 1875 to surpass seven thousand by 1904. William M. Tsutsui, "The Pelagic Empire: Reconsidering Japanese Expansion," in *Japan at Nature's Edge: The Environmental Context of a Global Power*, ed. Ian Jared Miller, Julia Adeney Thomas, and Brett L. Walker (Honolulu: University of Hawai'i Press, 2013), 23.

66. *Japan Weekly Mail*, July 12, 1890, "Measures to Restrain Poaching," 34.

67. December 30, 1893, "Mode of Dealing with Poaching Ships," *Japan Weekly Mail: A Review of Japanese Commerce, Politics, Literature, and Art*, vol. XX (July–December, 1893), 777.

68. *Japan Weekly Mail*, July 15, 1893, 63. A revised treaty with Great Britain was signed in 1894 and would soon be followed by the others. The revised treaties went into effect in July 1899 and Japan regained full tariff autonomy in 1911–12.

Chapter 9

1. Charlotte Attwood, "Seaweed: Zanzibar's 'Gift from the Ocean,'" *BBC World News*, March 27, 2014, https://www.bbc.com/news/world-africa-26770151; Mariana Zavery, "Seaweed Center: Paje, Zanzibar," *The Mindful Sprout Blog*, September 8, 2014, http//www.themindfulsprout.net/travel/2014/9/2/seaweed-center-in-paje; Per Pettersson-Lofquist, "The Development of Open-Water Algae Farming in Zanzibar: Reflections on the Socioeconomic Impact," *Ambio* 24, no. 7/8 (1995): 487–91; Marilyn Porter et al., "Globalization and Women in Coastal Communities in Tanzania," *Development* 51 (2008), 193–98.

2. Rachel Clara Reed, "Fighting to Farm: Zanzibar's Seaweed Growers Face a Changing Climate," *ABP News*, July 10, 2017, http://abeautifulperspective.com/2017/07/10/fighting-to-farm-zanzibars-seaweed-growers-face-a-changing-climate/; Sara Frocklin et al., "Seaweed Mariculture as a Development Project in Zanzibar, East Africa: A Price Too High to Pay?" *Aquaculture* 356–57 (2012): 30—39.

3. Rosemary Ommer and Gerald Panting, eds., *Working Men Who Got Wet* (St. Johns, NL: Maritime History Research Group, Memorial University of Newfoundland, 1980).

4. See, e.g., Paul Thompson, "Women in the Fishing: The Roots of Power Between the Sexes," *Comparative Studies in Society and History* 27, no. 1 (January 1985): 3–32, which primarily discusses his own research on women and men in Scottish and East Anglian fishing communities from about 1800 to the mid-twentieth century, but also refers to ethnographic studies of other fishing communities in the Baltic, Japan, Malaysia, India, and elsewhere. See also Paul Thompson with Tony Wailey and Trevor Lummis, *Living the Fishing* (London: Routledge & Kegan Paul, 1983); Bela Gunda, ed., *The Fishing Culture of the World: Studies in Ethnology, Cultural Ecology and Folklore*, 2 vols. (Budapest: Akademiai Kiado, 1984); Jane Nadel-Klein and Dona Lee Davis, eds., *To Work and to Weep* (St. John's, NL: Institute of Social and Economic Research, 1988); Raoul Andersen, ed., *North Atlantic Maritime Cultures: Anthropologic Essays on Changing Adaptations* (The Hague: Mouton, 1979); Dona Lee Davis and Jane Nadel-Klein, "Gender, Culture and the Sea: Contemporary Theoretical Approaches," *Society and Natural Resources* 5 (1992): 135–47; "Special Issue: Gender and Resource Crisis

in the North Atlantic Fisheries," *Women's Studies International Forum* 23, no. 3 (May–June 2000); "Forum: Fish/Wives: Gender, Representation, and Agency in Coastal Communities," *Signs: Journal of Women in Culture and Society* 37, no. 3 (Spring 2012); and Margaret Chapman, "Women's Fishing in Oceania," *Human Ecology* 15, no. 3 (September 1987): 267–88.

5. On women swimming, diving, boat handling, and navigating around the world, see, e.g., Kevin Dawson, *Undercurrents of Power: Aquatic Culture in the African Diaspora* (Philadelphia: University of Pennsylvania Press, 2018); Elise Huffer, "Women and Navigation: Does the Exception Confirm the Rule?" *International Journal of Maritime History*, 20, no. 2 (December 2008): 265–84; Dianne Newell, *Tangled Webs of History: Indians and the Law in Canada's Pacific Coast Fisheries* (Toronto: University of Toronto Press, 1993), esp. chaps. 2–4; Dorothy Jean Ray, *The Eskimos of Bering Strait, 1650–1898* (Seattle: University of Washington Press, 1975); Thompson, "Women in the Fishing"; Beatrice Moring, "Nordic Coastal Communities in Historical Perspective: The Interaction of Economic Activity and the Household," *International Journal of Maritime History* 14, no. 2 (December 2002): 145–65; Chapman, "Women's Fishing in Oceania"; and Paul D'Arcy, *The People of the Sea: Environment, Identity and History in Oceania* (Honolulu: University of Hawai'i Press, 2006).

6. Valerie Burton, "Introduction, Forum: Fish/Wives: Gender, Representation, and Agency in Coastal Communities," *Signs: Journal of Women in Culture and Society* 37, no. 3 (Spring 2012): 530. See also the other contributions to the 2012 *Signs* "Forum: Fish/Wives"; Jesse Ransley, "Boats Are for Boys: Queering Maritime Archaeology," *World Archaeology* 37, no. 4 (December 2005): 621–29; Margaret Creighton and Lisa Norling, "Introduction," in *Iron Men, Wooden Women: Gender and Seafaring in the Atlantic World, 1750–1920*, ed. Margaret Creighton and Lisa Norling (Baltimore, MD: Johns Hopkins University Press, 1996).

7. Many studies of gender and sexuality in Oceania and Native America bear this out; see, e.g., Patricia O'Brien, "Gender," in *Pacific Histories: Ocean, Land, People*, ed. David Armitage and Alison Bashford (Basingstoke: Palgrave Macmillan, 2014), 282–304; Matt Matsuda, *Pacific Worlds: A History of Seas, Peoples, and Cultures* (Cambridge: Cambridge University Press, 2012); and D'Arcy, *The People of the Sea.*

8. Thompson, "Women in the Fishing," 28.

9. W. Jeffrey Bolster, "Putting the Ocean in Atlantic History: Maritime Communities and Marine Ecology in the Northwest Atlantic, 1500–1800," *American Historical Review* 113, no. 1 (February 2008): 19–47. See also his more extended discussion in Bolster, *The Mortal Sea: Fishing the Atlantic in the Age of Sail* (Cambridge, MA: Harvard University Press, 2012).

10. I surveyed relevant scholarly literature in English that has appeared since such pioneering studies as Andersen, ed., *North Atlantic Maritime Cultures*; Thompson et al., *Living the Fishing*; and Nadel-Klein and Davis, *To Work and to Weep.* The scholarship is scattered across multiple disciplines, ranging from history and archaeology to anthropology, rural sociology, geography, women's studies, developmental economics, ecology, resource management, and conservation, and represents wildly different questions, methods, sources, and publication venues. Interdisciplinarity can be an asset, but it also complicates interpretation. Several authors refer to "traditional" practices, but only a few try to provide any more concrete temporal background. There has been little attention to change over time in as specific terms as we historians would like; when there is, the time period covered is generally recent. In addition, much of the work in English that addresses early modern history focuses on either the North Atlantic or East and Southeast Asia. Paul D'Arcy observes that maritime histories

of Oceania "are oriented toward the initial exploration and colonization of the region" and "a host of ethnographies . . . emphasize longer-term continuities rather than short-term change, so there is little historically specific detail in them." See D'Arcy, *The People of the Sea*, 1–2 and *passim*. (D'Arcy's book focuses on the period 1770 to 1870.) I noticed the same characteristics in almost all of the ethnographic studies of women and/or gender dynamics in fishing communities in other parts of the world, as well. See also Davis and Nadel-Klein, "Gender, Culture, and the Sea," which found in 1992 that the preponderance of the anthropological literature on women, gender, and fisheries focuses on either the North Atlantic or Southeast Asia and Oceania (137).

11. Danish marine archaeologist Christer Westerdahl emphasizes "the penetration and interdependence of land and sea in coastal zones" in his article "The Maritime Cultural Landscape," *International Journal of Nautical Archaeology* 21, no. 1 (February 1992): 5–14.

Michael Pearson has called for historians to focus more directly on littoral societies that surround the oceans and seas: Pearson, "Littoral Society: The Concept and the Problems," *Journal of World History* 17, no. 4 (December 2006): 353–73. Many historians and anthropologists have agreed: see, e.g., Gérard Le Bouëdec, "Small Ports from the Sixteenth to the Early Twentieth Century and the Local Economy of the French Atlantic Coast," *International Journal of Maritime History* 21, no. 1 (December 2009): 103–125; Jennifer L. Gaynor, "Flexible Fishing: Gender and the New Spatial Division of Labor in Eastern Indonesia's Rural Littoral," *Radical History Review* 107 (Spring 2010): 74–100; Greg Dening, *Islands and Beaches: Discourse on a Silent Land: Marquesas, 1774–1880* (Honolulu: University of Hawai'i Press, 1980) and Dening, *Beach Crossings: Voyaging Across Times, Cultures, and Self* (Philadelphia: University of Pennsylvania Press, 2004); John Gillis, *The Human Shore: Seacoasts in History* (Chicago: University of Chicago Press, 2012); Kären Wigen, "AHR Forum: Oceans of History: Introduction," *American Historical Review* 111, no. 3 (June 2006): 717–21; and John R. Stilgoe, *Alongshore* (New Haven, CT: Yale University Press, 1994), among others. Yet, still, few maritime or oceanic scholars appear to have answered the call.

12. See, e.g., several of the essays in Alexander Spoehr, ed., *Maritime Adaptations: Essays on Contemporary Fishing Communities* (Pittsburgh, PA: University of Pittsburgh Press, 1980). Controlling access to fishing grounds, regulating who can take what, when, and where from riverbank and ocean shore to distant pelagic zones, has been important throughout human history and prehistory. The variations and changes over time in regulation and enforcement no doubt have been a critical element in the gendering of fishing labor, but are sufficiently complex to preclude discussion in this essay, as are ancillary maritime industries such as salt production.

13. Bolster, "Putting the Ocean in Atlantic History," 22.

14. Chapman, "Women's Fishing in Oceania," 267–88; Thomas Ryan, "Fishing in Transition on Niue," *Journal de la Société des Océanistes* 37, no. 72–73 (1981): 193–203.

15. I'm drawing here from a substantial number of sources including, for just a few examples in addition to those cited elsewhere : Luisa Muñoz Abeledo, "The Labour Market in the Spanish Fish-Canning Industry, 1880–1977," *International Journal of Maritime History* 17, no. 2 (December 2005); 211–30; Christina Folke Ax, "Greenland Whalers and Life on a Wadden Sea Island in the Eighteenth Century," *International Journal of Maritime History* 27, no. 4 (November 2015): 680–95; Rebecca Bliege Bird, "Fishing and the Sexual Division of Labor Among the Meriam," *American Anthropologist* 109, no. 3 (September 2007): 442–51; Reginald Byron, "The Maritime Household in Northern Europe," *Comparative Studies in Society and*

History 36, no. 2 (April 1994): 271–92; Sally Cole, *Women of the Praia: Work and Lives in a Portuguese Coastal Community* (Princeton, NJ: Princeton University Press, 1991); Carol Cooper, "Native Women of the Northern Pacific Coast: An Historical Perspective, 1830–1900," *Journal of Canadian Studies/Revue d'Etudes Canadiennes* 27, no. 4 (Winter 1992–93): 44–75.

16. Chapman, "Women's Fishing in Oceania," 272-280; quotations 267, 268.

17. Chapman, "Women's Fishing in Oceania," 269.

18. Carol Jane Jolles, *Faith, Food, and Family in a Yupik Whaling Community* (Seattle: University of Washington Press, 2002), 50–92, 274–309, and *passim*. See also J. R. Bockstoce, *Eskimos of Northwest Alaska in the Early Nineteenth Century*, Pitt Rivers Museum Monograph Series No. 1 (Oxford: University of Oxford Press, 1977); Ray, *The Eskimos of Bering Strait*.

19. Jolles, *Faith, Food, and Family*, 291.

20. Fred Bruemmer, "The Last of the Umiaks," *Natural History Magazine*, October 1992, http://www.naturalhistorymag.com/htmlsite/master.html?http://www.naturalhistorymag.com/htmlsite/editors_pick/1992_10_pick.html.

21. James Francis Warren, *The Sulu Zone: The Dynamics of External Trade, Slavery and Ethnicity in the Transformation of a Southeast Asian Maritime State, 1768–1898* (Singapore: National University of Singapore Press, 2007); Clifford Sather, *The Bajau Laut: Adaptation, History, and Fate in a Maritime Fishing Society of South-Eastern Sabah* (Kuala Lumpur: Oxford University Press, 1997); Barbara Watson Andaya, *The Flaming Womb: Repositioning Women in Early Modern Southeast Asia* (Honolulu: University of Hawai'i Press, 2006); Gaynor, "Flexible Fishing." A recent newspaper article reports on recent scientific studies of the Bajau Laut: Carl Zimmer, "Bodies Remodeled for a Life at Sea," *New York Times*, April 19, 2018, D5. The terms *Bajau Laut* and *Sama Dilaut*, used by Sather and others, refers to the same subgroup of the widely dispersed ethnolinguistic Sama-Bajau speakers, the subgroup "of the sea" or *laut* who lived exclusively on boats in the Sulu Archipelago (see Sather, *The Bajau Laut*, 2–12). Padbrugge translated and quoted in Andaya, *The Flaming Womb*, 105.

22. Sather, *The Bajau Laut*, 111–21.

23. See Orvar Löfgren, "Marine Ecotypes in Preindustrial Sweden: A Comparative Discussion of Swedish Peasant Fishermen," in *North Atlantic Maritime Cultures* (1979): 83–109; and Moring, "Nordic Coastal Communities in Historical Perspective," 145–65, for mention of the traditional Swedish phrase "one green foot and one blue foot."

24. Bolster, "Putting the Ocean in Atlantic History," 26.

25. Bolster, "Putting the Ocean in Atlantic History"; also Moring, "Nordic Coastal Communities in Historical Perspective," 145–65, among other sources cited in this essay.

26. See Kathleen J. Bragdon, *Native People of Southern New England, 1500–1650* (Norman: University of Oklahoma Press, 1996), 59-69 and *passim*. See also Andrew Lipman, *The Saltwater Frontier: Indians and the Contest for the American Coast* (New Haven, CT: Yale University Press, 2015); Christopher L. Pastore, *Between Land and Sea: The Atlantic Coast and the Transformation of New England* (Cambridge, MA: Harvard University Press, 2014); Cheryl P. Claassen, "Gender, Shellfishing, and the Shell Mound Archaic," in *Engendering Archaeology*, ed. Joan M. Gero and Margaret W. Conkey (London: Basil Blackwell, 1991), 276–300.

27. Bragdon quotes Cheryl P. Claassen that "women are universally acknowledged as shellfish gatherers" and that because of the wide identification of women with shellfishing, shellfish and molluscs held a reputation as a "low priority foodstuff." Bragdon, *Native People of Southern New England, 1500–1650*, 77–112.

28. Bragdon, *Native People of Southern New England, 1500–1650*, 112, 118, 120.

29. Sophia Perdikaris and Thomas McGovern, "Viking Age Economics and the Origins of Commercial Cod Fisheries in the North Atlantic," in *Beyond the Catch: Fisheries of the North Atlantic, the North Sea and the Baltic, 900–1850*, ed. Louis Sicking and Darlene Abreu-Ferreira (Leiden: Brill, 2009), 61–90. See also Thompson, "Women in the Fishing," 7; Löfgren, "Marine Ecotypes in Preindustrial Sweden," 83–109; and Sicking and Abreu-Ferreira, "Introduction," in *Beyond the Catch*.

30. James Barrett, Alison Locker, and Callum Roberts, "The Origins of Intensive Marine Fishing in Medieval Europe: The English Evidence," *Proceedings of the Royal Society of London* B 271 (2004): 2417–21; Perdikaris and McGovern, "Viking Age Economics."

31. Maryanne Kowaleski, "Women, Family, and Seamen in Later Medieval England," unpublished paper presented at the University of Minnesota Center for Early Modern History conference, "The Social History of the Sea," May 2008, Minneapolis, MN.

32. Perdikaris and McGovern, "Viking Age Economics"; Carsten Jahnke, "The Medieval Herring Fishery in the Western Baltic," also in *Beyond the Catch*, 157–86 (quotation 177–78); Kowaleski, "Women, Family, and Seamen in Later Medieval England"; Thompson, "Women in the Fishing," 7; Löfgren, "Marine Ecotypes in Preindustrial Sweden."

33. Peter E. Pope, *Fish into Wine: The Newfoundland Plantation in the Seventeenth Century* (Chapel Hill: University of North Carolina Press for the Omohundro Institute of Early American History and Culture, 2004); Bolster, *The Mortal Sea*; Sicking and Abreu-Ferreira, "Introduction," in *Beyond the Catch*.

34. Captain Wheler quoted in Pope, *Fish into Wine*, 215.

35. Bolster, "Putting the Ocean into Atlantic History"; Kathleen Bragdon, *Native People of Southern New England, 1650–1775* (Norman: University of Oklahoma Press, 2009); Lipman, *The Saltwater Frontier*; Pastore, *Between Land and Sea*. On Native American men's employment as crew on Anglo-American whaling voyages, see Daniel Vickers, "The First Whalemen of Nantucket," *William & Mary Quarterly*, 3d ser., 40 (1983): 560–83; and Nancy Shoemaker, *Native American Whalemen and the World: Indigenous Encounters and the Contingency of Race* (Chapel Hill: University of North Carolina Press, 2015).

36. Moring, "Nordic Coastal Communities in Historical Perspective," 145–65. Note: The article does not focus directly on questions about gender and women's roles.

37. Danielle van den Heuvel, "The Multiple Identities of Early Modern Dutch Fishwives," *Signs: Journal of Women in Culture and Society* 37, no. 3 (2012): 587–94.

38. Darlene Abreu-Ferreira, "Fishmongers and Shipowners: Women in Maritime Communities of Early Modern Portugal," *Sixteenth Century Journal* 31, no. 1 (Spring 2000): 7–23. See also Abreu-Ferreira, "Neighbors and Traders in a Seventeenth-Century Port Town," *Signs* 37, no. 3 (Spring 2012): 581–87.

39. Abreu-Ferreira, "Fishmongers and Shipowners."

40. Ax, "Greenland Whalers and Life on a Wadden Sea Island," 680–95.

41. Ax, "Greenland Whalers and Life on a Wadden Sea Island," 685–88. I found a very similar pattern with the whale fishery on eighteenth-century Nantucket, with the interesting exception of the inheritance strategies. This difference may reflect the fact that there were very few family farms on Nantucket, where most of the land was held in common as a pasture for sheep. See Lisa Norling, *Captain Ahab Had a Wife: New England Women and the Whalefishery, 1720–1870* (Chapel Hill: University of North Carolina Press, 2000).

42. Molly A. Warsh, "A Political Ecology in the Early Spanish Caribbean," *William & Mary Quarterly* 71, no. 4 (October 2014): 517–48; and Warsh, "Enslaved Pearl Divers in the Sixteenth Century Caribbean," *Slavery & Abolition* 31, no. 3 (September 2010): 345–62.

43. Quoted in Warsh, "Enslaved Pearl Divers," 349.

44. Warsh, personal email communication with author, January 20, 2016; Dawson, *Undercurrents of Power*, 57–84.

45. Barbara Watson Andaya and Leonard Y. Andaya, *A History of Early Modern Southeast Asia, 1400–1830* (Cambridge: Cambridge University Press, 2015); Warren, *The Sulu Zone*, xix–xxvi, 35–37, and *passim*; Sather, *The Bajau Laut*, 41, 111–26; Edward A. Alpers, *The Indian Ocean in World History* (New York: Oxford University Press, 2014), 40–97.

46. Warren, *The Sulu Zone*; Sather, *The Bajau Laut*; Andaya, *The Flaming Womb*.

47. Arne Kalland, *Fishing Villages in Tokugawa Japan* (Honolulu: University of Hawai'i Press, 1995): 1–16, 45–50, 162–79; David L. Howell, *Capitalism from Within: Economy, Society, and the State in a Japanese Fishery* (Berkeley: University of California Press, 1995); David W. Plath and Jacquetta Hill, "The Reefs of Rivalry: Expertise and Competition Among Japanese Shellfish Divers," *Ethnology* 26, no. 3 (July 1987), 151–63.

48. Carrie L. Yodanis, "Constructing Gender and Occupational Segregation: A Study of Women and Work in Fishing Communities," *Qualitative Sociology* 23, no. 3 (September 2000): 268–69.

49. Burton, "Introduction, Forum: Fish/Wives," 530. Burton observes: "While it is true that perspectives on binaries are now more nuanced, the consistency with which gendered divisions of labor are reproduced in maritime worlds is striking. Men and women work apart even in the most recent[ly] (re)organized of fisheries. Seas and lakes are constituted as environments of primary economic agency where men generate products for the household and the market through direct harvesting of resources. Boundary crossings by women are rare, and transgressors risk a loss of status and reputation. . . . it is men who venture farther into dangerous maritime realms."

50. Attwood, "Zanzibar's 'Gift from the Ocean'"; Reed, "Fighting to Farm."

Afterword

1. See the introduction in this volume for a more detailed overview of the historiography.

2. Recently made available in English translation as *Land and Sea: A World Historical Meditation*, ed. Russell A. Berman and Samuel Garrett Zeitlin (Candor, NY: Telos Press, 2015). Based on a series of articles that Schmitt wrote for the Nazi weekly publication *Das Reich* in 1940 and 1941, *Land and Sea* elaborated on some of the central ideas of Schmitt's better-known *The Nomos of the Earth in the International Law of the Jus Publicum Europaeum*, trans. G. L. Ulmen (Candor, NY: Telos Press, 2003). For an overview of Schmitt's spatial analysis, see Stephen Legg and Alexander Vasudevan, "Introduction: Geographies of the Nomos," in *Spatiality, Sovereignty and Carl Schmitt: Geographies of the Nomos*, ed. Stephen Legg (London and New York: Routledge, 2011), 2–24. According to Schmitt, Jews were sea people because they had no homeland, a condition that rendered them as less than human. Britain's sea orientation placed it outside the orbit of international law, thus validating German aggression against Britain. Schmitt characterizes the war as the culmination of an epic conflict between the improving impulses of great land empires and the rapaciousness of European (non-German) overseas empires (Schmitt, *Land and Sea*, 11). Edits by Schmitt

after the war to remove openly anti-Semitic passages do little to disguise its pro-Nazi sentiments. See Samuel Garrett Zeitlin, "Propaganda and Critique: An Introduction to *Land and Sea*," Schmitt, *Land and Sea*.

3. Schmitt, *Land and Sea*, 47. This discussion fits with Schmitt's introduction elsewhere of the concept of *Grossraum* (Great Space) to capture the political effects that Schmitt saw as flowing from great power disruptions of the spatial order. On *Grossraum*, see Stuart Elden, "Reading Schmitt Geopolitically: *Nomos*, Territory and *Grossraum*," *Radical Philosophy* 161 (May/June 2010): 18–28.

4. Schmitt identifies the first global spatial revolution as the "British maritime appropriation of the world's oceans," a phenomenon linked to the industrial revolution and to Britons acting as "corsair capitalists." These patterns accompanied the prevailing juridical definition of the sea as free and only the land as subject to ownership. Schmitt, *Land and Sea*, 40, 59–60, 76. German expansion promised a second global spatial revolution that would restore the status of the sea as a "space [*Raum*] of human activity" like any other and inaugurate an era focused on the control of air space.

5. Schmitt, *The Nomos of the Earth*, 72–76.

6. Grotius's *Mare liberum* (The Free Sea), published in 1609, presents only a portion of a set of more nuanced arguments he made in the longer, posthumously published work of which it formed a chapter, *De iure praedae* (The Law of Prize), and his *De iure belli ac pacis* (The Rights of War and Peace), which appeared in 1625. Passages in the longer works describe the sea as an interimperial realm in which polities can exercise jurisdiction. See Lauren A. Benton, *A Search for Sovereignty: Law and Geography in European Empires, 1400–1900* (Cambridge: Cambridge University Press, 2010), 131–36.

7. Bernhard Klein and Gesa Mackenthun, "Introduction," in *Sea Changes: Historicizing the Ocean,* ed. Bernhard Klein and Gesa Mackenthun (New York: Routledge, 2004), 2.

8. On this point, see Berman, "Geography, Warfare, and the Critique of Liberalism in Carl Schmitt's *Land and Sea*" and Zeitlin, "Propaganda and Critique," in Schmitt, *Land and Sea.*

9. See Michel Foucault, "Of Other Spaces," trans. Jay Miskowiec, *Diacritics* 16, no. 1 (1986): 22–27.

10. William Langewiesche, *The Outlaw Sea: A World of Freedom, Chaos, and Crime* (New York: North Point Press, 2004); Michael High, "Pirates without Piracy: Criminality, Rebellion, and Anarcho-Libertarianism in the Pirate Film," *Jump Cut* 56 (Winter 2014–2015)

11. See the introduction to this volume. And as an example, on the similarities of practices of raiding and discourses of protection, see Lauren Benton and Adam Clulow, "Empires and Protection: Making Interpolity Law in the Early Modern World," *Journal of Global History* 12, no. 1 (March 2017): 74–92.

12. On this point, see Benton, *A Search for Sovereignty*, chap. 3.

13. We note some commonalities between our approach and that endorsed by Bashford for the study of "terraqueous histories." Yet, whereas she recommends collapsing the categories of land and sea, we emphasize processes that span these spaces, often while preserving their distinctions. The approach allows us to go beyond Bashford's characterization of land-sea zones as "meeting places" and to focus on the generation of geographic and regulatory frameworks encompassing land and sea. Alison Bashford, "Terraqueous Histories," *Historical Journal* 60, no. 2 (June 2017): 253–72, 262.

14. See, e.g., Lauren Benton, "Legal Problems of Empire in Gentili's *Hispanica Advocatio*," in *The Roman Foundations of the Law of Nations*, ed. Benedict Kingsbury and Benjamin Straumann (Oxford: Oxford University Press, 2010), 269–82.

15. Some studies of proximate seas and coasts as interpolitical zones are Renaud Morieux, *The Channel: England, France and the Construction of a Maritime Border in the Eighteenth Century* (Cambridge: Cambridge University Press, 2016); Christopher L. Pastore, *Between Land and Sea: The Atlantic Coast and the Transformation of New England* (Cambridge, MA: Harvard University Press, 2014); and Francesca Trivellato, "Amphibious Power: The Law of Wreck, Maritime Customs, and Sovereignty in Richelieu's France," *Law and History Review* 33, no. 4 (November 2015): 915–44. Works that develop similar ideas of land-sea formations include Lauren Benton and Adam Clulow, "Empires and Protection: Making Interpolity Law in the Early Modern World," *Journal of Global History* 12, no. 1 (March 2017): 74–92; Benton and Jeppe Mulich, "The Space Between Empires: Coastal and Insular Microregions in the Early Nineteenth-Century World," in *The Uses of Space in Early Modern History, 1500–1850*, ed. Paul Stock (New York: Palgrave Macmillan, 2015), 151–71; and Alison Bashford, "Terraqueous Histories," *Historical Journal* 60, no. 2 (June 2017): 253–72. On jurisdictional uncertainties of the "soaking ecologies" of urban wetlands and harbors, see Debanji Bhattacharyya, *Empire and Ecology in the Bengal Delta: The Making of Calcutta* (New York: Cambridge University Press, 2018).

16. Klein and Mackenthun, "Introduction," in *Sea Changes: Historicizing the Ocean*, 2.

17. On the diversity of Atlantic British spaces, see, e.g., Stephen J. Hornsby, *British Atlantic, American Frontier: Spaces of Power in Early Modern British America* (Lebanon, NH: University Press of New England, 2004).

18. See also Denver Brunsman, *The Evil Necessity: British Naval Impressment in the Eighteenth-Century Atlantic World* (Charlottesville: University of Virginia Press, 2013).

19. For a discussion of the modular qualities of empires, see Kerry Ward, *Networks of Empire: Forced Migration in the Dutch East India Company* (Cambridge: Cambridge University Press, 2008), 56.

20. Matilde Cazzola, "Space as Gravitational Field: The Empire and the Atlantic in the Political Thought of Thomas Pownall," *Global Intellectual History* 3, no. 2 (May 2018): 178–201, 180.

21. Cazzola, "Space as Gravitational Field," 189; on the patchy Atlantic order, see Lauren Benton and Lisa Ford, *Rage for Order; The British Empire and the Origins of International Law, 1800–1850* (New York: Cambridge University Press, 2016), chap. 5.

22. See, e.g., Andrew Phillips and Jason C. Sharman, *International Order in Diversity: War, Trade and Rule in the Indian Ocean* (Cambridge: Cambridge University Press, 2015); Gregory T. Cushman, *Guano and the Opening of the Pacific World: A Global Ecological History* (New York: Cambridge University Press, 2013).

23. Janice E. Thomson, *Mercenaries, Pirates, and Sovereigns: State-Building and Extraterritorial Violence in Early Modern Europe* (Princeton, NJ: Princeton University Press, 1994).

24. The strategy is exemplified by Benton and Ford's study of legal reform in the British empire and its regional and global imprint (Benton and Ford, *Rage for Order*) and in a study that begins with European bills of exchange and ends with their "distant echoes," Francesca Trivellato, *The Promise and Peril of Credit* (Princeton, NJ: Princeton University Press, 2019).

25. Raffaele Laudani, "Mare e terra. Sui fondamenti spaziali della sovrantità moderna," *Filosofia Politica* 29, no. 3 (December 2015): 513–30.

26. Nathan Perl-Rosenthal, *Citizen Sailors: Becoming American in the Age of Revolution* (Cambridge, MA: Belknap Press of Harvard University Press, 2015); Kevin Arlyck, "Plaintiffs v. Privateers: Litigation and Foreign Affairs in the Federal Courts, 1816–1822," *Law and History Review* 30, no. 1 (February 2012): 245–78; Gautham Rao, *National Duties: Custom Houses and the Making of the American State* (Chicago: University of Chicago Press, 2016); Ernesto Bassi, *An Acqueous Territory: Sailor Geographies and New Granada's Transimperial Greater Caribbean World* (Durham, NC: Duke University Press, 2017); and Michael A. Schoeppner, *Moral Contagion: Black Atlantic Sailors, Citizenship and Diplomacy in Antebellum America* (New York: Cambridge University Press, 2019).

Contributors

Lauren Benton is Nelson O. Tyrone, Jr. Professor of History and Professor of Law at Vanderbilt University. Her books include *Rage for Order: The British Empire and the Origins of International Law* (coauthored with Lisa Ford, 2016) and *A Search for Sovereignty: Law and Geography in European Empires, 1400–1900* (2010).

Adam Clulow is associate professor of history at the University of Texas at Austin. He is the author of *The Company and the Shogun: The Dutch Encounter with Tokugawa Japan* (2013), which was awarded multiple prizes, and *Amboina, 1623: Conspiracy and Fear on the Edge of Empire* (2019).

Xing Hang is associate professor of history at Brandeis University. He is the author of *Conflict and Commerce in Maritime East Asia: The Zheng Family and the Shaping of the Modern World, c. 1620–1720* (2016).

David Igler is professor of history at the University of California, Irvine. He is the author and editor of numerous books, including *The Great Ocean: Pacific Worlds from Captain Cook to the Gold Rush* (2013).

Jeppe Mulich is a teaching associate in the Faculty of History at Cambridge University. His book *In a Sea of Empires: Networks and Crossings in the Revolutionary Caribbean* is forthcoming from Cambridge University Press.

Lisa Norling is professor emerita of history at the University of Minnesota. She is author of the award-winning *Captain Ahab Had a Wife: New England Women and the Whalefishery 1740–1870* (2000) and co-editor (with Margaret Creighton) of *Iron Men, Wooden Women: Gender and Seafaring in the Atlantic World, 1700–1920* (1996).

Nathan Perl-Rosenthal is associate professor of history, spatial sciences and law at the University of Southern California. He is the author of *Citizen Sailors: Becoming American in the Age of Revolution* (2015).

Carla Rahn Phillips is Union Pacific Professor Emerita in Comparative Early Modern History at the University of Minnesota. She is the author of numerous books and articles on the history of Spain and its empire, including the award-winning books *Six Galleons for the King of Spain: Imperial Defense in the Early Seventeenth Century* (1986) and *The Treasure of the* San José*: Death at Sea in the War of the Spanish Succession* (2007).

Catherine Phipps is associate professor of history and director of the International and Global Studies Program at the University of Memphis. She is the author of *Empires on the Waterfront: Japan's Ports and Power, 1858–1899* (2015).

Matthew Taylor Raffety is professor of history at the University of Redlands. He is the author of *The Republic Afloat: Law, Honor, and Citizenship in Maritime America* (2013).

Margaret Schotte is associate professor of history at York University. She is the author of *Sailing School: Navigating Science and Skill, 1550–1800* (2019).

Index

The term (fig.) indicates a figure.

Acknowledgments

It has been a pleasure working together to edit this volume of original scholarship on a topic so central to each of our scholarly pursuits. The book would not have been possible without the help and support of a number of organizations, institutions, and people, and we gratefully acknowledge their contributions.

The USC-Huntington Early Modern Studies Institute provided generous funding for the conference "Global Maritime History," held at the Huntington Library in Pasadena in March 2016. The far-ranging conversations at the conference gave impetus to this volume, and we are grateful to the scholars who participated in those discussions. Amy Braden, associate director of the institute, offered superb organizational leadership for the conference. Peter Mancall, Andrew W. Mellon Professor of the Humanities, and Linda and Harlan Martens Director of the Early Modern Studies Institute, not only participated in the scholarly conversations at the conference but also served as an invaluable interlocutor as the volume took shape.

Our editor at Penn Press, Robert Lockhart, has been enthusiastic about this project since we first discussed it with him several years ago, and we deeply appreciate his keen editorial eye and collaborative spirit. We also benefited enormously from the comments of two anonymous reviewers for the press.

Our greatest debt is to the authors, including several who did not attend the conference, for entrusting their chapters to us. We hope we have fulfilled the promise to make the sum greater than its parts.

Last, we thank our families for insisting, repeatedly and often, that we set aside maritime and global history to enjoy the view from other portals.